John Churchman

An Account of the Gospel Labours

And Christian Experiences of a Faithful Minister of Christ, John Churchman

John Churchman

An Account of the Gospel Labours
And Christian Experiences of a Faithful Minister of Christ, John Churchman

ISBN/EAN: 9783337161736

Printed in Europe, USA, Canada, Australia, Japan

Cover: Foto ©ninafisch / pixelio.de

More available books at **www.hansebooks.com**

AN

ACCOUNT

OF THE

GOSPEL LABOURS,

AND

CHRISTIAN EXPERIENCES

OF A

FAITHFUL MINISTER

OF CHRIST,

JOHN CHURCHMAN,

Late of Nottingham, in Pennsylvania, deceased.

TO WHICH IS ADDED,

A short MEMORIAL of the Life and Death of a Fellow Labourer in the Church, our valuable Friend JOSEPH WHITE, late of BUCKS COUNTY.

DANIEL xi. 33. xii. 4.
" And they that understand among the People shall instruct many.
" Many shall run to and fro, and Knowledge shall be increased."

PHILADELPHIA, Printed.

LONDON: Reprinted
By JAMES PHILLIPS, George-Yard, Lombard-Street.

M.DCC.LXXX.

TO THE

READER.

IN the perufal of the following pages thou wilt receive a pious man's plain account of his beginning in the weighty work of religion, and his progrefs in a life devoted to promote the caufe of righteoufnefs, and the real happinefs of mankind.

Having experienced the fpiritual baptifm, which is effential to falvation, and abiding in a ftate of watchfulnefs and humility, he became, under the Lord's anointing, a well qualified inftrument for the inftruction and edification of others in the way of godlinefs; and, by attending to the gift of gofpel miniftry committed to his truft, and performing the duties required of him, he witneffed a growth from ftature to ftature, and attained to be an upright elder and father in the church, *being an example to the believers in word, in converfation, in fpirit, in faith, and charity.*

It is not for form fake, or from a mere motive of commendation, that any thing is here premifed refpecting the deceafed; but, as the enfuing narrative will be likely to come under the obfervation of many to whom he was either little known, or wholly a ftranger, it feems neceffary, for the information of fuch enquirers, to make known the eftimation in which he was held by his brethren with whom he was connected in religious fociety; who have given full declaration of their Chriftian unity and fellowfhip with him, and that his life and conduct adorned the doctrine of the gofpel, which he was concerned to publifh.

The monthly and quarterly-meetings of which he was a member from their firft eftablifhment, and who were many years partakers of his pious example and labours, after recounting divers of his vifits abroad, which are fully related by himfelf, teftify, that

'Although he was of a weakly conftitu-
' tion, and often infirm, efpecially in the
' latter part of his life, yet he appeared to
' be much devoted to the fervice of truth
' and the good of mankind, and gave up his
' time for that purpofe, when he apprehended
' it was required of him, being favoured
' with a fufficiency of outward things; and
' we believe he ftood loofe from the world,
' and its connections, not feeking, but re-
' fraining opportunities he might have had
' to get outward riches. He vifited neigh-
' bouring yearly, quarterly, and other meet-
' ings of friends, at times, to his laft year,
' and was truly ufeful in the difcipline of
' the

'the church, having a valuable gift in that
'respect; and was a good example, in a di-
'ligent care to attend all the meetings, both
'for worship and discipline, to which he be-
'longed; cautious of being forward in his
'publick appearances, and, for the most part,
'exampled us to silence in our meetings at
'home, especially in the latter part of his
'time: yet when he did appear in testimony,
'we think it may be truly said, his doctrine
'dropped as the dew, being lively, and edi-
'fying to the honest-hearted, though close
'and searching to the careless professors, as
'well as to the profane and hypocritical.'

'The elders who have ruled well are to
'be accounted honourable; so the remem-
'brance of the fatherly, diligent, humble,
'upright, honest, and self-denying example
'of this our deceased friend, as also his va-
'rious services in our meetings and neigh-
'bourhood, remain fresh, and of a pleasant
'favour to many minds.'

Abstract from the testimony of the monthly-meeting of Nottingham, dated fourth
month twenty-seventh, 1776, and signed
by Samuel England, clerk.

Which is certified to be read and approved
in the Western quarterly-meeting held
at London-Grove, in Chester county,
the nineteenth of the eighth month,
1776, by Isaac Jackson, clerk.

In confirmation of the truth of which memorial concerning him, many others of his brethren, in various places, can freely subscribe.

His deportment was grave and reverent, his judgment sound and clear, in matters of a spiritual or temporal concern; and his natural disposition being chearful, he sometimes discovered a turn of pleasantry in conversation, which, being careful to circumscribe within due limitations, rendered his company innocently agreeable and instructive.

Being deeply sensible of the weight and solemnity of the gospel ministry, he manifested great circumspection and care, that it might be preserved pure and unblemished from mistaken or false appearances, in himself or others; and in the exercise of his gift, his declarations were plain, familiar, and concise, accompanied with a fervent concern that his fellow-believers, and all others, might be brought to the sure knowledge of an holy living principle given to direct and lead into true devotion of heart, and the practice of self-denial, consistent with the doctrine and precepts of Christ Jesus our Lord; for the prevalence and enlargement of whose peaceable kingdom he was earnestly engaged, as the following narrative also makes evident, that with a degree of propriety he might have adopted the language of an eminent minister in the early age of the Christian church, addressed to the believers, " Know-
" ing

" ing that shortly I must put off this my
" tabernacle, even as our Lord Jesus Christ
" hath shewn me: moreover, I will endea-
" vour that you may be able after my de-
" cease to have these things in remembrance;
" for we have not followed cunningly de-
" vised fables, when we made known unto
" you the power and coming of our Lord
" Jesus Christ." 2 Pet. i. 14, 15, 16.

What he hath written, and left us, is now recommended to thy perusal and consideration; in which, if thou art seriously attentive, and not superficial, thou mayest, under the Divine blessing, receive profitable instruction in righteousness, which is the intent of the publication.

PHILADELPHIA, 9th month, 1779.

AN ACCOUNT

OF THE

LIFE AND TRAVELS

OF

JOHN CHURCHMAN.

CHAP. I.

His early sense of the impressions of divine love, and spiritual conflicts in his youth—Death of his father—His marriage—The settlement of a monthly meeting at Nottingham—His joining with other friends in visiting of families the first and second time—His being appointed an Elder, and first appearance in the ministry, &c.

I WAS born in the township of Nottingham, in the county of Chester, and province of Pennsylvania, on the Fourth day of the Sixth month, 1705; and was tenderly brought up in profession of the Truth by my parents, JOHN and HANNAH CHURCHMAN; who were diligent attenders of of Religious Meetings, both on the first, and other days of the week, and encouragers of their children in that practice; which is certainly a duty in parents to do, and often owned by the reaches of Divine Love, even to those who are very young in years, of which I am a living witness. For though I early felt reproof for bad words and actions, yet knew not whence it came, until about the age of eight years, as I sat in a small meeting, the Lord, by the reachings of his heavenly love and goodness, so overcame and tendered my heart, and by his glorious light discovered to me the knowledge of himself, that I saw myself, and what I had been doing, and what it was which had reproved me for evil; and I was made in the secret of my heart to confess, that childhood and youth, and the foolish actions and words to which they are propense, are truly vanity; yet blessed for ever be the name of the Lord! who, in his infinite mercy and goodness, clearly informed me, that, if I would mind the discoveries of his Truth and pure Light for the future, what I had done in the time of my ignorance he would wink at and forgive. And Oh! the stream of Love which filled my heart with solid joy at that time, and lasted for many days, is beyond all expression. Indeed I was early taught to think different from such who hold the perdition of infants, and am since confirmed in fully believing that the sin of our first parents is

not

not imputed to us, (though as their offspring we are by nature prone to evil, which brings wrath) until, by the difcovery of light and grace, we are taught to diftinguifh between good and evil, and in the feed and inward principle that fheweth the evil, we feel the enmity placed againft the evil, and the author thereof, the devil, or wicked one. If we afterwards commit thofe things which we faw to be evil, we then fall under condemnation and wrath: and here every foul that fins muft die to the fin he hath committed, and witnefs the being raifed again by the power of God into newnefs of life in Chrift Jefus, not to live to himfelf, to fulfil the will of the flefh, but to live unto him who died to take away fin.

I may not forget to relate this one thing: my father fent me about three miles on an errand; I rode a mare which had a colt, perhaps half a year old; on my return home the colt ran away from the mare, to a company of wild horfes, which were feeding not far from the path I was in; fo I went home without the colt. My father afked me where the colt was; I told him where it went from me; he bid me go to the place with fpeed, that it might follow the mare home. I went, and found the wild horfes feeding on a piece of ground where the timber trees had been killed, perhaps about two or three years; but, before I went among the dead trees, a mighty wind arofe, which blew

blew some down, and many limbs flew about. I stood still, with my mind turned inward to the Lord, who I believed was able to preserve me from hurt; so I passed among the trees without fear, save the fear of the Lord; which fills the hearts of his humble depending children with love that is stronger than death. I found the colt, which readily followed the mare, and I returned home, with great bowedness of heart, and thankfulness to the Lord, for his mercy and goodness to me on this occasion.

It was my practice when I went to bed to examine how I had spent the past day, and to endeavour to feel the presence of the Lord near, which I did for some considerable time prefer to all other things, and I found this practice a great help to sleep sweetly; and by long experience I can recommend it to children, and to those also of riper age.

I suppose that no one living knew my condition; for I delighted to keep hidden, yet quick to observe the conduct of others. I remember that a person once at my father's, who spake about religious matters with an affected tone, as if he was a good man; when he went away I was near him; and when he mounted his horse, taking a dislike to some of his motions, he called him an ugly dumb beast, with such an accent as bespake great displeasure, and grieved me much; for I did believe that a man whose mind was sweetened with divine love truly,
would

would not speak wrathfully or diminutively, even of the beasts of the field, which were given to man for his use; he did not make them himself. I relate this instance that it may be a warning to all, that they be careful of giving offence to the little ones.

Notwithstanding I had been favoured as before mentioned, yet, as I grew in years, I was much given to play, and began to delight again in several things for which I had before been reproved, and still, by the divine witness in my mind, was brought under judgment for: but having lost my innocence and covering of the pure blessed spirit, I endeavoured through fear to fly from the voice of the holy spirit in my own heart. The enemy persuaded me that I could never be restored to my former state, because I had sinned against so great knowledge; or if I was, the judgment through which I must pass would be intolerable to bear, so that I had better be chearful, and take my ease and delight. But when I was about nine years old my father sent me to school to learn to read, (having been taught to know my letters and spell a little at home) in which I took great delight, and thereby diverted myself from feeling my pain of mind, for the great loss of my innocence which I had sustained. And although the man by whom I was taught was poor, and sat in his loom, being a weaver, while the children read to him, I improved very fast, and he soon put me to writing;

writing; and, finding my capacity full as ripe as is common in boys of that age, he began to teach me arithmetick: yet gracious goodness still favoured me with conviction, and by his spirit was witness against me. And in mercy the Lord visited me with a sore fit of sickness, and by his rod of correction brought me a little more to myself. This was in the fore part of the winter, when I was between nine and ten years of age. And being pretty well recovered for some weeks, I had in the following spring a relapse of the same disorder, (the pleurisy) in which, by outward correction with sickness and inward judgment, the Lord was pleased to draw me to himself; which caused me to renew my covenant with him, and I did hope never more to stray from him, to follow lying vanities, whose sweets I had experienced to be bitter, yea exceeding bitterness in the end. I had taken great delight from a child to play with whistles, and pipes, made of the bark of small branches of trees, and of straws of wheat and rye, but now it grieved me to observe children delight therein, and I ventured to tell my mind to some of them concerning such things.

Man is distinguished from other creatures not only by his voice, but by varying the breath, together with the orderly motion of tongue and lips, that voice is made to convey the ideas of the mind and thoughts of the heart to his fellow-creatures; and as he was created

created to glorify his Maker, the end and intention of his voice should be directed to promote his glory among men, whether in things natural or spiritual, that is, of this life, or that to come. Musick, as now commonly used, and whistling and singing, have no such tendency, but are rather diversions of the mind from what it ought to be employed about, and therefore a base consumption of precious time, which man must be accountable for; which, if enough regarded, instead of musick, whistling and singing merry, foolish, and prophane songs, many would have occasion to lament and weep for their mispent time. I leave it as a caution to parents, to beware of indulging their dear children in any thing which may impress their tender minds with a desire after music, or such diversion, when they grow in years; but that, instead thereof, by living in the pure fear of the Lord, and near the spirit of truth in their own hearts, they may be furnished with example and precept to direct the minds of their offspring to attend to the voice of him who called to Samuel in days of old, and remains to be the same teacher to his people in this age. May his holy name be magnified for ever and ever!

I retained my care and circumspection for some time, but through unwatchfulness and a desire for play, which led into lightness and forgetfulness, I lost this state before I was twelve years of age; and though the

Lord was near, and followed me by his reproof, in order to bring me under judgment, I fled from it as much as I could; having let in a belief, that as I had been favoured to taste, in so wonderful a manner, " of " the good word of life, and power of the " world to come, and had so shamefully fal- " len away, there remained for me no more " sacrifice for sin, but a fearful looking for " of judgment, and fiery indignation;" which, as I thought, seemed to burn in me to that degree, that I was afraid to be alone; for it seemed to be loudly proclaimed in me, that whether I eat or drank, waked or slept, I was accursed. When alone I abhorred myself; but when in company used my utmost endeavours to hide my condition, by being chearful and arch in my discourse, and was thought by most young people to have a knack, as they called it, at jesting and witty turns; yet even in this time I entertained such a value for religion, that I was not willing to reveal my situation, lest I should be a reproach thereto, or discourage others from seeking happiness. But when night came, and I went to bed, no tongue can express the anguish I felt; afraid to lay awake, and afraid to desire sleep, lest I should be cut off from the land of the living, and my portion appointed in utter darkness. I so far neglected my learning, that when about thirteen years old I could not read but in a poor manner, though once noted to be a

ready

ready reader. I was not willing that good friends should take notice of me, or look me steadily in the face; for I thought they would discern my wickedness, and it would be a trouble to them, or by their reproving me, add to my distress. I seemed to be left without any power to resist what I knew to be evil, and being ashamed that I had so lost my little learning, I sought to divert myself by endeavouring to regain it. My former genius and delight so returned, that when I was about fifteen years of age I had made great improvement, not only in reading, but in writing and arithmetick, and several branches of the mathematicks, and began to value myself in some degree thereon; and so I got over the convictions of the divine witness, which spoke trouble in me. Nevertheless, during this time I kept close in attending meetings, hoping, at seasons, that perhaps the Lord would condescend once more to visit me: for a saying of an eminent pious man was revived in my remembrance, " That if there remained a desire in the " heart after redemption, as it was kept to, " the Lord would again assuredly visit such " in his own time." So that I was fearful of neglecting meetings, if my parents had not forwarded me, lest I might miss of the good intended for me. Yet the subtle workings of the power of darkness was at times very great; suggesting to me that all things came by nature, and that there was no God, no heaven, no devil; no punishment for evil; religion a jest, and painful care about futurity a silly whim, propagated to deprive people of pleasure. But, blessed be the Lord! he preserved me from that snare: for while I felt his judgment for sin, I believed in his being and holiness. And I am indeed fully of the mind, that no man can be an atheist before he acts contrary to knowledge, when, to allay the horror and anguish of mind he feels for the commission of sin, he closes in with this temptation. At other times the same subtle power would tempt me to despair of mercy, which, if given way to, would lead to distraction; but the hand of the Lord was underneath, though for my disobedience he suffered me to remain in the wilderness, and to dwell among fiery serpents, until he had wasted that in me, which lusted after forbidden things.

In this state I continued until I was about nineteen years of age; and as I was walking one day to meeting, thinking on my forlorn condition, and remembering the bread in my heavenly Father's house, when I was a dutiful child, and that by straying from him, and spending my portion, I had been eight years in grievous want; I inwardly cried, if thou art pleased again to visit me, I beseech thee, O Lord! visit my body with sickness, or pain, or whatever thou may please, so that the will of the old man may be slain with the transgression, and every thing in me
that

that thy controverfy is againft; that I may be made a fanctified veffel by thy power; fpare only my life, until my redemption is wrought, and my peace made with thee!

About this time my father died, in the tenth month, 1724, which was a great lofs to our whole family; and as he had allotted me to live with and take care of my mother, it became my duty to keep moftly at home. I fpent near a year much in the condition above-mentioned, often out of hope of ever attaining to that ftate I had witneffed when very young; but in the fall of the year after I had arrived to the age of twenty years, it pleafed the Lord to remember me, who had been an exile, in captivity under the old tafkmafter in Egypt fpiritually, and by his righteous judgments, mixed with unfpeakable mercies, to make way for my deliverance. I was vifited with a fore fit of ficknefs, which in a few days fo fully awakened me, that I had no hope of ever being again intrufted with health. My mifpent time, and all my tranfgreffions, were brought to my remembrance, and heavy judgment was upon me for them: I was met with in this narrow path, and could no longer fly from God and his fpirit in my confcience, whofe fore difpleafure I had juftly incurred. I had heard of men who had been notorious offenders, and fled from the juftice of the common law, until they became outlawed; such in a fpiritual fenfe my cafe appeared to be. I
thought

thought I had as it were heard an act of grace and free pardon repeatedly proclaimed, if I would return and live uprightly for the future; but in the time of such visitations I concluded it was only to bring me under judgment to take me from my pleasure, for that mine offences would never be pardoned, and so I had withstood or neglected those visitations. I now saw clearly that herein I had followed the lying suggestions of Satan mine enemy. At this time my old will in the fallen nature gave up its life, and I cried, ' I am not worthy to live or enjoy favour; ' yet, O Lord! if thou wilt be pleased to ' look on me with an eye of pity, do what ' thou wilt with me, magnify thy own ' name, prepare me by thy judgments and ' power, that thy mercy may be shewn in ' and by me, whether thou cut the thread ' of my life, or shall grant me more days, ' which is only in thy power.' Now my heart was made exceedingly tender, I wept much, and an evidence was given me that the Lord had heard my cry, and in mercy looked down on me from his holy habitation; and a willing heart and patience was given me to bear his chastisements, and the working of his eternal word of power, which created all things at the beginning, and by which poor fallen man only is created anew in the heavenly image, and prepared to praise him with acceptance, who lives for ever and ever.

Whilst

Whilst I lay in this condition perhaps I was thought, by those who watched with me, to be near expiring, but though I said little or nothing, I believe I was quite sensible, yet exceedingly weakened, having for about twenty-four hours felt more inward and inexpressible anguish than outward pain, which was no doubt great. I take it to be toward the morning of the fifth day and night of my illness, that I felt the incomes and owning of divine love in a greater degree than ever; for the prospect I had of so great forgiveness made me love the more: for love is ever reciprocal. I remember that I saw the morning light, and thought all things looked new and sweet. I lay where the sun shone near or on my bed, and have sometimes since thought that, being weak, the strength of the light, and too much company hurt me. I leave this hint to excite nurses and those who have the care of very weak indisposed people to beware of letting over much light come upon them, or many visitors, except they be such who are sensible of the weak by being inward and quiet, waiting to feel the sympathy which truth gives; the company of such being truly refreshing.

It pleased the Lord so to restore me, that I recovered my usual strength, and was frequently humbled under a sense of the tender dealings of a merciful God, whose goodness and owning love I felt to be very near. I then loved retirement, and inwardly to feel

after

after the incomes of life, and was often fearful left I should again fall away. In this time it was manifested to me, that if in patience I stood faithful I should be called to the work of the ministry. I loved to attend religious meetings, especially those for discipline; and it was clearly shewn me, that all who attend those meetings should inwardly wait, in great awfulness, to know the immediate presence of Christ, the head of the Church, to give them an understanding what their several services are, and for ability to answer the requirings of truth; for it is by the light and spirit thereof that the Lord's work is done with acceptance, and none should presume to speak or act without its motion or direction: for they who act and speak without it do often darken counsel, mislead the weak, and expose their own folly, to the burthen and grief of sensible friends. It was in great fear that I attempted to speak in these meetings, and as I kept low, with an eye single to the honour of truth, I felt peace and inward strength to increase from time to time: and it is good for all who are concerned to speak to matters in meetings for discipline, in the first place to take heed that their own spirits do not prompt thereto, and to mind the time when to speak fitly: for a word in season from a pure heart is precious, and frequently prevents debates instead of ministering contention; and when they have spoken

to

to business, they should turn inward to feel whether the pure truth owns them, and in that rest, without an over anxious care whether it succeeds at that time or not: so friends will be preserved from being lifted up because their service is immediately owned; or if it should be rejected or slighted, in this inward humble state the labour is felt and seen to be the Lord's.

It is a great favour from the Lord that he is pleased to cover his children with his pure fear, and array their souls with the garment of humility, that they may stand in his presence with acceptance, waiting to be taught of his ways, in meekness to be guided in judgment: these only feel the necessity of minding that excellent exhortation, " Be ye " stedfast, immoveable, always abounding in " the work of the Lord." In a degree of reverent thankfulness I bless the name of the Lord through his beloved Son, that I then, according to my measure, knew what I now write: it was a time of growing with me; I rarely passed a day without feeling the incomes of divine life, and was favoured strongly to desire " the sincere milk of the " holy word," that in humility I might grow thereby in substance. But afterwards I was left and withdrawn from, so that for days, yea, many days together, I was without inward refreshment, and ready to fear that I had offended my gracious Redeemer; and being thoughtful, and inwardly engaged to know the cause, I had to consider that children, though they may be thriving, and darlings of their natural parents, are not fit for much business until they are weaned, and although they grow finely, they are gradually taught to wait the appointed time between meals before they have much care of their father's business, and are further prepared, so as to miss a set meal, or be a longer time without outward food, before they are fit for a journey. And with these thoughts (leaving the reader to judge from whence they came) a hope began to revive in me that I was not forsaken, which, indeed, as I kept patient, I was abundantly sensible of at times, even those times which are in the Lord's hand: for his children experience that the times of refreshment come from him, who, when he hath exercised and proved them, in his infinite kindness is pleased to cause them to sit down, and condescends himself to serve them. Blessed for ever be the name of the Lord! who knows how to prepare his soldiers to remain faithful, and to indure with patience what the natural man would account hardness.

I had strong desires that elderly friends should be good examples to the youth, not only in word and conversation, but in meetings for the worship of God, and it grieved me exceedingly to see any of them overcome with sleep; and my concern for one friend on that account was so great, that I knew
not

not what was best to do, and reasoned after this manner: Lord! thou knowest that I am young, and he an elderly man, he will not take it well that I should speak to him, and perhaps I may yet fall, and if so, the more I take upon me the greater my fall will be. Besides, though I have spoken in meetings for discipline, when truth hath been strong upon me, yet out of meetings I am not fit to reprove, or speak to particulars. For I was cautious, indeed, in those days, of talking about religion or good things, from a fear of getting a habit thereof, and so not know the true motion, which I thought I had observed to be the failing of some. In this streight it came into my mind to go to the person in the night, as the most private time and manner: for if I took him aside before or after a meeting, others might wonder for what, and I might betray my weakness, and reproach the good cause, and do no good; and if the friend should be displeased with me, he might publickly shew what otherwise he would conceal after a private deliberation. So in the evening I went, desiring the Lord to go with me and guide me, if it was a motion from him. When I came to the house it was dark; I called, and the friend came out to see who was there, and invited me in. I told him I was in haste to go home, but wanted to speak with him if he pleased, and so passed quietly toward home, to draw him from the door, and then told him my concern for him, in a clofe, honeft, plain manner, and, without ftaying to reafon much, left him in a tender loving difpofition, as I believe. I returned home with great inward peace. " When thou doeft or giveft " alms, let not thy left hand know what thy " right doth," was an excellent precept: that left hand of felf fhould not act in fuch things; no matter how privately they are done, they often anfwer the end better; neither is it a fault to lay things low and familiar, the truth will have its own weight, and accompany what it dictates with its own evidence. My intention in writing this is to encourage the humbled careful traveller in the way of his duty. At fome times it appeared to be likely to do moft good to write my mind to fome, which I did with fuccefs, as I aimed only at a difcharge of duty in the moft private manner, and the good of thofe to whom I wrote.

When I had entered the twenty-fifth year of my age I accomplifhed marriage with Margaret Brown, a virtuous young woman, whom I had loved as a fifter for feveral years, becaufe I believed fhe loved religion. I think I may fay fafely it was in a good degree of the Lord's pure fear, and a fenfe of the pointings of truth, on both fides, that we took each other, on the 27th day of the eleventh month 1729, (old ftile) in an appointed meeting at Eaft Nottingham, and I thought that our Heavenly Father owned us

with

with his presence at that time. The covenants made in marriage are exceeding great, and I think they can never be rightly kept and truly performed without Divine assistance; and am convinced, if all who enter into a marriage state would in the Lord's fear truly seek his assistance, they would know their own tempers kept down; and instead of jarring and discord, unity of spirit, harmony of conduct, and a concern to be exemplary to their offspring, would increase and be maintained.

The summer following, in the year 1730, a monthly-meeting was settled at Nottingham,. (being before a branch of New-garden monthly-meeting) by the advice and appointment of the quarterly-meeting. This brought a fear and weighty concern upon me and many others, that the affairs of truth might be managed to the honour thereof; for we had but few substantial elderly friends. In a sense of our weakness, it was the breathing desire of my soul that the Lord would be pleased, for his own sake, and the honour of his great name, to be near to his children, and inspire them with wisdom and judgment for his own work; and, blessed for ever be his holy name! I believe he heard our cry, and in measure answered our prayers: being kept low and humble, it was a growing time to several. My affection for friends of New-garden monthly-meeting was so great, that for many months after we parted from them, I seldom missed attending it, and therein had great satisfaction; and some of their members frequently attended ours, for our love towards each other was mutual.

When I was about twenty-six years of age some friends were appointed to perform a family visit, and being desirous of my company, I joined with them, and therein felt the ownings of truth in some degree: but notwithstanding I saw at times the states of families and particulars, yet not in so clear a manner as I thought necessary to become my duty to open my mouth in the service, save now and then, in a private way to particulars, of which none knew, except those to whom I spake. At one house the friends on the service had a good opportunity, several young folks, some of whom were not of the family, being present. I felt the Divine presence to be very near, and a motion to conclude that sitting in supplication and thanksgiving to the Lord, but was not hasty, for fear of doing what was not required of me: so omitted it, and afterwards asked an experienced worthy minister if he had ever known any friend appear in a meeting in publick prayer before they had ever appeared in publick testimony? which enquiry I made in such a manner, as to give him no mistrust of me. He answered, "nay; I believe it "would be very uncommon." It struck me pretty closely, but I kept my condition very private, having been exceedingly fearful

ful of deception, and now began to doubt whether it was not a delusion for me to entertain an apprehension that I should be called to the work of the ministry, the concern whereof had been at times very heavy upon me, though no motion that felt like a gentle command to break silence, until at the house before mentioned. Now I let in reasoning, and so departed for a time from my inward guide and safest counsellor, as all assuredly will, who place their dependence on man for instruction to perform duties required of them, or who forbear, or reason against the humbling gentle motions and leadings of the spirit of truth. Much safer it is to attend steadily thereunto for instruction and ability to perform religious services, which, when so performed in meekness, we ought to be tender of the sentiments of our brethren concerning them, and not over confident of our call and commission; for our brethren have a measure of the same spirit by which we are taught, and have a sense and right thereby given, to judge of our service. A becoming diffidence of ourselves, and a readiness to attend to the advice of such, is ever the badge of true discipleship: humbling Divine Love teaches to esteem others rather than ourselves.

This was an exercising time to me, but I did not discover it to any one: I seemed to be quite forsaken, though not sensible of much judgment for my omission of duty;

for I could with sincerity appeal to him who knoweth all things, that it did not proceed from wilful disobedience, but a fear of following a wrong spirit; and a secret hope revived, that my gracious Lord and Master would not quite cast me off: and, blessed be his holy name! he did not leave me very long before I was favoured as usual, but had no motion of the same kind.

When this visit was over I kept much at home, yet was careful to attend meetings on the first and other days of the week, and found work enough to watch against a lukewarm, indolent spirit, which would come over me when I sat down to wait upon God. Though I came to the meeting in a lively warm engagement of mind, I found the warfare against lukewarmness, sleepiness, and a roving mind, must be steadily maintained; and if none of these hindrances were given way to, the Lord, when he had proved his children, would arise for their help, and scatter his and their enemies, which my soul hath experienced many times beyond expression. The Lord alone is all-powerful, and worthy to be waited upon and worshipped in humility and reverent adoration of soul for ever. Indolence and lukewarmness bring darkness and death over a meeting, and, when generally given way to, occasion hard work for even the most livingly exercised friends to get from under the burthen and weight thereof. It was a mercy that I was preserved
seeking,

seeking, and could not be satisfied without feeling the renewings of Divine favour, by which I rather grew in the root of religion, though I thought very slow, but had hope it would be lasting.

The love of truth, I believe it was, and a desire that the discipline and good order of the church might be maintained, made me willing to take considerable pains to attend neighbouring monthly-meetings, which I think was a blessing to me in some good degree, being thereby often instructed; and I have often admired at the slackness of some, that suffer trifling things to keep them from their meetings for worship on week days and first days; for though curiosity brings such to monthly-meetings, they are seldom of any real service when they come, not being sensible of that pure Divine Love in which the church, through its several members, edifieth itself: and as any become truly sensible thereof, they will delight to wait upon God with their brethren and sisters, who is the fountain of pure Love, and so fills the hearts of his humble depending children therewith, that by it they are known to be his disciples.

In the year 1731 our ancient and worthy friend William Brown, who had been in the station of an elder many years, growing feeble and incapable to attend the quarterly-meeting of ministers and elders, friends of our particular meeting proposed me to the monthly-

monthly-meeting for that service; which brought a close exercise upon me, considering myself a youth, and the weight of the service: but, after a solid consideration, I found most peace in submitting to the meeting, with fervent inward desires that the Lord would be pleased to be with me therein, to preserve me from acting or judging in my own will and spirit, knowing that the service could not be performed but by wisdom, understanding and ability from him. When I attended those large and weighty meetings of ministers and elders, the care and fear that was upon me is not easily expressed: and may I never forget the gracious condescension of kind Providence, who was pleased to own me by the shedding abroad of his love in my heart, that I verily thought they resembled the school of the prophets; the High Priest, great Prophet, and Bishop of Souls, our Lord Jesus Christ, being president among them.

An apprehension that I should be called to the ministry, and a concern on that account, had been at times for several years weightily on my mind; but I now again thought I was mistaken in that belief, and that it was only a preparative to qualify me for the station of an elder, and thereby my exercise became somewhat lighter for a time. The tenderness and love I felt to those engaged in publick ministry was very great, and I believe I was made helpful to some,

by

by giving private hints, when and to whom I thought there was occasion, in plainness, simplicity, and fear, which often afforded instruction to myself, as well as to them.

In 1733 I accompanied friends on another visit to families, wherein, at times, I felt the opening of truth in the love of it, and a few words to speak to the states of some; though in great fear, lest I should put my hand to that weighty work without the real requiring of duty: and at one family, on a morning pretty early, being the first we went to on that day, I thought it would be better for the whole family, in a religious sense, if the heads of it were more zealous in attending meetings. I saw the necessity of being examples to children and servants, by a careful attendance of meetings for worship on the first and other days of the week, but I was so weak and poor, that I doubted whether it was my duty to mention any thing thereof to them, so concluded to omit it; by which I hoped to judge of what I had been about before, and so grew easy in my mind: and as we were on the way to the next house, I began to judge, that I had no real business to have said any thing at any house; and having forborne in my own will, I was now left to my own judgment for a time. At the next house friends were particularly opened, and tenderly concerned to speak to several states, and of several matters which I thought instructive; but I sat dry and

and poor, and so remained during our passage to the next house, where I fared no better, but worse, my feeling and judgment being quite gone, as to the service in which we were engaged; and though I did not say any thing to the other friends how it fared with me, yet they were affected therewith, as I apprehended. I was in great darkness and distress, and sometimes thought of leaving the company privately, and go home; but again concluded that would not only be a disappointment to my friends, but dishonourable to truth, which made me determine to go forward, and endure my own pain, as much undiscovered as possible. My companions, as I before observed, were affected, and all, save one, seemed closed up from doing the service, and in the evening of the same day, at the last house, all of them were silent. There was a school-house near, the master being a friend, and the children mostly belonging to friends, whom some of our company appeared willing to visit, but others being doubtful, we omitted it; which now some thought was not right, and that therefore this cloud of darkness and distress came upon us, and we were willing to meet at the school-house next morning, to try if we could recover our former strength in the ownings of truth; which being agreed to, each took his way home. It being now night, and I alone, I rode slow, under a deep exercise of mind and humble inquiry into

the

the cause of my own distress; and after some time, being favoured with great calmness and quietude of mind, I was inwardly instructed after this manner: 'Thou sawest what was wanting in a family this morning, and would not exhort to more diligence or amendment in that respect, and therefore if they continue to do wrong, it shall be required of thee;' on which I became broken in spirit, and cried in secret; May I not perform it yet, and be restored to thy favour? O Lord! I am now willing to do whatsoever thou requirest of me, if thou wilt be pleased to be-with me. And, blessed be his name! in mercy he heard my supplication, and I was fully persuaded that I must go to the house again, which I concluded to do next morning, and went home with a degree of comfort, and, being weary in body and mind, slept sweetly, and awoke in the morning quiet and easy in spirit; and now began to conclude, that I might meet my company and be excused; but my covenant of going was brought to my remembrance, and I was given to believe that peace was restored on condition of my performance; therefore I went to the house, though several miles distant, before sun-rise. The man of the house was up; he invited me in, and I followed him, and sitting down by the fire (being cool weather) with my mind retired, I felt that I must not speak before the rest of the family, but rather in private,

yet

yet was fearful of calling him out, being unwilling to discover any thing to them. In the mean time he went out, and walked the way I was to go; I followed, and told him how I felt when we were at his house the morning before, and could not be easy without exhorting him to be more careful in several respects, and a better example to his family in his attendance of meetings; he seemed affected, and said he hoped he should mind my advice. I then left him, and met my companions at the school-house, and enjoyed great peace. I leave this remark to excite all to dwell in meekness and fear, and to beware of the will of the creature, and the reasonings of flesh and blood, which lead into doubting and disobedience. They who are faithful in small things, shall truly know an increase in that wisdom and knowledge which is from above.

Before we had gone through this visit I attended the quarterly-meeting of ministers and elders at Concord, and as I sat therein, the unwearied adversary renewed a former charge against me, by suggesting to my mind that I might know I had been wrong, and under a delusion, in entertaining a belief that I should be called to the work of the ministry; for that all who had ever been rightly engaged therein, it was in a cross greatly to the will of the creature, which was not my case, for I was willing. This I felt to be true, and was therefore now exceedingly dis-

distressed, not considering that I was made willing by the weight of the exercise, which had been several years at times very heavy upon me, until it seemed as a fire in my bones, and as though "I was dumb with "silence, I held my peace, even from good; "and my sorrow was stirred; my heart "was hot within me; while I was musing, "the fire burned," Psal. xxxix. 2, 3. While under this conflict, a friend stood up with these words: "Also I heard the voice of "the Lord, saying, whom shall I send, and "who will go for us? Then said I, here "am I, send me," Isa. vi. 8. shewing, that 'to them whose will was rightly sub-'jected to the Lord, it became their meat 'and drink to do the will of him who had 'subjected them by his divine power, and 'influenced their hearts with his love to 'mankind:' by which I was relieved, and my spirit humbled and made thankful. Next morning, being the first day of the week, I went to Kennet meeting, and toward the close thereof something appeared to my mind to offer, but was fearful that the motion for speaking was not enough powerful, and had like to have forborne, but remembering what I had suffered by neglecting a weak motion in a family visit, as already related, I stood up, and spake a few sentences in great fear and brokenness of spirit, and had solid satisfaction. I attended the quarterly-meeting of business at Concord on second day, on
my

my return from whence I let in the old reasoner, who suggested to me, that if I was called to the publick ministry, I had not waited for a sufficient commission to speak; for some had been raised up with great power and authority they could not withstand, but that I might have been still and quiet, the motion was so gentle and low; and that I must not think to speak in publick testimony in great meetings with so small a motion, and in so doing I had committed a sin that would not be readily forgiven, perhaps a sin against the Holy Ghost. My exercise was great, but as I endeavoured to be quiet in my mind, seeking to know the truth of my present condition, I was secretly drawn to follow and attend to something that spoke inwardly, after this manner, 'If thou wast to take a lad, an entire
' stranger to thy language and business, how-
' ever likely he appeared for service, thou
' must speak loud and distinctly to him, and
' perhaps with an accent or tone that might
' shew thee to be in earnest, to engage his
' attention, and point out the business; but
' thou wouldst expect it should be otherwise
' with a child brought up in thine house,
' who knew thy language, and with whom
' thou hadst been familiar: thou wouldst
' expect him to wait by thee, and watch
' thy motions, so as to be instructed by thine
' eye looking upon him, or pointing thy fin-
' ger, and wouldst rebuke or correct such an
' one

' one, if he did not obey thy will on such a
' small intelligent information.' I was instantly relieved thereby, and leave my reader to judge from whence this intimation came, believing it would be no crime in me to judge it to be from the Spirit of Truth, that was to lead and guide into all Truth.

When this meeting was over, being in the ninth month, 1733, we proceeded to finish our family visit. The part which remained was on the west side of Susquehanna, at Bush river, and a few families begun to settle near Deer-creek. We were remarkably favoured with the presence of our great and good Master, who opened the states of families to us, and gave ability to speak thereto: may his his holy name be praised! The visit being finished, we returned home; and in a short time after, as I sat in a week day meeting, I had a few words fresh before me, with a gentle motion to deliver them, which I feared to omit, still remembering what followed a former neglect; so I expressed what was on my mind, and therein had peace, and afterwards was silent for several weeks, in which time I let in a fear I was forsaken by my dear Lord and Master, whom I loved above all things. For I had no openings in heavenly things, as I thought, but was left poor and needy; yet I loved friends, and, remembering a saying of a minister formerly, " We know that we are passed from death " unto life, because we love the brethren,"

1 John

1 John iii. 14. I hoped that I was not quite forgotten. Some remarkable sentences had fixed in my mind sometime before, which I now began to understand more sensibly. 'Ministry should be of necessity, and not of choice, and there is no living by silence, or by preaching merely.' For something in me was ready to wish to be employed, that I might have bread; for when I found a motion to speak I had the owning love of the heavenly Father, which is and ever will be bread to his children. The creaturely will would choose, and would be busy with questioning, Is it not, or may it not be so and so? This is that womanish part, which is not permitted to speak in the church.: it runs first into transgression, for want of learning of the husband at home, or being in subjection to him; which if Eve had literally done, instead of reasoning with the serpent that tempted, she might have been preserved from being a tempter. Our strength, preservation, health, and peace, stand in our entire subjection to the will of the Lord, whether in silence or speaking, suffering or reigning, still dwelling with the seed (Christ) in our own hearts, humbly waiting for and feeling after his power to arise, who is the Resurrection and the Life, and when he is pleased to appear, his children partake in measure of his glory.

I continued in the station of an elder, and sometimes delivered a few sentences in publick

lick teſtimony, which occaſioned me to apprehend that I ſhould not be in my proper place, except I requeſted to be releaſed from my elderſhip. After a time of weighty conſideration, I modeſtly requeſted that friends would conſider my caſe; for inſtead of taking care of the miniſtry of others, I ſtood in need of the care of others, and that it would be relieving to my mind, if they would nominate an elder in my room; which was taken into conſideration for a time, friends waiting, I ſuppoſe, to ſee what proof I ſhould make of my miniſtry. I attended the winter quarterly-meeting of miniſters and elders, and had to give an account of the miniſtry at our meeting. The elders being called to anſwer one after another in order, according to the ſettlement of the meetings they belonged to, a fear ſtruck me left a form of words was too much in general obſerved, particularly, ' that the miniſtry was well re-
' ceived.' When my turn came, I could not be eaſy without varying that part, and inſtead of ſaying ' the miniſtry of the miniſters is well received,' I ſaid that I believed the miniſtry of the publick friends was generally approved of; and added, that I did wiſh that the miniſtry of all the miniſtring friends was better received than I conceived it was. Whereupon I was aſked what I meant; and, under the weight I felt on my mind, I replied it was not from a thought of bearing hard on the ſervice of the publick friends,

but from the difference of approving thereof, becaufe they believed it to be right, and attending no further, which would not do the work; but to put in practice what they heard recommended, was only well receiving of it, and if that was really the cafe, our fociety would appear more beautiful than at prefent. Thus the matter clofed, and I had peace in the remark. I think this was the laft meeting I attended as an elder: before the next quarterly-meeting in the fecond month, 1734, another was recommended in my place.

About this time, as I fat in one of our own meetings, I felt a flow of affection to the people; for many not of our fociety came there, perhaps out of curiofity, feveral young minifters having come forth in publick teftimony. In which extraordinary flow of affection I had a very bright opening, as I thought, and expected to ftand up with it very foon, but being willing to weigh it carefully was not very forward, viewing its decreafing brightnefs, until fomething faid, as it were within me, ' Is the woe in it? is ' neceffity laid upon thee? 1 Cor. ix. 16. and therefore woe if thou preach not the gofpel?' This put me to a ftand, and made me feel after the living prefence of him, in whofe name and power I defired to fpeak, if I appeared in teftimony; and not feeling the pure life and power of truth, fo as to ftand up, the brightnefs of the vifion faded, and

left

left me quiet, humble, and thankful for this preservation. The drawing strength and lusting desire of the unstable, who centre not to the pure gift in themselves, are as the many waters, or sea of mystery Babylon, for her merchants to sail their ships and trade upon. This was a time of inward growing to me, the welfare of the churches was strongly desired, and the extendings of the love of the Heavenly Father I felt at times to reach over sea and land, to my great admiration; but however my heart was enlarged, I believed it was my duty to retire inward, and wait with patience until my friends should so approve of my ministry, as to recommend me as a minister, before I made any request to go much abroad; though I went to some neighbouring meetings, such as I could go to in a morning, and return home at night, but not without acquainting some elderly friends therewith, and desiring their company, which I generally had.

In the winter 1735-6, William Brown, my brother-in-law, my sister, Dinah Brown, (then a widow) and myself, were all recommended to the meeting of ministers and elders as ministers, and at this meeting I let a certain friend know that for some time I had a desire to visit friends at Newtown, Middletown, Goshen, Caln, and Bradford meetings, hoping that he would go with me; for without some suitable companion I was not easy to go, because it would be necessary

cessary that notice should be given, to answer the end of a visit; which he also thought necessary, and let me know that he would take the needful care, which I supposed was previously to inform some friends of each meeting, in order that they might acquaint their neighbours, if they had freedom, and I was easy, not knowing but he would bear me company. On third day I was at the general meeting of worship held at Providence, and at the breaking up thereof, the friend whom I had spoken to stood up, and gave public notice that I intended to sit with friends at the meetings aforesaid, and named the days in order, and requested friends would take proper care to give notice; at which I was exceedingly surprized, and repented that I had spoken thereof. I would have gladly ran home, but for fear of bringing a reproach, and to me it seemed likely it would be the case if I pursued the tract laid out for me: in this strait I was humbled, even to weeping. A sympathizing experienced friend came to me, and spake affectionately, bidding me not to be cast down, for it was heard with gladness that it was in my heart to visit those meetings; and that if I lived, and did well, I must meet with greater trials. I suppose friends of those meetings knew more of me than I expected, for I had carefully attended meetings of discipline several years, and had been sometimes active therein: the meetings were generally pretty full

full, and I believe truth owned my service. In this little journey friends were very kind to me, and I was afraid too free in manifesting of it. Indeed there are many indulgent nurses, many forward instructors, but too few fathers in the church; who, having been acquainted with him the Great Alpha in their tender beginning, and by dwelling in his holy counsel and fear, have the care of the members at heart, and in the wisdom of truth know how to instruct, advise, and conduct themselves towards such who are called to the Lord's work, according to their several dispositions, growths, and gifts received; in order that they might be preserved growing in and by him, the Alpha, experiencing him, their beginning, to be with them, and to be the Omega in their conclusion; the First and the Last, all in all, the Lord God over all, blessed in himself and the Son of his love, our holy High Priest and Instructor. For want of proper caution herein some have valued themselves above what they ought, and thereby reduced their credit with others.

In the summer following I felt a secret gentle draft to visit the meetings in the back parts of Chester, Philadelphia and Bucks counties; which continuing with me, and my brother-in-law William Brown having the like concern, we acquainted friends at our monthly-meeting, late in the fall of the year, and had their concurrence, and I believe

lieve their good wishes for us. So in the tenth month, 1736, we proceeded, and went to Goshen, Radnor, and to a general meeting at Haverford, and to an evening meeting at a school-house in Upper Merion, and over Schuylkill to Plymouth: we had good satisfaction mostly. I could see that my brother grew in his gift; and after one of the meetings, a well-meaning friend told me that I was a seer, and knew the states of people better than they could inform me, at which I felt some secret pleasure, yet not without (as I thought) an humble fear, knowing that flattery or unguarded commendation, if listened to, is a kind of poison to young ministers, and sometimes makes them swell beyond the proper size. At Plymouth I had an open meeting, and it seemed to me as if what I had to say was received freely by the people, and after meeting I was filled with joy to such a degree that I wept, and dropped behind my company (to keep undiscovered) in our going to a friend's house; inwardly praying that it might be taken from me, for I feared that, by the natural part in me, it was taken to excess. Next day we had a small meeting in Job Pugh's house, where I thought I saw the states of particulars very clear, and had something to say, which perhaps I delivered in too strong terms, considering my age and experience in the ministry: a becoming fear and modesty in expression is very ornamental and safe for ministers,

nisters, both young and old. After meeting we went home with Edward Evans to North Wales, who conversed but little with us, but was grave and solid, and therein a good example to me; for sometimes young ministers hurt themselves by too much talking, and draw from others of like freedom things not convenient for them to hear. The next day we were at North Wales meeting, which was large, being first day. My brother William Brown appeared in the fore part, and had good service; afterwards I stood up, with a large and good opening as I thought, but found hard work, and sat down again without much relief, which being a little unusual, I ventured to stand up again, and, with a zeal that exceeded my childish knowledge, laid on some strokes with the strength of the man's part more than with the humbling power of truth: for if we deliver hard things to the people, we should ever remember that we are flesh and blood, and by nature subject to the same frailties. This would lead us closely to attend to the power, and to minister only in the ability of truth, in the meekness, gentleness, and wisdom which it inspires. I soon sat down again, and in a moment felt myself left in great darkness, and friends broke up the meeting in a minute or two after, which I soon thought was rather unkind, as it seemed to shew a publick dislike, when a private admonition, which I believed was my due,

would have anfwered the end better. But when I knew they held an afternoon meeting, I judged I had infringed on the time, and the weight of the trial fettled ftill deeper on my mind. In the afternoon I fat filent, and was very much dejected, and my good friend Evan Evans, an experienced minifter and father in the church, bid me be fteady and inward, looking to the Lord, who knew how to deal with his children, and gently correct, as well when they went too faft as too flow. This fatherly tender hint fully opened my eyes; for before I was in fome doubt wherein I had miffed: I now believed he faw I was too zealous and forward, and believed alfo that he had judgment of truth, this was enough for me; I abhorred myfelf, and was in great fear that I fhould not be forgiven. Another friend told me, that I only felt an oppofing fpirit in fome, whofe ftates had been remarkably fpoken to by me, and defired me not to be too much caft down, for I had the mind of truth. This, inftead of relieving, rather added to my affliction; for I faw it would have a tendency, if heeded, to take me from under the hand of the Lord, which was heavy upon me; and fomething in me faid, ' Let God be true, and every man a liar;' ' keep to the witnefs in thine own heart;' ' attend to the Spirit of Truth there, and ' mind its reproof.' Man, through natural affection and fympathy, may err, and adminifter

nifter false instruction, but the other proceeds from the God of Truth. I would have given all that I had to have been at home; for I greatly feared that I should bring a reproach on the truth, the honour whereof was dear to me. I hid my distress as much as possible, and proceeded to attend meetings with my brother, whom I greatly preferred, and was afraid to discourage by my complaints.

We were at a meeting at Skippack, and at another at Perkioming or New Providence, in each whereof I had so much light and understanding as to offer a few words, but the service lay chiefly on my brother. From thence we went to Oley, where I had a few things to deliver in a friend's house in an evening, sitting with his family, which was large. The friend in great tenderness observed afterward, that revelation was not ceased, for their states were very exactly spoken to; at which I marvelled, for I was greatly reduced, and thought myself one of the poorest and most unqualified that ever travelled in that great service in which we were now engaged. This dispensation, though sorrowful to wade through, was very humbling and profitable to me, who perhaps but a little before was ready to think I knew something about preaching, but now knew nothing, that I might more fully understand that he who thinketh of himself " he know-
" eth any thing, knoweth nothing as he
" ought

"ought to know;" to wit, that all pure knowledge is sealed up in him who is the Fountain of Wisdom and Knowledge, to be only opened by himself to his dependant children, by the revelation of his own Spirit, when and to whom he pleases.

From hence we went to Maiden Creek, and to Richland in Bucks county, being still low in my mind, yet favoured for a few minutes in meetings, in which I had a few sentences, and then was closed up again. I was like one who having learned a few things or rules in literal knowledge, was again turned back again to his beginning.

From thence we went to Plumstead in Bucks county, (here I was rather more enlarged) and to Buckingham, Wrightstown, Falls, Middletown, Bristol, and over on the ice to Burlington in New Jersey, the weather being exceeding cold, and came back again on the ice over Delaware the same evening to Bristol, and thence proceeded to Byberry and Horsham meetings; and by this time I was relieved from the depression of spirit I felt before, yet was under an humble reverent fear, not forgetting the meeting at North Wales: I was in some degree again admitted to behold the lifting up of the Heavenly Father's countenance, which makes the solitary rejoice. From Horsham we went to a meeting appointed at William Hallowell's. The company of the man who undertook to shew us the way not being agreeable, we
persuaded

persuaded him to return, and so were left, not knowing the way to the house, which made me very thoughtful, lest we should miss our way, and friends would then be blamed for neglect of duty towards us. As I was thus pondering in my mind a faith arose that Providence could direct, and that moment I beheld the track of a man who had crossed the road we were in, and felt a sudden turn of mind to follow the same, which made me quite easy. It brought us to a field, where we found the fence down on both sides, and led to the house where friends were gathered, and we were not discovered to be without a guide; for which I was thankful, believing it to be the secret direction of kind Providence, and not barely chance. I relate this with a view to excite such as may meet with difficulties to rely on him alone who can shew the way, and give faith to follow; but man must be humble and quiet in mind, to understand the inward gentle sense that truth favours with. This small gathering was owned in a good degree with the Divine presence.

From thence we passed to Abington and Frankfort meetings, and to Philadelphia; and after visiting of those meetings we turned to Germantown, and so over Schuylkill to Merion meeting, where we met our worthy friend John Fothergill, who had great and good service therein, with whom my brother William Brown returned to Philadelphia,

phia, to the quarterly-meeting, which began next day; and while he was absent from me, I attended Springfield and Newtown meetings, when he again came to me. We attended some other meetings until our quarterly-meeting began, at which was our friend John Cadwalader from Horsham, who had good service. After which I returned home, and was glad to sit with friends in our own meeting, wherein I did not see it was my place to say much, but by example to recommend silence.

Early this spring (1737) the Lord was pleased to try me with poverty and inward want, which brought me into great searchings of heart, and secret enquiry into the cause; but I could not understand that I had wilfully disobeyed, neither stood convicted in my mind for doing amiss; but my poverty and inward want increased, with distress and doubting to that degree, that I began to fear I had mistaken, and took error for truth, and in my own imagination formed a religion, and for the rebellion of my youth was suffered to go on until now; and all that ever I had done was brought into judgment and reduced to nothing; and the enemy endeavoured to stir me up to impatience, and to persuade me that my transgressions would never be forgiven. Many days of sorrow and nights of sore distress I passed through, and began to despair of ever beholding

holding the light of the Heavenly countenance lifted up towards me again.

Towards the laſt of the third month I went to Sadſbury, to ſettle a diſpute about the bounds of land; and having ſomething to do near Samuel Nutt's iron works on French Creek, as I was going thither, being alone, and my inward ſorrow and diſtreſs very great, I thought I would now endeavour to vent it, were it but in mournful groans; and drawing in my breath, in order to vent it in a groan, my inward anguiſh ſeemed to burn like fire, and I was inſtantly ſtaid from breaking forth; for I was perſuaded my paſſion of grief, if given way unto, would go beyond bounds, to the tearing of my cloaths, if no further: my heart not being tender, I could not weep, which brought me to a more calm pauſe than I had known for ſome time, and therein was ready to ſay, Can the good hand be ſtill near to ſtay me? O that I may have patience given, and reſolution ſtrengthened to continue ſeeking, and if at laſt I ſhould periſh, that it may be at his footſtool! For a ſmall ſpace I had ſome hope of beholding again him whom my ſoul once loved above all things; but in a few miles riding it began to look pleaſant to me to go into ſome remote place, where I ſhould not be known. When reflecting thus—what! abandon mine acquaintance! violate my marriage covenant, and leave my deareſt connections! I ſuddenly
knew

knew this prospect of pleasure was from the evil one, and something in me abhorred it as wicked, and as it were closed my eyes therefrom; so that evening I went to the house of a former intimate acquaintance to lodge, who received me kindly, and in the evening brought a book containing some astronomical problems, and began to converse very freely thereon, supposing it would be pleasant to me as aforetime; but I was heavy in my spirit, and inwardly thoughtful about something of another nature, and he soon perceiving his conversation on that subject was disagreeable, proposed my going to bed, as fittest for a weary man, judging that to be my present ailment; I was glad of the offer, and immediately accepted thereof. I now saw clearly that when my mind was turned from delighting in that wherein our former friendship consisted, my company was rather unpleasant to him. I soon left his house in the morning, dispatched my business, and returned home with as much speed as I could, without the least inclination to go elsewhere. I believe my prayer was heard, for I had patience granted to me; I say granted, because no man can endue himself therewith, and I think my distress gradually abated after the time aforementioned.

When one has fasted, and suffered the want of natural food for a long season, men of prudence will portion out the food they give to such with care, that strength may be

be increased and the constitution preserved healthful and sound. The Lord, whose love and care to his children doth far exceed that of any natural parent to his offspring, dealt with me in his tender mercy, giving at times, by the gentle touches of his love, to feel that he had not forsaken me, which in a few minutes would be again withdrawn; but, though of short continuance, was sufficient for me to own it was worth all my sorrowful longing for; and hereby he was pleased to let me experimentally know the value of heavenly bread by the want of it. Having food and raiment, I was now taught to be therewith content: the renewing of heavenly favour, and the covering of the Holy Spirit, so as to be admitted to stand before him in humble reverence with gracious acceptance, was all my soul craved. I neither wanted this man's gift, nor the other man's popularity and eloquence, but to be in mercy admitted into the number of his family, and occupying mine own gift to his honour alone that gave it. When Peter was examined by his Lord, whom he had denied through fear, " Lovest thou me more than " these?" the third time answered, " Thou " knowest all things, thou knowest that I " love thee," he did not answer the question in its full extent, viz. *more than these*, with respect to the rest of the disciples, who had not denied their Lord and Master, as Peter had done, who was nevertheless looked
upon

upon with forgiving compassion, and therefore had need to love in proportion. Perhaps his honest confession and appeal to his Master's knowledge might shorten his answer. His threefold charge of feeding the sheep and lambs of his Lord was necessary, to gain his diligent attention to the work of him whom he had three times denied: he to whom much is forgiven loveth much, if he is not ungrateful. No marvel that I met with this trial of my love and affection, who so often (not through fear, but the desire of indulging my creaturely will) had denied or neglected to follow my Lord and Master, who had so early made me acquainted with his will, and who now had passed by mine offences, and called me to work in his vineyard. Now I was made thankful for favours which before had been scarcely owned as such: for to be preserved inwardly watchful, and quietly resigned to wait upon the Lord, though we partake not of immediate consolation by the renewing of life, is a great blessing, for which we ought to be thankful, as we cannot stay our own minds, nor curb our thoughts. And I did believe that labour was healthful, created an appetite, and sweetened the relish of rest and food in a spiritual as well as natural sense, and therefore I wanted not to eat the bread of idleness, and live on the labour of others.

After this trial, which continued most of the summer, I was much favoured with the incomes

incomes of Divine Love and Life, and in the winter following visited most of the meetings in Chester county, and some few in Philadelphia county. The weather was very cold, being about the middle of the tenth month when I set out, and in my journey went to visit a worthy friend who was indisposed, and lodged at his house; and as we sat together in the evening he asked me why I chose the winter season to visit my friends, for many infirm folks could hardly attend meetings, and said he was sometimes ready to query whether publick friends do not take that time to serve their Master, because they could do but little for themselves. I was thoughtful and low in my mind before, and had some reasoning, whether it had not been better that I had staid at home, than ventured out on the service at that time of the year. Though I thought I had an engagement sufficient when I set out, this query of his made me more thoughtful, and added to my reasoning; but I soon recovered strength, and it came fresh in my mind to ask him whether friends could eat to supply and sustain their bodies in the summer, and partake also of spiritual food for their souls in that season, so as not to labour in the winter, and care for the sustenance of their bodies; or assemble and attend meetings to worship and wait upon God for spiritual food for their souls? He acknowledged I had by this query

query satisfied him to the full, and said he was glad of my visit, and hoped his talking as he did would not discourage me; for I believe he saw it brought a damp over me at first. This answer I believe was given to me for mine own help, and was encouragement to me through this journey, in which I had most of the time Joshua Johnson of Londongrove for a companion, who was very agreeable, and in my return home I felt great peace.

CHAP. II.

His journey with Robert Jordan to the Western part of Maryland in the year 1738. Also to the Quarterly-meeting at Shrewsbury in New Jersey—And with John Hunt through that province—His visit to the Eastern shore of Maryland—His journey to Fairfax and Hopewell in Virginia, in company with a committee of friends—And a second time to the Eastern shore of Maryland, with John Cadwalader and companion—And his visit to New-England, in company with Samuel Hopwood, in 1742.

IN the summer following I went with Robert Jordan to West-river yearly-meeting, in Maryland, and we visited most of the meetings of friends in that province, and his company was profitably instructive to me, who was but young in the miniſtry. I think I knew him well: he had a good gift of the miniſtry, and was highly favoured in the living openings of truth, but was often low in mind, and very humble in ſpirit. One time, as we were riding together, he lagged behind for ſeveral miles; I aſked him why he rode ſo ſlow, he made no reply, whereupon I ſtopped until he came up: his countenance was ſolid, and looked as if he had been weeping; I aſked what ailed him. After ſome time he told me that he had been thinking of the great favours which man partook of, particularly in being placed over the beaſts of the field, and how eaſily they were broke and made ſubject to his will; what a ſmall turn with the bridle would put them to the right hand or the left, and on a gentle motion would amend or ſlacken their pace, at the will or pleaſure of the rider; and that man, the moſt noble and intelligent creature, ſhould ſo far neglect the duty of a willing ſubjection to his Maker, who ſo highly has favoured him with temporal bleſſings, and the knowledge of heavenly things. I had been at that meeting about three years before, having had ſome buſineſs to do for a friend of mine on the Eaſtern ſhore of Cheſapeak, and croſſed over the bay to the Weſtern ſhore, and was at the yearly-meeting; and being grieved at the conduct of ſome of the elders, whoſe age, if they had kept to the truth, and had been zealous for the honour thereof, would have made them better examples, I spoke my mind plainly to them, but not without proper caution (as I thought) both with respect to my youth and their age; but some seemed a little warmed thereby, and asked for my certificate, if I had any. I honestly told them the principal business that brought me from home was temporal, which having accommodated, I thought I might attend that meeting without offence, if I did not misbehave myself. William Richardson desired friends to consider what I had said, for he believed if they did they would perceive the young man had a certificate with him, that might answer for one of a neighbouring province to attend such a meeting:

It may not be unseasonable to relate that in the year 1736, one night, as I lay in bed, my mind was uncommonly affected with the incomes of Divine Love and Life, and therein I had a view of the churches in New-Jersey, with a clear prospect that I should visit them: and in that prospect and the strength of affection which I then felt, I said in my heart, It is enough, I will prepare for the journey as soon as I can hear of a suitable companion; for I do not expect that I shall have a clearer sight than I now have. I soon heard of a friend who had a visit to New-Jersey before him; I spoke to him about my concern; he let me know that he knew of a companion, and they had agreed
upon

upon a time to proceed. After I had mentioned it to him and some other friends, my concern seemed to die away; but I remembered the resolution that I took up, and that I then had thought I would not look to be bidden again; and was fearful something had drawn my mind from the proper attention to that opening, which was the reason it seemed to go off; but the more I strove to look after it, the duller it grew. I then sorely repented that I had spoken about it, and thought it should be a warning to me in future: for I began to see there was a difference between seeing what was to be done, and being bidden to do the thing shewn. Besides this, I had to consider there was a time to bud, a time to blossom, a time for fruit to set and appear, and a time for it to ripen.

And in the fore part of the winter, 1738, I thought it seemed to revive, and when I saw John Hunt, a friend from England, I believed I should go with him when he went through New-Jersey, and told him what I thought, at which he rejoiced, for we were nearly united. So we appointed a time to meet at Philadelphia, and when we had so far concluded, being about six weeks beforehand, my concern, as I thought, soon withered away, and I began to be in great fear that I had been again too forward therein; but after some time of humbling exercise on that account, the Lord, whom I feared,

feared, from the love with which he was pleased to enrich my heart, gave me to remember, that when I made the appointment with my friend, it was in his fear, and great abasement of self, and, as I had seen clearly to make the appointment, it was my place to attend in humble reliance on him for ability to perform the embassy; for the Lord, who calleth and sendeth forth his own, will also provide all things convenient for them.

When the time came, I set forward very poor and needy, which continued until we entered our service. We took a few meetings before our general spring meeting, and after attending that we went to Woodberry, Piles-grove, Salem, Alloways-creek, Cohansie, and so to Cape May, and had some close work, but in the main satisfactory to ourselves at least. After having several meetings at and near the Capes, we went to Great-Egg-harbour, and had a meeting there, and another at the house of our friend Japhet Leeds, and so over the Marshes to Little-Egg-harbour river, and had two meetings with friends, in one of which I stood up with a large opening, as I thought; but after a short introduction it closed up, and I sat down again, which was some mortification to me as a man, though very profitable, being thereby taught to know that he that would speak as the oracle of God must, under the gentle burden of the word, in humble

ble fear wait for wisdom, utterance and ability, to perform the service to the edification of the church and his own inward peace, and not to look after large and specious openings, sometimes desirable to the creaturely part, both in ourselves and others, which must suffer famine.

At one of the meetings in these parts, coming very early, a friend belonging thereto invited us to go to his house, not far off, and he would put up our horses to hay during the time of the meeting, saying, that we must go to his house to dine; but I felt a stop in my mind, and told him that our horses could stand very well there until after meeting. It so fell out that neither of us said any thing in the meeting, which nevertheless was to us satisfactory; for we had a sense, that the people had been fed with words, and had a hunger thereafter, more than for the instruction of the pure word of Power and Life nigh in the heart and mouth, that they might not only hear it, but be found doers thereof. After the meeting no one asked us to dine, but went away and left us, and had it not been for the care of our kind guide, that came from the meeting we were last at, we should have been at a loss to have got forward. I mention this to shew how unacceptable silence is to such whose ears itch after words.

From hence we went through the desert to Upper Springfield, where we had a satisfactory

factory meeting; then taking the meetings northward to Stonybrook and Trenton, we returned to Bordentown, and so crossed Delaware. Some of the meetings were large, and very satisfactory under the owning of truth, the power whereof was in dominion, and the name of the Lord praised, who is worthy for ever; and some were remarkably close and hard, which made me remember a saying of that experienced minister and elder John Fothergill, that, 'When he was first 'in this country, he had some extraordinary 'meetings hereaway, the people being in- 'dustrious in a natural as well as spiritual 'sense, some of whom were now removed, 'and their children possessed the temporal 'estates of their fathers; and though their 'outward habitations looked spacious, their 'meetings for worship were dull and heavy, 'by reason of a worldly spirit, and their 'indifference about heavenly treasure.' One meeting which we were at was remarkably hard; my companion John Hunt was exceedingly exercised, under a sense that the people were too rich, full, and whole in their own eyes. He sat the meeting through, and suffered in silence; but I had something to say very close and particular, and felt a degree of the strength and power of truth to clear myself in an innocent and loving manner, and, remembering they were brethren, did not preach myself out of charity towards them, and so had peace. We went home

home with an elderly friend, who, in a stern manner, asked me from whence I came, and said I was a stranger to him. I answered him with a cheerful boldness. He asked me what my calling was; I told him husbandry. He farther queried if I was used to splitting of wood; I let him know I had practised it for many years. He again asked me, if I knew the meaning of a common saying of those who were used to that business, ' 'Tis soft 'knocks must enter hard blocks:' I told him I knew it well; but there was some old wood, that was rather decayed at heart, and to strike with a soft or gentle blow at a wedge in such blocks, would drive it to the head without rending them, and the labour would be lost, when a few smart lively strokes would burst them asunder. Whereupon he laid his hand on my shoulder, saying, ' Well, my lad; I perceive thou art ' born for a warrior, and I commend thee.' And thus we came off better than we expected; for I thought he pointed at my service that day. He was ever afterward very loving to me, and I was inwardly thankful that the Lord was near to me, for which I praise his sacred name! To be becomingly bold in the cause of truth, at times is particularly necessary; otherwise the weight of the testimony thereof would be lessened, and a carping spirit set over it.

From Bordentown we went to Plumstead, in Bucks-county, and on a first day had a

pretty

pretty good meeting, and to a monthly-meeting at Buckingham, then to Wrights-town, the Falls, and Middletown, which meetings were in a good degree satisfactory, the reaches of the Power of Truth being felt to extend, for which we were thankful. Though in some of them there is too great a want of faithful members to put the discipline in practice against those that were disorderly, and thereby brought a reproach on the truth. We then went to Philadelphia, and next day to Chester, from whence I went home the same day.

In the fall of the year 1740, I had some drawings in my mind to attend the quarterly-meeting at Shrewsbury, and was at several meetings on my way thither; at one of which a friend appeared, who I thought had good service in the fore part of his testimony; but as truth did not rise into dominion so high as he expected, perhaps in too much zeal and creaturely warmth, he laid on a little too fast, and continued until the life rather abated, and some tender minds were hurt. For it often happens, that such to whom hard things belong, will put them off, and those who are more tender, and least deserving of such doctrine, will take it to themselves, to their own hurt. Oh! how careful ministers ought to be whilst they are in their service, that they may be favoured with an inward feeling sense of the states to which they minister, and be influenced with Wisdom

dom from above, to divide the word aright, in meekness, gentleness, and holy fear, then truth will have its own weight, authority, and power. After the friend sat down, it became the concern of another, in a few words, as it were to number the slain, and search for the wounded, and set close and hard things where they belonged, by describing their several dispositions in choosing and refusing to take hard things. Afterwards, being in company with the friend above hinted, and he being down in his mind, and perhaps not fully knowing the cause, asked me what I thought of the meeting, to which I was not forward to answer. He said, 'Tell me what I have done this day.' Whereupon I asked him privately, and in a pleasant manner, what Gideon did to the men of Succoth; Jud. viii. 16. at which he was greatly humbled, fully understanding what I meant, and did not in the least resent the hint; which I thought was truly great in him, and very becoming a minister: for if we would instruct others, we should be examplary in taking instruction ourselves when necessary.

On my way falling in company with Robert Jordan, we had a freedom to propose a meeting to the Anabaptists at Middletown, to which they readily consented, and we had a profitable opportunity with them in their meeting-house, and on the same evening a meeting at the house of Hugh Hartshorne,

horne, to which several Baptists came. This was a time of favour, and I hope of service; it was concluded by Robert Jordan in solemn prayer and thanksgiving to the Lord, who is worthy for ever and ever. Just as the meeting broke up, I felt myself poor and inwardly weak, to as great a degree as ever I had done, and looking towards my said friend, I saw he was in the same condition; for it seemed as if we had hardly strength to stand: but a query of our dear Lord's came suddenly into my mind, and ministered relief, viz. "Who hath touched "me?" Whereupon, leaning toward my companion, I repeated it to him, being my belief that it was as much for his relief as my own. He understood the meaning instantly, without further explanation, and was thereby also relieved. Perhaps some, who may hereafter peruse these lines, may think this is too bold for a mortal man to mention; but having by a degree of experience known, that when the healing virtue of truth, from the holy Physician of Souls, has flowed through an humble servant, to the relief of some of the infirm and poor amongst the people, who have followed physicians of no value, and spent all their living thereby, and no cure wrought, notwithstanding virtue has gone through them, as instruments or conduits, they have felt inwardly weak for a time, that in humble abasement of soul they might be taught to acknowledge, that the

king-

kingdom, power, and glory, doth belong to him alone, who is God over all, blessed for ever and ever.

From thence we went to William Hartshorne's, at Sandy-hook, and so to the quarterly-meeting at Shrewsbury, which was large in the several sittings, in which was felt the power of truth in a good degree; but many loose and rude people of the neighbourhood, and parts adjacent, coming together at such times, to drink, carouse, and ride races, are very hurtful to each other, and disturbing to friends. Then going homeward, I had several meetings on the way, and enjoyed great inward peace, and could therefore rejoice, and ascribe the praise to the Lord, who had called and enabled me to perform this service.

Having a concern on my mind to visit the meetings of friends on the Eastern shore in Maryland, I laid it before our monthly-meeting, and obtained a certificate on the tenth month; my brother-in-law, James Brown, bearing me company; and we were at Cæcil monthly-meeting, held at Chester, in the eleventh month. Before meeting a friend informed me, that he thought it would be best for me to cross Chester river, and go directly southward. I told him it might be so, but I could say little to it at present. But some friends consulting about it, and one being there who lived near the meeting-house in Queen Ann's county, they thought
he

he could give notice on first day to several meetings. So a friend ventured to speak publickly thereof at the close of the meeting for worship, without letting me know what he intended to do. I had been uncommonly distressed as I sat in the meeting, from an apprehension that but few of the friends belonging to that particular meeting were there, and when he published where it was proposed I should be the ensuing week, I felt my mind opened and turned another way, and stood up and told friends, that I did believe they thought it most for my ease to lay out the meetings after that manner; but if friends at that particular meeting would favour me so far as to meet there next day, I should be glad to sit with them, provided they would please to let other friends and neighbours, who were absent, know of it: for if I had a right sense, there were several members not present, and I should be willing to be at Cæcil meeting on first day, and Sassafrass on second day, which was directly back, and therefore told them it seemed easiest to my mind, though it would occasion more riding. This being agreed to, we had a much larger meeting next day; for many before were absent, as I had thought, and I had a full opportunity to discharge myself toward the lukewarm and indifferent, and disorderly walkers, and had peace. I visited several families on seventh day to good satisfaction, and was at Cæcil meeting on first day, and the next day

day at Saffafrafs, and had to believe it was by the fecret direction of the good Shepherd, who never faileth his dependent children, that I was turned this way: for he was pleafed to own my fervice in thefe meetings by his prefence in a good degree, to the praife of his own name, which is worthy for ever. From thence we paffed over the head of Chefter, by the bridge, John Browning, a friend from Saffafrafs, going with us as a guide, who fome time before had been convinced of the bleffed Truth by the inward operation of the Holy Spirit, without any inftrumental means. He had been a member of the church of England, fo called, and for his fobriety was chofen a veftryman; but after a time felt a fcruple in his mind about taking off his hat when he entered the church-yard, fo called, fearing it was a fuperftitious adoration of the ground, from its fuppofed holinefs; but would take it off when he entered the worfhip houfe, and walk uncovered to his pew: but after a time he could not uncover his head, till what they call Divine Service began; which, as he kept inwardly attentive to the fcruple in his mind, became very lifelefs to him, who was inwardly feeking for fubftance and life, and therefore withdrew therefrom, and after fome time went to one of our meetings, rather out of curiofity than expecting any good, but felt himfelf owned, and had a tafte of the peace which the world cannot give,

give, and from that time became a conſtant attender of our meetings.

We had a meeting at Queen Ann's, amongſt a people who, for want of keeping to the life of religion, had almoſt loſt the form. In converſation at a certain houſe in the evening, I aſked a friend whether ſhe was a friend's child, or one convinced of our principles. Her reply was, that when ſhe was young ſhe lived at a friend's houſe, and took a notion of going to meeting with them, which ſhe had done ever ſince. Alas! when notion changes the will, and not that faith which works by love to the purifying of the heart, the religion is without reformation, empty, and dead. From thence we went to Tuckaho meeting, and the weather being very cold, and rivers frozen up, ſeveral maſters of veſſels and ſailors came there, and divers others, people of faſhion, with gay cloathing. In the fore part of the meeting there was an appearance made which grieved me, for my heart yearned towards the people. The words that he began with were, "Wo, wo, to the crown of pride, "and drunkards in Ephraim;" and with very little application ſat down. It appeared to me as if the appearance of gaiety had fired the creaturely zeal, which was the chief motion to this ſhort ſermon. This, with the cold wind blowing in at the door, much unſettled the meeting, it being at the time when that remarkable ſnow fell, which
laid

laid so long in deep drifts this winter. Whereupon I desired the door might be shut, which being done, the house became more comfortable, and the meeting settled, and I stood up with an heart filled with affection, having that passage of scripture before me, in which the apostle declared the universality of the Love of God; " I perceive of a " truth that God is no respecter of persons," &c. and was much enlarged thereon, to my own admiration, and I believe satisfaction of the people. The meeting ended sweetly with thanksgiving and prayer to the Lord, for the continuance of his mercy, who is the alone author of all good, and worthy of adoration and worship for ever! After which, we attended the several neighbouring meetings, though very severe cold weather, and the houses being very open, and unprovided with the means of keeping them warm, of which there is too manifest a neglect in those parts, they were uncomfortable and unsettled. In this journey my companion appeared in a few words in several families and meetings. We reached home just before our quarterly-meeting in the twelfth month.

In this journey, travelling in Talbot county, an elderly man asked us if we saw some posts standing, pointing to them, and added, the first meeting George Fox had on this side of Chesepeak Bay, was held in a tobacco-house there, which was then new: the posts that were standing were made of walnut.

walnut. At which John Browning abovementioned rode to them, and sat on his horse very still and quiet; then returning to us again, with more speed than he went, I asked him what he saw among those old posts; he answered, 'I would not have missed of
' what I saw for five pounds; for I saw the
' root and grounds of idolatry. Before I
' went, I thought perhaps I might have felt
' some secret virtue in the place where
' George Fox had stood and preached, whom
' I believe to have been a good man; but
' whilst I stood there, I was secretly in-
' formed, that if George was a good man
' he was in heaven, and not there, and vir-
' tue is not to be communicated by dead
' things, whether posts, earth, or curious
' pictures, but by the power of God, who
' is the fountain of living virtue.' A lesson which, if rightly learned, would wean from the worship of images, and adoration of reliques.

I was not many miles from home this summer, save to attend our own quarterly and yearly-meetings; but in the fall, having some drawings in my mind to visit friends in the New-settlement in Virginia, I went with a committee of the quarterly-meeting, appointed to inspect whether friends at Fairfax were in number and weight sufficient to have a meeting settled amongst them, to the reputation of truth; and we visited all the families of friends there, and had a meeting among
them

them to satisfaction. From thence we went to a place called Providence, or Tuskarora, from whence Mordecai Yarnal, who was one of the number, went home, having heard that his wife was dead, or likely to die. We had a meeting with the friends there, who were glad to see us, and then went to Hopewell monthly-meeting, to some satisfaction. From whence I went to a few families settled up Shanondoa, above the Three-topt Mountain, so called, and had a meeting amongst them. They were pretty much tendered, and received the visit kindly, especially such who did not make profession of the truth with us. I admired how they had notice, for many came to it, and some ten miles or more. I believe that the delight in hunting, and a roving idle life, drew most of them under our name to settle there. So having discharged myself in a plain, yet loving manner, I returned to Robert M'Coy junior's, and having had several other meetings thereaway, I went home with peace of mind and thankfulness of heart to him who alone enables his children to answer his requirings; having rode in this journey above four hundred miles.

This winter John Cadwalader and Zebulon Heston, in their return from a religious visit to friends in Maryland, Virginia, and Carolina, were at my house, and being desirous to visit some meetings on the Eastern-shore of Maryland, I went with them to

Sassafrass-meeting, and called to see the widow and children of John Browning, who had been dead about a month, and she gave me in substance the following account of him, viz.

'My husband was not long sick, but said
'that he believed he should not recover,
'and charged me to endeavour that his
'children should be brought up in the way
'of Truth, which friends profess; and if
'they incline to have trades, to put them
'apprentice to real friends, not barely no-
'minal ones, (which she said she was wil-
'ling to do, though she had never yet joined
'to friends) and desired she would not trust
'her own judgment, and named some
'friends with whom she should advise in
'choosing masters. Then said, when I am
'dead, bury me by my father and mother,
'in the grave-yard belonging to our family;
'and thou knowest that I put a large grave-
'stone at my father's grave, and there is
'one ready for my mother's grave, which I
'did not put there, because I began to
'think they were more for grandeur than
'service. I sent for them from England,
'(not at the request of my father) they are
'mine, and now I have a full testimony
'against such formal tokens of respect;
'therefore when I am buried, before the
'company leaves the grave, inform them
'what my will is, and desire their help to
'take the grave-stone from my father's
'grave,

'grave, and carry it out of the yard, that
'it may be brought home, and lay one in
'one hearth, and the other in the other
'hearth of this new house, and they will
'be of real service there*; which she pro-
'mised him to observe, and told me she had
'complied therewith. He remained sensi-
'ble to near the last, and departed in a
'quiet resigned frame of mind.'

How weak are the arguments of such who make profession with us, and plead for those grand marks of memorial, or other tokens of distinction, set up at or on the graves of their deceased relations; and how soon would they subside, did they but live so near the pure truth, as to feel the mind thereof; as I fully believe this our friend did, knowing that the name of the righteous will not perish, but be had in everlasting remembrance, because their portion is life for evermore, having entered into that kingdom prepared for the blessed before the foundation of the world.

This spring of the year, 1742, I felt strong drawings of mind to visit friends in New-England, having had some view thereof several years before; and, having obtained a certificate, I set forward in the third month, and after visiting several meetings in New-Jersey, and one in New-York, I at-

---

* He had built a new brick house, and the hearth not fully laid.

tended the yearly-meeting on Long-Island, wherein the power of truth was felt, and a great openness to those of other societies, many of whom were present, particularly the last day, and two priests, who behaved solidly.

I then went with Samuel Hopwood (a ministering friend from England, with whom I had travelled in this journey through part of New-Jersey) to Ryewood, and had a meeting there, where were a few solid friends, but others too talkative. And being at Old Sea-brook, had a meeting in an inn, on the first day of the week. The people being chiefly Presbyterians, few attended besides ourselves, and those of the family, who were kind and civil to us. Then going to Conanicut, we had a meeting with friends on that island, and proceeded to Newport on Rhode-Island, and on the fifth day of the week attended the meeting at Portsmouth, where we met with Lydia Dean from Pennsylvania, who was on a religious visit to friends in New-England, and many other friends, coming to be at the yearly-meeting on this island. It began on the sixth day of the week, with a meeting of ministers and elders, and two meetings for publick worship, one in the forenoon, and the other in the afternoon, and were held in the same order until the second day of the next week, when the meeting for discipline began. This large yearly-meeting

ing in the several settings thereof was generally solid and satisfactory. After which, taking divers meetings in our way, namely, Portsmouth, Tiverton, Seconnet, Accoakeset, and Aponigangset, and attending their monthly-meeting there, all which were in a good degree satisfactory, Samuel Hopwood and myself embarked for Nantucket, and through the mercy of kind Providence arrived safe there, after a passage of three days and two nights, occasioned by scant winds, and an easterly storm, which tore our sails very much, being old and rotten; so that if some watchful friends on the island had not seen us in distress, and come with three whale boats, and took all the passengers, being twenty-four of us, from the vessel, we should have been in great danger. For being near a sand-bar, the vessel struck ground soon after we left her, and by the violence of the wind was driven on shore. We looked on this deliverance as a mercy from God, to whom several of us were bowed in humble thankfulness for this particular favour. On the twenty-second day of the fourth month the yearly-meeting began, which though small on this day, by reason of the storm, was comfortable. The other sittings were mostly large, and in a good degree owned by the power and virtue of Truth.

My friend Samuel Hopwood, apprehending himself clear, inclined to return to the

Main-land, but no paſſage offered; and notwithſtanding the meetings had been generally attended by moſt of the inhabitants of the iſland, and large, yet I was not eaſy without endeavouring to have ſome opportunities with friends by themſelves, as much as could be, which I obtained, beſides attending their uſual week day meetings; and in theſe ſittings it pleaſed the Lord to open my way to deliver ſeveral things which had lain heavy on my mind. For although ſome ſolid tender-ſpirited friends lived on this iſland, yet I ſaw there was a libertine ſpirit ſecretly at work amongſt ſome others, to draw away from the pure inward life of religion, and the ſimplicity of truth, into eaſe and liberty. After which I had great peace, and my mind was made thankful to the Lord, who had owned my labour by a good degree of his preſence and power.

Being now fully clear, and a paſſage offering, on the ſecond of the fifth month we took leave of our friends, and landed the ſame day in the evening at Seconnet, and on ſeventh day Samuel Hopwood and I went to the quarterly-meeting at Sandwich, and were at their firſt day meeting alſo: after which I went back to Seconnet, and had a meeting at Benjamin Boreman's, then returned to Sandwich, where I again met Samuel Hopwood, and on third day we had a meeting at Yarmouth; and returning to Humphry Wady's, we from thence went towards

wards Boston, taking a meeting with friends at Pembrook; reached that town on sixth day, and attended their morning and afternoon meetings on first day, also one at a friend's house in the evening. I have here little to remark, save that religion seems to be at a low ebb. From Boston I went to Lynn, but Samuel Hopwood returned towards Rhode-Island. I had a meeting at Lynn, also at Salem, Newberry, and Dover, being the monthly-meeting. The next day at Cachecy, and in the afternoon again at Dover, at the burial of Mary Whitehouse, who was ninety-five years of age; and on second day morning I was secretly drawn to have a meeting over the river on the Kettery shore, among friends, which was satisfactory to myself and them, there being a tender people there. On third day morning, as I lay in bed, I felt my mind drawn towards the north-west, which was an exercise to me; for I had before thought myself at liberty to return towards Boston. I arose about sun-rise, and asked the friend where I lodged, whether any friends lived at a distance on that quarter; for that I had a draft that way? He answered no; and asked how far I thought to go. I told him it did not seem to me to be more than ten miles. He said there was a people about eight miles distant, which he supposed was the place to which I felt the draft. I desired him to send a lad with a few lines to some person that

that he knew, to inform them that a stranger would be glad to have a meeting among them at the eleventh hour of that day, if they were free to grant it; which he did, and with his wife went with me: so that we got to the place near the time proposed, and found a considerable gathering of people, that I wondered how it could be in so short a time, not more than three hour's warning. They were preparing seats, by laying boards on blocks in a pretty large new house, and soon sat down in an orderly manner. I went in great fear and inward weakness; and at the sight of such a gathering of people, and none of our profession among them, except the friend and his wife who accompanied me, and two others who joined us in the way, my spirit was greatly bowed, and my heart filled with secret cries to the Lord, that he would be pleased to magnify his own power: and, blessed for ever be his holy name! he heard my cry, and furnished with wisdom and strength to declare his word to the people, among whom there were some very tender seekers after the true knowledge of God; and the doctrine of Truth flowed freely towards them, the universality of the love of God being set forth, in opposition to the common Predestinarian notion of election and reprobation. When the meeting was over I felt an uncommon freedom to leave them, for they began to shew their satisfaction with the opportunity in many

many words. So speaking to the friend that went with me, we withdrew, and went to our horses; and I immediately mounting, beheld the man of the house where the meeting was held running to me, who, taking hold of the bridle, told me I must not go away without dining with them. I looked stedfastly on him, and told him, that I did believe this was a visitation for their good, but I was fearful that they, by talking too freely and too much, would be in danger of losing the benefit thereof, and miss of the good that the Lord intended for them; and my going away was in order to example them to go home to their own houses, and turn inward, and retire to that of God in their own hearts, which was the only way to grow in religion. So I left him, and returned with my friend Joseph Eastees and his wife. Next day I was again at Cachecy meeting, where Lydia Dean, and her companion Eliphal Harper, met me; it was a good meeting. From thence we went to Dover, and had a meeting, and another the same evening at the house of John Kenny; and being clear in my mind of those parts, I returned, having meetings at Hampton, Salisbury, Aimsbury, and Haverhill, at which last place several persons were assembled with us, who had never heard the preaching of any friend before. There was great openness among them, and we had a good meeting together, for which I was thankful to the

holy

holy author of all good. Next day I again met with Lydia Dean and Eliphal Harper, at Stephen Sawyer's, near Newberry, where we had a meeting; at which I was concerned to speak in a brief manner of the beginning of the reformation from the errors of the church of Rome, and the sufferings of the Protestants, particularly in England, some of whose successors turned persecutors, and were very cruel to those whom they called Sectarians; amongst whom the Presbyterians having suffered persecution, in order to be eased therefrom, came into America, and settled in New-England, expecting there to enjoy that reasonable right, the liberty of their conscience; and in this their ease, forgetting the golden rule of doing to others as they would be done unto, became, to their lasting ignominy, persecutors of Quakers, so called, even to the death of several of them. And I had to speak of the nature and ground of persecution, and the great inconsistency thereof with Christianity. Several of the Presbyterians were present; and an ancient man from Newberry, one of their leaders, and an elder among them, when the meeting was over, desired he might speak with me. I being withdrawn into a little parlour, friend Sawyer came and informed me, that the old man wanted to be admitted to me, to which I felt no objection, being quiet and easy in my mind, though I expected he would be for disputing.

ing. When he came in, he let me know that he had some observations to make to me: viz. 'he supposed I was a man that 'had read much, or I could not be so fully 'acquainted with the reformation, and that 'he also supposed I had a college education.' As to the last, I told him that I had never been at a school, but about three months, and the man I went to being a weaver, sat in his loom, and heard his scholars read. That I was so far from having a popular education, that I was born in a wilderness place, where a few families had settled many miles remote from other inhabitants. At which, lifting up his hands, he blessed himself, and added, 'Heaven has then anointed you to 'preach the gospel, and you have this day 'preached the truth; but I can assure you, 'though I have been a parish officer, I ne-'ver did take any thing from your friends 'the Quakers, for I am against persecution; 'so God bless you with a good journey.'

The next day I had a meeting at Ipswich, in the house of Benjamin Hoeg, none professing with us living in that town, but himself and family; though there was a friendly man, who, as I came late to the town the evening before, invited me to lodge at his house, of which I accepted, and being weary, slept well. In the morning I heard a noise of high words in the street, and getting up, I opened the door of the parlour where I lodged, and through a passage into the kitchen,

kitchen, saw a woman, whom I took to be the mistress of the house, and went toward her, but, with a look of exceeding displeasure, she immediately shut the door; so I turned into my room again. After a while the landlord came to me, and told me that he had been with the burgess, who had given leave that a meeting might be held in the town-hall; but the priest and his two sons had since been with the burgess, and forbad him, and that, rather than displease them, he had withrawn the leave. The priest asserted that the Quakers were hereticks, and had gone about the town to forewarn his hearers against going to the meeting, which was the meaning of the noise I heard in the street. I felt very easy, and desired that he would not trouble himself any further than to inform them, that the meeting would be held at the house of Benjamin Hoeg; for I did believe that the railing of the priest would raise the curiosity of the people the more to come, and so it proved. I asked him to shew me the way to the house, that I might be assistant in making provision for seats, if occasion required. He said I must take breakfast with him, which was soon brought in by the woman, who had shut the door, as before mentioned. I asked him if she was his wife; he told me she was; on which I arose from my seat, and offered her my hand, asking her how she did; but she in displeasure refused, and, saying not a word, directly left the room.

room. After breakfast we went to the house where the meeting was to be held, and there soon came a great number of people, and the priest also very near the door, where he stood, cautioning his hearers; but several came by an alley to the back door, and others seemed little to regard him; so that after a time he went away; and through the goodness of the Lord we had a solid profitable meeting: for I believe many were there, whose hearts were reached and tendered by the love and power of the gospel of Christ, and among them I saw my scornful landlady. It seems a woman whom she valued had persuaded her to come with her. Before the meeting ended, I perceived her countenance was changed, and her stout heart tendered; and after it she came to me with her husband, and kindly invited me to dine with them; I owned their love, and desired them to mind the truth by which they had been reached. So in humble thankfulness of heart to the great Author of all living mercies, I left them, and went that night to Salem; and tarrying one meeting, the next day passed on to Marblehead, and had a meeting in the town-hall, the magistrates readily granting it, which was large. I had to speak on morality, the nature and necessity thereof, shewing that a man could not be a true Christian without being a good moralist. I thought they had need of a reformation in their morals, though they
professed

professed Christianity in a high manner. One thing is worthy of remarking, the select men and officers were very careful to keep the rude boys and people that came to the door from making disturbance: several of them walked to the door, and spoke to them, and rapped some on their heads with their canes, to make them still. The meeting ended to satisfaction, without the least opposition. From thence, taking a meeting at Lynn by the way, I went to Boston, and was at their meetings on first day in the forenoon and afternoon, at both which several came that were not in profession with us, and truth opened the doctrine thereof to the people pretty freely. But I was not easy to leave this town without having an opportunity with friends by themselves, for which purpose it was held at Benjamin Bagnall's, and therein I was deeply bowed under a sense of the state of ease, in which some were delighting themselves in their imaginary attainments, whilst the pure seed lay under suffering; but blessed be the Lord! who was graciously pleased to endue with a spirit of love and tender compassion, and thereby enabled me to discharge myself fully, and I was released from what had lain very heavy upon me for several days. The next day I had an opportunity with several friends at Samuel Pope's, and then left Boston pretty easy in my mind, and went to Samuel Thayre's at Mendham, who accompanied

panied me the next day to Uxbridge, where we had a meeting with a few raw, talkative people, which, through the goodnefs of God, was neverthelefs to fome degree of fatisfaction. I returned with Samuel Thayre to his houfe, where I met with Hannah Jenkinfon from Pennfylvania, and we were at Mendam meeting together. She then went towards Bofton, and I to Wainfokett, and Providence-Town, and had a meeting at each place; the latter of which was a poor meeting, the people looking for words, and not waiting for the word of life in their own hearts. From thence I went to and had a large and good meeting at Nefhanticut, the Lord's prefence being felt to his own praife, and another at Greenwich. Then proceeded to Smithfield and Taunton, taking a meeting at each to fome good degree of fatisfaction. From thence to Swanfey, Free-Town, Rochefter, and Cufhnet, having a meeting at each; at one of which, after I ftood up to fpeak a few words in great fear, life being low, and, as I apprehended, the feed under fuffering, I heard a kind of fighing by one in the gallery, which feemed to bring death rather than to raife life; and after I had fpoken a fentence or two it became exceedingly burdenfome, whereupon it came frefh in my mind to fay, ' Can an
' Ifraelite fing a true Hebrew fong whilft
' the feed is in captivity, and under fuffer-
' ing? an attempt of the kind fhews igno-
' rance;'

'rance;' at which there was a great silence, and the sighing ended, and I received strength to deliver what was on my mind, and truth was felt in a good degree to arise. The meeting ended well, and several friends expressed their satisfaction with the service on that day. Being clear of those parts, I went to Rhode-Island, and, in a sense of the goodness and mercy of the Lord, who had helped me in my travels in his work, my soul worshipped before him.

On the twenty-second of the sixth month I sat with friends at Newport in their fore and afternoon meetings, and next morning left Rhode-Island with a heavy heart, and had a meeting at South Kingston, where I met with Susannah Morris, and her sister Hannah Hurford, and the same day had a meeting at James Parry's; and the day following we had one at Thomas Stanton's, in Westerly, among a mixed people of several societies, to whom I felt a stream of gospel love; but the meeting was hurt by several appearances of one present, who lived at no great distance. Our manner of sitting in silence is so very different from the common practice of most other religious societies, that it is no marvel if it should be as time mispent to some, and fill others with wonder, which was the case this day: and for want of a deep inward attention to the living word of truth, instead of instructing the people in the true way of worship, in the
love

love of the gospel, there may be a warm censuring of them for what they understand not, and thereby raise a dislike in them, to the foreclosing of other service: and I have sometimes observed hurt done by this means, by some who appeared in the impatience, not having the weight of the work upon them. Custom had taught the people to look for words, and they were offended by words spoken not in season, and therefore not fitly spoken. I left this meeting with sorrow; and after I mounted my horse, the person who had appeared there three times came to me, and said, ' he hoped he had not ' hindered my service in it.' I reminded him that he had informed the people in that meeting, their looking for words had been one reason why the Lord had shut up the testimony of truth in the hearts of his servants, which I told him I did believe was not then the case; but that his forward appearances had mudded the waters, unsettled the people, and marred the service; so we parted. And feeling my mind drawn back towards Newport, I went that evening to James Congdon's, and the next day to Newport, calling in my way at James Parry's, where I found Lydia Dean, very sick, she being so far on her journey towards home; and on the fifth day of the week I was at two satisfactory meetings there; and on seventh day had a small meeting at Nicholas Easton's, and on first day two large good meetings at Newport; and next day hearing that Lydia Dean was come to Samuel Clark's, on Conanicut-Island, I went with several others to see her, and she returned with us to Newport; where, after a very short notice, we had a large evening meeting, wherein the Lord was pleased mercifully to favour us with his immediate presence, to the glory and praise of his own eternal name, which is worthy for ever! After attending their monthly-meeting at Portsmouth, finding my mind clear and easy to proceed homeward, Lydia Dean, Patience Barker, John Easton, and myself, set out from Newport, taking leave of friends in a tender manner on both sides, and were the first day following at a meeting in Westerly, which was in a good degree satisfactory; and passing through Connecticut to New-Milford, Oblong, and Ninepartners, had meetings in each place. And having a great desire to be at our yearly-meeting for Pennsylvania and New-Jersey, to be held at Burlington, which was near approaching, we passed on, and took a meeting at Samuel Field's, to which several not of our society came, and the opportunity was, through the goodness of the Lord, profitable. We then proceeded as fast as convenient, and reached Burlington on first day, in the time of the yearly-meeting, where many friends were gathered, and Michael Lightfoot, in his return from Great Britain, with whom came John Haslam

lam and Edmund Peckover, on a visit to friends in America. This meeting was large and solid; at which I also met my dear wife, to our mutual thankful rejoicing. After the meeting I went home, where I found things as to the outward in good order; for which I was humbly thankful to the Lord, who had not only been with me by his heavenly presence in this journey, and brought me safe home to my family, but had supported them in my absence; blessed be his holy name for ever!

CHAP. III.

His visit to Long-Island—Visit with others to the families of friends in Nottingham—and to some families in Philadelphia, and to the mayor of that city—also to the assembly of Pennsylvania in the year 1748.—His journey with Michael Lightfoot to the yearly-meeting at West River in Maryland—and accompanied by Joshua Brown to divers Meetings in Pennsylvania and New-Jersey. —His considerations on apprehending it his duty to visit friends in Europe, and proceedings in preparing to enter upon that weighty service, to the time of his leaving home, in order to take shipping for London.

IN the spring of the year 1743, having drawings in my mind to make a general visit to friends on Long-Island, I sat out in the third month, in order to be at the yearly-meeting at Flushing, which began on the sixth day of the week, and continued until the second of the week following: it was large, and signally owned by the power of truth in each sitting. The publick service in the ministry lay mostly on Edmund Peckover, who was there in his way to New-England. On first day I thought I had an engagement to stand up, and considerable matter before me, and after speaking three or or four sentences, which came with weight, all closed up, and I stood still and silent for several minutes, and saw nothing more, not one word to speak: I perceived the eyes of most of the people were upon me, they as well as myself expecting more; but nothing further appearing, I sat down, I think I may say, in reverent fear and humble resignation; when that remarkable sentence of Job, chap. i. 21. was presented to my mind: "Naked "came I out of my mother's womb, and "naked shall I return: the Lord gave, and "the Lord hath taken away; blessed be the "name of the Lord:" and for, I suppose, near a quarter of an hour I remained in a silent quiet; but afterwards let in great reasonings and fear, lest I had not waited the right time to stand up, and so was suffered to fall into reproach. For the adversary, who is ever busy, and unwearied in his attempts to devour, persuaded me to believe that the people would laugh me to scorn, and I might as well return home immediately and privately, as attempt any further visit on the island. After meeting I hid my inward exercise and distress as much as I could. When night came I lodged with a sympathizing friend and experienced elder, who began to speak encouragingly to me; but I said to him, that I hoped he would not take it amiss if I desired him to forbear saying any thing: for if he should say good things, I had no capacity to believe, and if otherwife, I could not then underftand fo as to be profitably corrected or inftructed, and after fome time fell afleep. When I awoke, I remembered that the fentences I had delivered in the meeting were felf-evident truths, which could not be wrefted to the difadvantage of friends, or difhonour of the caufe of truth, though they might look like roots, or fomething to paraphrafe upon; and although my ftanding fome time filent before I fat down might occafion the people to think me a filly fellow, yet they had not caufe to blame me for delivering words without fenfe or life. Thus I became very quiet, and not much depreffed, and was favoured with an humble refignation of mind, and a defire that the Lord would be pleafed to magnify his own name and truth, and preferve me from bringing any reproach thereon. So I ventured to have meetings appointed, and my particular friend and intimate acquaintance Caleb Raper, of Burlington, being at that meeting, went as companion with me, of whofe company I was glad, he being a valuable elder. We went firft to Rockaway, then to Jamaica, Sequetague, Setakit, Matinicock, Cowneck, and Weftbury meetings, and at moft of them I had good fatisfaction; the good prefence of the Lord, in whom I delighted above all things, being witneffed to my comfort, and I believe to the edification and comfort of the fincere in heart: but the teftimony

of

of truth went particularly sharp to the lukewarm professors and libertines in our society. That humbling time I had at Flushing was of singular service to me; being thereby made willingly subject to the Divine openings of truth, and motion of the eternal spirit and pure word of life, in speaking to the several states of those who were present in the meetings; and life came into dominion, and the power thereof overshadowed at times, to my humble admiration: blessed be the name of the Lord, who is worthy, for ever and ever!

Then crossing Whitestone-Ferry, we had meetings at West-Chester, Memarineck, Rywoods, and Long-Reach, which were mostly to good satisfaction. We then went to New-York, and were at their meeting, and in the evening had a select one with friends, which gave me considerable relief, and I believe satisfaction to them; and we were made thankful together in the renewings of the covenant of life. From thence we went to a meeting at Newtown on Long-Island, and to the monthly-meeting at Flushing; where friends gave me a certificate in return to that I brought from home, in which they signified their unity with my service on the island. Then taking leave of friends in sweetness of mind and inward peace, being clear of those parts, I returned homewards, and went to the Narrows that night, but could not get over: next morning

ing early crossed the ferry, when there was a great swell, occasioned by the stormy weather in the evening and night before, and having now no wind, were obliged to row the boat over. In the passage I remembered, that in crossing this ferry when coming on this visit, I thought myself never much poorer, having only a secret hope and trust in the holy arm of power: and being now inwardly sensible of my own weakness, I had to acknowledge that I went not forth on this embassy in my own will and strength; and therefore craved only that my blessed Lord and Master would blot out mine offences, and yet enable me so to walk in humble obedience the residue of my time, as to be favoured with the answer of "well "done" at the conclusion: and knowing the nature and treachery of self, did not want to be intrusted with much reward at present, choosing rather that the Lord, in his infinite wisdom and mercy, should deal out to me my daily bread according to his own pleasure. " I passed over this Jordan with " my staff, and now I am become two " bands," was the saying of Jacob, Gen. xxxii. 10. As this saying of the good patriarch came fresh in my mind, I thought, that although I could not see myself much increased in heavenly treasure, I came poor, and had only the staff of faith to lean upon, yet I had to bless the Lord that he was now pleased to favour me with the same staff in
my

my return, on the never failing strength whereof I might with safety evermore rely; and in holy resignation I had to praise his worthy name. I proceeded with my friend Caleb Raper to Burlington, where we parted in much love and nearness, in which we had travelled together. I reached home about wheat harvest, and found my dear wife and family well.

I went not much abroad the residue of this summer, and the year following, but was careful to attend our own and many neighbouring meetings; also monthly, quarterly, and yearly-meetings, in this and the adjacent province. Some business of a publick nature, together with my own circumstances, necessarily engaged me for several years; in which time, viz. in the spring of the year 1745, my dear wife having drawings in her mind to visit the meetings of friends in Virginia, Maryland, and North Carolina, obtained a certificate of the unity of friends with her, to travel in that service with Jane Hoskins, of Chester. And in the same year I was nominated, with several other friends, to visit the families belonging to our monthly-meeting, which being large, and many friends living at a distance, it was a laborious work, and not fully performed until the fall of the year 1747, when account was given that the service was perfected to a good degree of satisfaction. In the winter following I had it on my mind to visit all the families of the particular meeting of Newark near Brandywine, who seemed to be in a declining state as to religion, having dropped their week-day meeting, and often much neglected to attend their first-day meeting, many of the elderly friends being deceased, and their children almost turned to the world, and united to the spirit, pleasures, and pastimes thereof. My brother William Brown, and his wife, and mine, were with me on this service, and great plainness was used in opening to many particulars the cause of their declension; and as the love of truth engaged me in the service, I had peace and satisfaction, and those visited seemed to receive the visit kindly.

In the spring of the year 1748, I felt drawings in my mind to visit some families of friends in Philadelphia, of which I acquainted my brethren at home; and having their concurrence, in the fourth month I joined with some friends in the city, who were some time before appointed to the service, and we went in much love from house to house, the Lord, by his good presence, being with us, to our mutual comfort. And as I attended to the drawings of truth, I found a concern to go to the mayor of the city (accompanied by my good friend Israel Pemberton the elder,) and was engaged to lay before him the nature of his office as a magistrate, and exhorted him to take care that he bore not the sword in vain, but to put the laws in execution against evil doers, such as drunkards, profane swearers,

ers, &c. and to be, in his authority, a terror to the wicked, and an encourager of them that do well. He was loving and tender, and expressed his satisfaction with the visit.

While I was in the city, the governor called or summoned the members of assembly together, and in pressing terms laid before them the defenceless state of Pennsylvania, in order to prevail with the house to grant a sum of money, to station a ship of force at Delaware capes, also to encourage the building a battery below the city, which was begun some time before by subscription, but likely to be too heavy for the undertakers. One night, as I lay in my bed, it came very weightily upon me to go to the house of assembly, and lay before the members thereof the danger of departing from trusting in that divine arm of power which had hitherto protected the inhabitants of our land in peace and safety: the concern rested on me several days, which occasioned me with earnest breathings to seek the Lord, that if this was a motion from him, he would be pleased to direct my steps therein, so that I might be preserved from giving just cause of offence to any: for it seemed to be a very difficult time; many, even of our society, declaring their willingness that a sum of money should be given to the king, to shew our loyalty to him, and that they were willing to part with their substance for his use, though, as a people, we
had

had a testimony to bear against all outward wars and fightings. I made no man privy to my concern until a week had near passed, when one morning it became so heavy upon me, that I went to the house of an intimate friend, who, being just up, invited me to come in, and as we sat together, he had a sense that something of weight was upon me, and asked if I was concerned about the assembly. Whereupon I asked him, if he ever knew of any friends going to the assembly with a concern to speak to them? he answered, nay; adding, ' but I have often wondered that they have not; for I have understood that it was formerly a common practice for them to sit in silence a while, like solemn worship, before they proceeded to do business." I told him, that I had it on my mind to go to the house that morning, and should be glad of suitable company. He directed me to one whom he thought such, and I immediately went to him, and acquainted him with my concern; but as I spake, I felt that I had better go alone, and therefore told him, that if he did not feel clear and easy to go with me, I advised him to stay. He replied, ' Thy way is before thee, but I believe I must not go.' I therefore returned to my friend, who did not discourage me, though I had no company. Being pressed in mind, I went directly to the state-house, before I took breakfast, and got there just as the
speaker,

speaker, J. K. was going in. I beckoned to him, and he came to me. I told him I wanted to be admitted into the house, for I thought I had something to say to them, which seemed to me of importance. He said it was a critical time, and they had a difficult affair before them, and queried whether I had not better wait until the house parted; and another member being near, said he thought it would be best, and less liable to give offence, for there were divers members not of our society; and if I would wait until the house broke up, they would inform all the members that were friends, and did not doubt they would be willing to give me an opportunity to inform them what was on my mind. I told them that would give me no relief, for I had a particular desire that those members who were not of our society should be present; believing that it would be better for them to hear and judge for themselves than to have it at second hand, as it might be differently represented; at which they were a little silent. Then I requested the speaker that he would go in and inform the members, that a countryman was in waiting, who had a desire to be admitted, having something to communicate to them, and if they refused, he would be clear. He readily and affectionately answered he would, and soon brought me word that they were willing. There was a great awe over my mind when
I went

I went in, which I thought in some measure spread, and prevailed over the members, beyond my expectation. After a silence of perhaps ten or twelve minutes, I felt as though all fear of man was taken away, and my mind influenced to address them in substance after the following manner:

' My Countrymen, and Fellow-Subjects,
  ' Representatives of the Inhabitants of
  ' this Province.

' UNDER an apprehension of the dif-
  ' ficulties before you, I feel a strong
' sympathy with you, and have to remind
' you of a just and true saying of a great
' minister of Jesus Christ in his day, "The
" powers that be are ordained of God."
' Now if men in power and authority, in
' whatsoever station, would seek unto God
' (who will be a spirit of judgment to them
' that sit in judgment) for wisdom and
' counsel to act singly for him that ordained
' the power, and permitted them to be sta-
' tioned therein, that they should be his
' ministers, such will be a blessing, under
' God, to themselves and their country:
' but if those in authority do suffer their
' own fears, and the persuasions of others,
' to prevail with them to neglect such atten-
' tion, and so make or enact laws, in order
' to their own protection and defence by
' carnal weapons and fortifications, stiled
                                    ' human

'human prudence, he who is superintend-
' ant, by withdrawing the arm of his pow-
' er, may permit those evils they feared to
' come suddenly upon them, and that in
' his heavy displeasure. May it with grati-
' tude be ever remembered how remarkably
' we have been preserved in peace and tran-
' quility for more than fifty years! no inva-
' sion by foreign enemies; and the treaties
' of peace with the natives, wisely began
' by our worthy proprietor William Penn,
' preserved inviolate to this day.

' Though you now represent, and act for,
' a mixed people of various denominations,
' as to religion, yet remember the charter is
' the same as at first: beware therefore of
' acting to oppress tender consciences, for
' there are many of the inhabitants whom
' you now represent, that still hold forth
' the same religious principles with their
' predecessors, who were some of the first
' adventurers into this, at that time wilder-
' ness, land, who would be greatly grieved
' to see warlike preparations carried on, and
' encouraged by a law consented to by their
' brethren in profession, or others, contrary
' to the charter; still conscientiously con-
' cluding, that the reverent and true fear
' of God, with an humble trust in his an-
' cient arm of Power, would be our great-
' est defence and safety. And they who hold
' different principles, and are settled in this
' government, can have no just cause of

' reflection if warlike measures are forborn,
' because they knew the charter framed,
' and the peaceable constitution, and have
' ventured themselves therein.

' We may observe by sundry laws enacted
' in parliament, when the Reformation was
' but newly begun in England, our mother
' country, there seemed to be wisdom from
' above to influence their minds. May you
' be rightly directed at this time, many of
' whom do fully believe in the immediate
' influence of Christ, the wisdom of God,
' which is truly profitable to direct! It is not
' from disrespect to the king or government
' that I speak after this manner, for I am
' thankful in heart that the Lord in mercy
' hath vouchsafed, that the throne of Great
' Britain should be filled with our present
' benevolent prince, King George the Se-
' cond; may his reign be long and happy!'

I acknowledged their kindness in hearing me with so much patience, and, taking leave, withdrew. Several members followed me out, and expressed their satisfaction in an affectionate manner with my visit; and, embracing each other, we parted, in a sense of the love and power of Christ Jesus our Lord, who, with the Father, is worthy of all thanksgiving and praise for ever and ever.

After my service in Philadelphia was over, I returned home with peace and satisfaction,
and

and went not much abroad, save to our quarterly and yearly-meetings, until the spring following, in the year 1749, when I went with Michael Lightfoot to the yearly-meeting at West-river in Maryland; in which journey, the weather being hot, and some weakness of body attending, it threw me into a strong fever, and a stoppage in my breast, that it was with some difficulty I got home, and continued without any amendment a considerable time: and one evening, as I was preparing for bed, an imposthume broke, which I suppose was on my lights, because it came up my windpipe, almost strangling me for a considerable time, that I expected I was near expiring; but felt a resignation in this trying time beyond my expectation, which I took to be a great favour from the Lord: there is no support like the light of his countenance. I continued bleeding more or less many days, but gradually mended. In the eighth month, being pretty well recovered, in much love I felt drawings in my mind to visit some meetings in the back parts of Chester, Philadelphia, and Bucks counties, and part of New-Jersey, and laying my concern before my friends, had their concurrence, and was accompanied by my kinsman Joshua Brown through most of the journey. Our first appointed meeting was at Radnor, in which truth owned our service in a good degree, and passing over Schuylkill, we went to Plymouth, North Wales, Skippack,

Skippack, and New Providence, which laſt meeting, for want of more careful notice, was very ſmall; and not being eaſy in my mind, I had a ſingular freedom to let them know that I would endeavour to be at that place on the ſecond day following, and ſhould be glad they would pleaſe to give full notice thereof; and having a ſtrong draught in my mind to turn back to North Wales, I went the ſame evening to Robert Jones's at Skippack, and next day to ſee a friend who had been a long time indiſpoſed, with whom we had a good opportunity, which I believe was of advantage to the friend, through the goodneſs and mercy of the bleſſed Shepherd of Iſrael. I alſo viſited two other friends, and we were comforted together in the renewing of heavenly goodneſs: and on firſt day was at North Wales meeting, which was large and ſatisfactory, and at Providence again on ſecond day, where friends generally met, and I had an opportunity to clear myſelf in a particular manner. Then went to Evans's meeting, by the ſide of Schuylkill, and had a meeting the ſame evening at the houſe of Thomas May, both which were to ſome ſatisfaction. Afterwards went to Maiden-creek, Exeter, and Richmond, and from thence over Delaware to Kingwood, and viſited the meetings in Burlington, Gloucester, and Salem counties, as far down as Greenwich, and returned homewards by Haddonfield, from whence,

in

in my going down, my kinsman Joshua Brown left me, and went home. I called to visit Hannah Cooper, whose husband had not long been dead: she seemed under affliction of body and mind. I felt a near sympathy with her, and, though we did not converse much together, yet in the owning love of him who is a friend to the afflicted, we were mutually comforted. She expressed her satisfaction in a tender manner, saying, that soon after I came her exercise was lightened, and she was refreshed, in a sense of the kindness of the Lord, in affording a sympathy and inward feeling to the children of his family. My soul was humbled in reverent thankfulness to him, the Author of all good, who is praise worthy for ever. In the morning I had a passage over Delaware, about the tenth hour, which, by reason of ice, had not been passable for several days before. Tarrying in Philadelphia that night, I went next day to Derby meeting, and the day following got well home, and found my dear wife and family well.

On my leaving home to perform this visit, I felt great inward weakness, and in going from meeting to meeting, frequent humbling baptisms attended, in which the present state of the church was seen, and the conditions of many spoken to in the love of truth; which made me often think that it seemed like a farewell visit, at least for a long time.

I may now make a remark, which I hope will not be improper or unprofitable. As I passed along in this visit, I observed some people would earnestly press me to go home with them, and would say they would not take it kind if I did not; and friends did not use to serve them so, that is, pass by them; yet I thought there was not much of the innocent sweetness of truth to be felt at their houses, or even about them. Though they would say, 'Why, thou hast hit the 'nail on the head! there is just such people 'among us as thou hast spoken of;' and seemed to themselves safe and easy, when perhaps their religion lay much in thinking that good friends were familiar with them, and thought well of them. I also took notice of another sort, who, though they were not fond of having friends to go with them, would speak well of their service, and deal it out liberally to others in a censorious manner, and not look on themselves with a true prospect, which would have led them to smite on their own breasts, with a feeling, short prayer, rather than apprehend themselves better than others, when perhaps covetousness and a worldly spirit had almost destroyed charity, which is the sure product of true religion. A third sort I beheld humbled and bowed, whose words were few, and who would frequently, if they said any thing, lament the state of the society, and speak of their own weakness, and fear lest they

they should not walk in the uprightness of truth before their own families and the church: the dew rested on them in their humble situation. I was thankful in the sense I had that there were some few of these in almost every meeting; and I had a firm belief, that some among the youth were under the hand of the Great Preparer of men for his own work. These children are mostly modest, and diffident of themselves, sincerely affectionate, not over forward or fondling, but lovers of truth in heart, to whom I felt great nearness of spirit, believing they would grow in the root of life. I beheld some others among the youth, whom I feared had too great a delight to live on the labours of others, who nevertheless had been favoured with the reaches of Divine Love, but for want of dwelling deep and humble with the pure witness in themselves, ran out in the affectionate part, and were greatly delighted to hear truth's testimony, and valued instruments according to their own liking. These, though they appear as goodly flowers, for want of an humble abode in the vine, do sometimes wither away as grass on the housetop. " If you love me, keep my com- " mandments," was a precept of our holy Lord and Master. To keep his commandments, we must inwardly dwell with his grace in our hearts, by which the law of the spirit of life is known and understood, by the enlightening and everlasting sure word of prophecy, which will privately interpret, and secretly shew to every man his duty, and the calling of God, and abilitate to abide therein: and his " law is light," and his commandment as a lamp to the feet of his people for ever.

As I sat in a week day meeting in the winter (1748) which was held in a private house, (our meeting-house being burnt some time before) I felt great weakness and poverty attending my mind, which occasioned a deep inquiry into the cause; and after a time of inward waiting, the humbling Divine Presence was felt in reverent profound silence, yet the gentle operation of the Divine Power caused a secret inward trembling, and the following was uttered in a language intelligent to the inward man, ' Gather thyself from all the cumbers of ' the world, and be thou weaned from the ' popularity, love, and friendship thereof.' I believed this to be the voice of the Holy One of Israel, as a merciful warning to prepare for my final change, or to stand ready for some service which would separate me from temporal business, and the nearest connections in life; and from that time I endeavoured to settle my affairs, and contract my little business as well as I could. In the summer following I met with an unexpected trial; for without my knowledge my name was put in the new commission for
justices

justices of peace, and endeavours were used to persuade me to be qualified, in order to act in that station, and some of my particular friends told me it seemed providential, and they thought it was my place to accept thereof, as I might be helpful by way of example to some in the commission who were friends. For a short time I was exceedingly straitened, but my eye being fixed on the Lord for counsel, it pleased him in great condescension once more to revive the sentence before mentioned, ' Gather thyself ' from all the cumbers of the world,' &c. which to me settled the point, and I became easy in mind, and humbly thankful to my blessed Instructor, who had called me for other service.

After my return home from the visit to friends in New-Jersey, before related, I felt such an inward silence for about two or three weeks, that I thought I had done with the world, and also any further service in the church, and the preparing hint was brought to my mind, with thankfulness that I had endeavoured in a good degree to practise it. And one day, walking alone, I felt myself so inwardly weak and feeble, that I stood still, and, by the reverence that covered my mind, I knew that the hand of the Lord was on me, and his presence round about: the earth was silent, and all flesh brought into stillness, and light went forth with brightness, and shone on Great Britain, Ireland,

Ireland, and Holland, and my mind felt the gentle, yet strongly drawing cords of that love which is stronger than death, which made me say, 'Lord! go before, and 'strengthen me, and I will follow whither-'soever thou leadest.' I had seen this journey near fifteen years in a very plain manner, and at times, for ten years, thought the concern so strong upon me, that I must lay it before my friends for their advice, but was secretly restrained; being made to believe that an exercise of that sort would ripen best to be kept quiet in my own heart, to know the right time, by no means desiring to run without being sent. To see a thing is not a commission to do that thing: the time when, and judgment to know the acceptable time, are the gifts of God. The time I had to prepare for the journey was short, and therefore thought it was needful to employ my time to the best advantage; and as I had a desire to see friends of several particular meetings, namely Bradford, West and East Caln, Uwchland, Nantmill, and Goshen, my sister Dinah James went with me to those meetings, which through the goodness of the Lord were solidly profitable. We had also a meeting at Henry Hockley's, near French Creek Iron works, which was to some good satisfaction, and so to the quarterly meeting at Concord in the twelfth month, where I met my brother, William Brown, who queried of me where I had been,

been, and what I had been doing. I told him, I had been doing as he and every honeſt man ought to do, collecting little debts, and paying where I owed, and endeavouring to ſettle my affairs; for that ſuch care was neceſſary when one expected a great ſum would be immediately demanded. In a few days after my return from the quarterly-meeting I laid my concern before our preparative meeting, in order that friends might have a month to weigh and conſider it before I ſpoke for a certificate: for I wanted their feeling concurrence in this weighty undertaking, firmly believing that my great and good Maſter would not require any thing of me in which my dear friends could not concur; and though while the power of truth was upon me, I was made freely to give up, yet now home, and the near affection to a dear wife, only ſon, relations and friends, were exceedingly quick and affecting; and ſomething in me ſeemed to have a choice, that my friends would judge that I was too weakly and infirm in body, or not otherwiſe qualified for the ſervice, and if that ſhould be their mind, I thought I ſhould be clear. In the interval I viſited the neighbouring meetings, and carefully attended to the motion of truth therein: and in the firſt month, having the concurrence of the preparative meeting, I laid my concern before the monthly-meeting, and attended our general ſpring-meeting at Philadelphia.

ladelphia. And my brother, William Brown, having spoken for a certificate on the like concern, it seemed pleasant to think of crossing the ocean together, and friends were for proposing a passage, and what ship we should go in; but I felt a secret prohibition against being any ways concerned about a passage until I had a certificate, and knew that I was fully clear, so returned home. And having a desire to see friends in York county, over Susquehanna, I went there, accompanied by my brother, James Brown, to the meetings at Newberry, Warrington, Huntington, and Monallan, which were mostly to a good degree of satisfaction; and in my return, being humble and low in mind, and ruminating on my European journey, which was before me, my spirit seemed to sink, and my affection to my dear wife and family, and friends, so awakened upon me, that it looked to me impossible to part from them and live; but endeavouring to retire, blessed be the name of the Lord, the helper of his people! by whose power a silence was known, and by a gentle, instructive, inward voice, my attention was gained, and my mind diverted from its pain by the following query: 'Suppose thou shouldst
' lend a valuable thing to a neighbour of
' thine, to be returned on demand, and
' thou shouldst favour him therewith from
' time to time, not only one year, but se-
' ven, and then shouldst see cause to de-
                                    ' mand

'mand it to be refigned; wouldst thou not
'think that neighbour ungrateful, if he
'did not refign it chearfully, and with
'thankfulnefs and acknowledgment fuita-
'ble to thy kindnefs?' The propofition
demanded my affent, and my underftanding
was fully opened by the following application: 'All that thou enjoyeft is mine; doft
'thou love thefe things more than me? if
'not, why is it fo hard for thee to refign
'all to follow me?' which made me cry,
'Lord! enable me, and I will follow thee:
'it is only by thy ftrength I can do it."
And by the gracious goodnefs of Chrift, my
great and good Mafter, I felt an humble refignation to his will, who, being all things
to his people, is worthy to be followed and
obeyed for ever. Now I was led to believe
this was the inftruction of the bleffed Spirit
to me, and as I had much comfort and fatisfaction thereby, I am free to leave it as a
hint, that others under trials, of what kind
foever, may be encouraged to look unto him
for help, who is the Lord, mighty to fave,
and able to deliver to the uttermoft all who
fincerely truft in him.

I returned home, and my certificate being
figned in the fecond month, attended our
quarterly-meeting at Concord in the third
month, and went to Philadelphia to fee for
a paffage, and with my brother, William
Brown, found one to our liking, and to the
fatisfaction of friends, which we alfo valued.

lued. I then returned home, waiting until the ship was near ready to sail, and during that time visited several neighbouring meetings, taking leave of my neighbours and friends. And on the first day of the fourth month, (1750) taking leave of my dear wife and aged mother, I left home before sun rise, and went to Philadelphia that night, spent the next day in visiting some of my acquaintance, and on the first day of the week attended three meetings; in the morning at the Bank, which was a satisfactory good meeting, wherein friends were exhorted to attend on the gift of God for instruction and ability to perform every good word and work, and in the afternoon and evening at the High, or Market-street house, which, though not quite so open as the other, were in the main solid good meetings.

CHAP. IV.

His visit to Great Britain, Ireland and Holland, from the year 1750 to 1754, with divers observations on the state of our religious society in the course of his travels.

ON the fourth day of the fourth month, (1750) being the second of the week, we left Philadelphia, accompanied by several of our relations and friends to Chester,

and

and went on board the ship Carolina, Stephen Mesnard commander, (bound for London) where my brother, William Brown, and myself, took leave of them; and passing down Delaware, went out to sea in the afternoon of the sixth of the same month, and had a good passage, in which I was not sea sick, though my brother was most of the time. We landed at Dover on the sixth of the fifth month, being just five weeks from the time I left my own house; and we had to rejoice with humble thankfulness that, during the passage, we were careful to keep our meetings in the great cabin twice a week, in which we felt the presence of our great Lord and Master, and therein were comforted. On the day we landed we had a meeting at Dover, to good satisfaction; then took passage in a stage coach to Canterbury the same evening, and lodged at William Patterson's, who entertained us very kindly; rested there on seventh day, and on first day sat with friends in their morning and afternoon meetings, to some satisfaction. Though I had little to say to them, I thought there was a tender people in that city, and William Brown had an open time. Next morning taking our passage in a stage coach, we reached London the same evening, and continued in and about the city until the twenty-first of the sixth month, in which time I wrote divers letters to my wife, and particular friends in Pennsylvania;

Pennsylvania; and was several times at each of the meetings in the city, in which I sat mostly silent, under a great exercise of mind from a sense of a too forward ministry, which rather disturbed the solemn quiet thereof than ministered instruction to the humble waiting children, (of which number I thought there were many in that city) though it seemed delightful to those who loved to hear words eloquently delivered, and to have the itching ear pleased, yet who in heart were libertines, and in practice disorderly walkers. I sometimes thought, that my silent sitting was so ordered for an example to others, for a more steady waiting in their own gifts, to know life to rise into dominion in meetings. My exercise increased so, that my sleep seemed to depart from me, and I remained as one sealed up, as to ministry; nor had I freedom to go from house to house to dine, or to make many acquaintance: I was therefore censured by some, as singular and narrow. At length I felt great enlargement of heart towards other societies, though my mouth was shut towards our own: and for a time it seemed as if I must go and have meetings among those who did not profess with us. And one day, as I was walking towards Ratcliff fields, for the air, a draught of affection flowed so strong towards some in high stations in government, that I concluded, that I must declare the way of life and salvation
through

through Chrift Jefus our Lord among them, feeling a greater opennefs that way than to friends; but making a ftand, I fecretly cried, ' Ah, Lord! what then will become of the ' family whom thou dreweft me hither to ' vifit.' Then, after a little while, that charge came into my mind very frefh, Mat. x. 5, 6. "Go not into the way of the Gen- " tiles, and into any city of the Samaritans " enter ye not; but go rather to the loft " fheep of the houfe of Ifrael." Which brought great fweetnefs, and an increafing heart-yearning for, and love to, the houfhold, and made me acknowledge, Good art thou, O Lord God, for thy mercies endure for ever and ever. And I remembered that Nehemiah quietly viewed the ftate of Jeru- falem by night; and faw that if I had any fervice to do in London, the time for it was not yet come. I alfo remembered what came into my mind at the fecond meeting I was in after my landing, in which I had but a few fentences to fpeak, and the motion of life ceafed, and I fat down, (as I have always found it fafe to do) and felt inward poverty and weaknefs, yet a quiet and at- tentive mind; but my brother, William Brown, had good fervice, and an open time among the people, at which I did admire, and faid in my heart, he is fit to be fent abroad; but, alas! I am one of the meaneft fervants that was ever fent over the fea to preach the gofpel; when this gentle cau-

tion came before me: 'Mind thy own bu-
'finefs, and be faithful in thy gift; thou
'haft a great journey before thee, and thy
'ftore is fmall: live, therefore, frugally,
'and fpend carefully, and covet not ano-
'ther's, and thou fhalt not want what is
'convenient for thyfelf, and fomething to
'fpare to the needy.' Whereupon I defired, with an humble heart, to be preferved
in patience and meeknefs, becoming a dif-
ciple of my great Lord and Mafter, and
therein to wait for renewed inftruction and
ability, to labour in mine own gift without
repining, however fmall.

In a few days I felt fome opennefs towards the Weft of England, and informed
my brother, William Brown, thereof, who,
after a little paufe, told me that his way
opened Eaftward. One fome confideration
of the matter, we concluded it was beft
for each of us to mind the pointings of
truth, though in fome crofs to our own
wills; for this profpect feemed to part us:
and if we fhould endeavour to go together
for a time, and then part, fome might judge
there was a diflike, or want of unity between us, and on communing with fome of
our friends, they were of the fame mind.
So we refigned, and in much love and affection took leave of each other.

Underftanding there was a yearly-meeting to be held in Somerfetfhire for feveral
of the weftern counties, and having fome
drawings

drawings to attend it, I left London on the twenty-firſt of the ſixth month, in company with my friend John Hunt, at whoſe houſe I lodged, and John Pemberton, who came over ſea with us on account of his health, and had a meeting that day at Staines, which was pretty good and open; the next at Baſingſtoke, and ſo on to Saliſbury and Shaftſbury, the two laſt being dull meetings; (which is often the caſe where friends are not careful to live near to truth) and reached to Ivelcheſter, the place where the yearly-meeting began, on ſeventh day in the evening, the twenty-fifth of the month. On firſt day we had two meetings in the town-hall; and many people being there, meetings were held at the Market-croſs in the ſtreet at the ſame time. I ſat ſilent that day. On the next there was a meeting of miniſters and elders in the morning, in which I had ſome remarks to make reſpecting miniſtry. There were alſo two publick meetings the ſame day, one of which was dull, the other more open, and on third day two meetings rather better, when the yearly-meeting ended. Some meetings being laid out for me, John Hunt returned to London, but John Pemberton concluded to go with me a few days, and his company was kindly accepted of by me, he being a ſober, well inclined young man. We went to Ilminſter, the firſt appointed meeting, in which the good preſence was witneſſed much to my comfort: for I ſaw that the Lord was near, and helped me in my gift by opening the state of the meeting, bleſſed be his name for ever! I alſo had an evening meeting at Chard, and next day at Yeovil, which was large, and open for doctrine. Then at Sherborn, on the edge of Dorſetſhire. From thence went to viſit the wife and children of Jonah Thompſon, at Compton, he being in Pennſylvania, on a religious viſit. I had ſome good ſatisfaction in the family, and tarried there a day. Then went to the meetings at Long Sutton, Puddimore, Grinton, Glaſtonbury, Shipton-mallet, and Frome, in which I had moſtly cloſe and plain ſervice, yet not without a degree of the ſweetneſs and power of truth, in a ſenſe whereof I was often made humbly thankful to the Lord. Then proceeding to Bath, was at the forenoon and afternoon meetings there, and had an evening meeting at Caleb Tyley's, which were in ſome good degree owned by truth; but there is a want of weighty ſolid friends in this place, which is much frequented by moſt ſorts of people, on account of the waters. From thence we went to Bradford and Pickwick meetings; but not being clear at the firſt, I returned, and had an evening meeting there, to which many came, and it ended to ſatisfaction. Here I may note, that having a deſire to ſee friends by themſelves, and ſomething on my mind in a cloſe manner to the ſociety, when I ſtood up and began

began to speak, the house was soon almost filled by others, who would wait without, setting some one to watch when there was any thing spoken. Upon their coming in the subject in my view closed, and an opening in a doctrinal way presented, and my mind turned to it, and I believe it was to the satisfaction of some seeking people present. After I sat down a few minutes, finding no ease respecting my concern towards friends, I had a freedom to inform the people, that the publick service of that meeting was now over, but I had a desire that the members of the meeting would stay a little while. On which a friend went to the door, and when the others had gone out shut it, and the friends mostly kept their seats, and in a little time the state of the meeting came fresh before me again, and I had an opportunity to clear myself in a very plain manner; shewing that the greatest enemies to the truth were the professors of it, who did not observe the instructions of truth, or grace of God, in their own hearts; for although the doctrine thereof, when declared by qualified instruments, was clear and powerfully convincing, having the love and sweetening evidence of truth with it, reaching the witness in their hearts; yet when the eyes of such so reached were turned to behold the steps and conduct of the libertine professors among us, they were stumbled by their example, and such were an offence to the little ones, and their portion, by way of comparison, is hinted at by our Lord, when he says, Mat. xviii. 6. "But whoso shall offend one of these little ones, who believe in me, it were better for him that a millstone were hanged about his neck, and that he were drowned in the depth of the sea." From thence we went to Westbury and Lavington meetings, and to the quarterly-meeting for Wiltshire, held at Devizes, which began on the first day of the week, two meetings for publick worship, and one in the evening for ministers and elders, and next day for worship and business; but I could see no time, nor room to clear myself to advantage, for want of more stillness. The service of meetings may be hurt for want of silence, and the minds of the people become too unsettled to understand and hear to profit. In a sense whereof I left this place, with an heavy heart, and went to Chippenham, Corsham, Charlcot, and Melksham meetings; besides which had three evening meetings, one at Pickwick, in a school-house belonging to Thomas Bennet, with his boarding scholars, and others; one at John Fry's, of Sutton Benjar; and the other at Samuel Rutty's; some of which were good meetings. Then leaving Wiltshire, we passed through Bradford and Bath, and came to Bristol on the twenty-second of the month, where I tarried until first day, the seventh of the eighth month,

month, constantly attending their meetings as they came in course, and visiting several families, as truth opened my way. My mind and spirit was bowed very low in this city, under a sense of too general a declension and falling away from truth, into pride, high-mindedness, and the spirit of the world, and a conformity to the vain customs and fashions thereof, of which I frequently made mention amongst them. I was at their two weeks meeting for business, and quarterly-meeting for inspecting the affairs of truth, and laboured much to encourage them to hold weekly-meetings for ministers and elders, in order to enquire how meetings for worship were attended by publick friends, and whether their ministry was acceptable, and the lives and conversations of ministers and elders correspondent with their doctrine and profession; which care they had dropped for some time. I was at sixteen meetings in this city, and one at Frenchay, and visited Anthony Purver's boarding-school at that place. And being easy to leave Bristol for the present, we went to Chewmagna, in Somersetshire; and, after dining at John Hipsley's, had a religious opportunity in his family, and the next day a meeting at Portishead, an evening meeting at James Player's; then to Claverham, Sidcot, and Mark, some of which were good meetings. A few elderly friends here live near truth, and there was a visitation to the youth, several of whom

whom appeared tender and growing in religion; though many professors are seeking after the gain, love, and friendship of the world, not enough considering that godliness with contentment is the best gain. Our next meeting was at Bridgewater, then at Taunton; and we were comforted together with friends in their morning and afternoon meetings. In the Divine presence there is life; and the living are made able to praise the Lord, who is worthy. From thence passing to Minehead, Milverton, Wellington, Spiceland, Columpton, having a meeting at each place, we came to Exeter, in Devonshire, and attended three meetings there on first day, in each of which I had something to offer; but was much depressed under an apprehension of the prevalence of a deistical spirit over some, which, with the indifference of others about religion, and a light forward zeal in some others, without the deep, inward, baptizing knowledge of truth, occasion the pure and ever blessed power thereof to be at a low ebb in that city. When the children of the Lord know him their Redeemer to live by his heavenly power in them, they know also that thereby they live, and feelingly know his truth and the precious testimony, and by this knowledge are influenced with an holy, humble zeal, in love and meekness to work in his vineyard the church, to the honour of God, and the edification and restoration one of another.

Leaving

Leaving Exeter, we went to Topsham, and had a dark, dull meeting; and staying at a friend's house to dine, one at the table, who, as I understood, could not spare time to attend the meeting, asked me if I was ever in New-England, and whether I could inform him what sort of a country it was: for, added he, I have heard people say, that the corn (that is wheat) will not ripen there, but is smitten with a rotting mildew, which blasts the wheat in the ear. I suddenly felt that I had need of being careful in answering, but knew not why. I answered with caution, that I had seen wheat in that country which looked to be well grown, but in the ear, where grain should be, there was little else but a black smut, in form of a grain. I have heard, said he, that it would bear full, good wheat formerly, and what can now be the cause why it is blasted; didst thou ever hear? On which I related to him a passage which I had heard, viz. two persons being in Boston, had a curiosity to see the old prison, from whence those friends were led to the place of execution who were hanged at Boston for their religious testimony and principles; and an inhabitant of the town going with them, brought them to the prison; and one of the men said to their guide, is this the old jail where the friends lay who were hanged? An old woman, who sat knitting at the door, though not spoken to, answered, Yes, it is, and we

feelingly

feelingly know it; for a curse has been on the land ever since, so that it will not bear wheat without a blasting, and we are beholden to other colonies for bread. He replied, with an air of jesting, I have heard so, but I believe nothing of it. I told him we might observe, that the Almighty had sometimes manifested his displeasure on a people or nation, by famine, the sword, or pestilence, for their transgressions, if we had a belief in the sacred writings of the Old Testament. He said it could not be, that the Almighty, who is love in perfection, and in himself infinitely happy for ever, should delight in severity, and take vengeance on man, the workmanship of his hand: some, who are narrow in their way of thinking, may believe such things, but, for his part, he had ideas more noble of the Deity, than to believe such notions. By which I perceived he was a Deist, and did not regard the scriptures, and that it would be vain to say much to him: having often thought it was very difficult to say any thing to reach those sort of low freethinkers, who exercise themselves in the wisdom which is from beneath, and dwell safely in their own imaginations and conceits, whose communication is often infectious to others, and to be perceived in the meetings and neighbourhoods where they reside.

From thence we went to Bovey, Newton-Bushel, Totness, and King's Bridge; at the last,

last, after the morning and afternoon meetings, we had one in the evening with friends selected, which was to satisfaction. And hearing of one family that lived many miles from any meeting, I had a desire to see them, and went thither. I let the friend know that I came there on purpose to see him and his family, and should be glad to have them come together, and be still a little while, desiring it might be soon, for we intended to go that night to Plymouth. He said it would not answer them at that time, his children being employed in pressing out cyder. I let him know that I hoped I should not detain them long, and if they lightened the press, the cyder would not run over: but could not prevail with him, though I informed him that I had left all my business, and had come some thousands of miles to see my friends in this nation; and hearing how remote he lived from meeting, had a particular mind to see him. He replied, that he should be glad if it had suited them, but could not put his business by at that time. So, with a heavy heart, I left his house, and went to Plymouth, where we had a meeting the next day. Then to Germain's, Liscard, Looe, Austil, and Denny's, (in Cornwall) at which last place the people are mostly employed in the tin mines, and we had a pretty good meeting, a visit from a friend being acceptable to them, and they willing to leave their business, though
poor

poor people. From hence we proceeded pretty direct to the land's-end, intending to take the meetings on our return, and were at Penzance meeting on sixth day. At this meeting my companion, John Pemberton, spoke a few words in way of testimony, tender and broken, being the first time, and I thought had a good degree of the favour of truth attending. And on seventh day went to visit an ancient friend sick and bed rid, near the land's-end, where formerly there had been a meeting, and returned in the evening to Penzance. On first day had a meeting at Marazion in the morning, and at Penzance in the evening. We then turned eastward, and attended a meeting at Falmouth, and five others in this county of Cornwall. Then passed through Devonshire, taking a meeting at Oakhampton, and twelve others in Somersetshire, some of which were large and open, for there came many seeking people to the meetings at Bridgewater, and I hope some of those opportunities were, through Divine favour, profitable to some of them. And not being easy in my mind to leave this county without being at the quarterly-meeting for business, to be held at Glastonbury, I returned thither, and was concerned to lay before friends the declining state of the society in that county, and to exhort them to put the discipline in practice, that the church might be cleared from disorders, which caused reproach. It was thought

thought by friends to be the most solid quarterly meeting which had been held in that county for many years. From thence we went to Calne, in Wiltshire, being about fifty miles, and were at their meeting on first day, the sixteenth of the tenth month; where we met our friend and countryman Daniel Stanton, from Philadelphia, in the course of his religious visit, and were glad in each other's company, though the meetings, both forenoon and afternoon, were but dull; the people looking for words were disappointed. The next day we went together to a monthly-meeting at Chippenham. The meeting for worship was held in the meeting-house; at the conclusion of which friends rose and went out. I asked them where they were going, for I felt very uneasy; they said to do the business of the meeting; and feeling a strong engagement to be with them while they transacted the affairs of the church, I followed them, though it rained very fast. They went into a spacious house, where a room was prepared for the purpose, and a good fire. I sat down with them, though sorely distressed. They seemed to do the business in a formal ready way; I endeavoured to press them to weightiness of spirit, that they might feel the state of the society, and the need there was to put the discipline in practice, for religion was at a low ebb in that county. They seemed not to understand me, and indeed I found but
little

little room or openness to say much to them. They soon finished their business; when I rose up, and moved for going away: they informed me, that friends staid to dine where the business was transacted, and that the friends of the house would think it very strange if I went away: so they told the woman that the friend was going away. She met me in the hall, and said I must not go before I took dinner. I told her I should, for I had not freedom to stay to eat or drink in the house. She asked me why. I pressingly desired her to enquire of the truth in her own heart, and she might find the cause; so I went away, and a friend followed me out, and shewed me the way to his house, where I left my horse, and there I found Daniel Stanton, and my companion, John Pemberton, who went not to the meeting for business. Daniel informed me, that he followed us to the door, but could not go in; for he thought he felt the life of truth struck at, or trampled upon in that house, and therefore returned to the other, where we had left our horses, and John Pemberton with him. I was glad that he had such a sense, and he expressed satisfaction that I did not stay to dine, so we dined together; after which Daniel went westward, and we towards London, taking several meetings in our way, and arrived there the thirty-first of the tenth month, and tarried in the city until the twenty-fifth of the eleventh month.

month. In the mean time I carefully visited all the meetings, in great awfulness, being bowed in spirit under a sense of a forward ministry, and sat chiefly in silence among them. I also attended their meetings for discipline, namely, one quarterly-meeting, the monthly, two weeks, second day morning meeting, and meeting for sufferings, and was in much heaviness of mind, having a sense of a great neglect in some who were active members, in not waiting for a true qualification to act for the honour of God and edification of the church. Nevertheless, there is a remnant who are concerned to seek his honour, and to wait for the influence of his Divine Spirit and Power, to whom I was, at times, concerned to speak by way of encouragement. To transact the weighty affairs of the church in as light and easy a manner as men commonly buy and sell in a market, will always rather bring death over a meeting than life.

We left London on the twenty-sixth of the eleventh month, and went to Chelmsford, in Essex, and the next day sat with friends in their forenoon and afternoon meetings, to pretty good satisfaction, through the goodness and power of the Lord, whose presence was measurably felt among us to the praise of his ever worthy name. Then taking meetings as regularly as we could, we visited that county in twenty-four days, and had twenty-three publick meetings, and
some

some family sittings. My service for truth in this county was in a close plain way, mostly with but few words; for it often appeared to me, that there was a greater desire to hear, than to put in practice those things they were exhorted to, for which I often mourned, and had a strong sympathy with the few sensible, baptized friends among them. For brevity sake I close this general account without further remark.

We then passed to Ipswich, in Suffolk, and had a meeting with friends there to some satisfaction; there being a tender sincere remnant among them. And taking the east part of the county, we had ten meetings, and visited several indisposed friends to good satisfaction. Then went to Yarmouth, in Norfolk, and after attending their meetings in the morning and afternoon on first day, had a large satisfactory one the same evening, many of the people of the town coming to it. Then going to Norwich, we tarried with friends there about a week, in which time I had four meetings in that city, and one at Lammas, near it; and also visited divers indisposed friends, and had satisfaction therein. Intending to visit all the meetings in Norfolk county, a friend undertook to lay them out for me, and made a list of them, of which he gave me a copy, and told me it was the way to take the meetings with the least travelling: but I felt a strait in my mind, which I had always

ways found it safe for me to attend to, until I saw a way open; and being thoughtful about it, I desired him to inform me what meeting bore most to the north-east from that place; he told me it was North-Walsham; I desired him to begin there, and name the meetings most regular afterwards; and I would tell him if the lift felt pleasant as he went on. He then proceeded, and we readily finished one that was easy to me; when I desired him to set down the distances, as he had done in the other, and, on comparing them, we found the last to be at least three miles less riding. He seemed to be pleased, and said it was not the usual way of taking those meetings. I was willing to lay out nine, but told him, I was not fully easy to venture the giving publick notice further; that perhaps the weather might be difficult. He said there would be a general meeting in a few days, when friends from many meetings would be together, and likely to have full notice very easily given for a few meetings further, which he thought I had best leave to him. So we went forward to North-Walsham, and had a satisfactory meeting, and taking the meetings in course, came to the quarterly-meeting of ministers and elders at Norwich. The friend who laid out the meetings informed me, that if I had taken them according to his first lift, I should have interfered with a publick friend at several, who was then on a visit,

K and

and he thought there was a hand of Providence remarkable in turning me: for as we were both strangers, we should have been straitened through a tender regard to each other's service. He likewise let me know, that he did not remember that their quarterly-meeting began the next day after the meeting beyond which I told him I was not free to appoint any; and that having sent the list to a friend, to publish at the general meeting before mentioned, he had been obliged to attend that meeting to stop the notice respecting the few meetings he talked of, otherwise I should have missed the quarterly-meeting; and he thought it would teach him to be more cautious in future. I mention this occurrence with a degree of reverent thankfulness and humility, with no other view than to encourage those ministers who are called forth to visit the churches, to diligently and innocently attend to the motion of truth, which, the more we are humbled and inwardly quiet, the clearer it is understood and felt: but as this is instruction for ourselves, it is safer for us to treasure it up in our own hearts, than to make it too cheap by talking thereof to others. This quarterly-meeting, both in respect to publick worship and transacting the affairs of truth, was held to satisfaction, through the Lord's favour, who will be near to them that diligently seek him, blessed be his name for ever!

Then

Then taking Ellingham meeting, we went to Thetford, and had a meeting with friends there, both which were diftreffing, from a fenfe of the prevalence of a ranting fpirit. Here it appeared expedient to lay out meetings for the enfuing week, in order that fuitable notice might be given; and as they were named to me in courfe by friends, I felt a remarkable defire to fee the friends of one certain meeting by themfelves, at or near the eleventh hour of the day, although quite a ftranger to their fituation, numbers, or ftate. And a friend being prefent belonging to that meeting, I requefted her care about it, and then went home with Richard Brewfter to Edmondfbury, and attended the meetings there on the firft day morning and afternoon, which were in the main fatisfactory, and in the evening had a meeting with a fick friend. In this town there is a confiderable number of hopeful friends. We then went to Rattlefden, Bardwell, and through Livermore to Brand, the place where I had the defire to fee friends by themfelves, as before mentioned, and coming to the friend's houfe whofe wife had been intrufted with the notice, I afked her if it was not time to go to the meeting; fhe faid, Thou muft afk my hufband, appearing to be diftreffed. I afked where he was; fhe replied in his warehoufe, and fent for him. He coming after a while, I fuppofe about twelve o'clock, I afked him the time of the meeting; he answered, At six in the evening, to be sure. I told him, that I had informed his wife of my desire that it should be at eleven; he replied, She said so; but I thought it would be dishonourable, for few only would attend it at that time; for the people of that town were chiefly such as were obliged to do their day's work, which would be finished at six in the evening, when the house would be nearly full. I told him I did desire to see friends by themselves, and supposed they could meet at any hour. He granted that they could have met at the time proposed; but said, he was a man of a more liberal spirit than to want to eat his morsel alone, but was desirous his neighbours should partake with him; and thought it his duty to endeavour to inform and help those whom he apprehended were backward or ignorant in the performance of their duty: and he said the end and intent of ministers going forth was to publish the gospel, and he thought to the more the better. I let him know that it was necessary for those who were called to the work of the ministry, to know also to whom they were called, or otherwise they might be mistaken, and go north instead of south, or to a different nation or country. He answered, that he believed if they were rightly called, the spirit would inform them where they were to go. I replied, very well; and when they are come to the right place, the spirit would

would let them know what they have to do. He said, I believe so too. Whereupon I told him, if I knew the language of that spirit which called me from my native land to Old England, it was the same that inclined me to see the friends of that town by themselves; and afterwards, if I felt an enlargement of mind, I could have proposed a publick meeting with the town's-people in the evening. And why not one opportunity for both, he queried; adding, 'for I
' should be willing that all the town might
' hear what thou canst have to say to us.'
I then said to him, ' If a certain great per-
' son, on whom thy prosperity in all things
' temporal did absolutely depend, should,
' in singular kindness to thee, send a mes-
' senger to acquaint or advise thee of some
' matter relating to thyself, in thy own par-
' ticular conduct, in which thy prosperity,
' peace, and interest would, without thy
' immediate care, be nearly affected, wouldst
' thou judge it prudent to say to the am-
' bassador of such a friend, deliver not thy
' message to me, until I call my neighbours
' and the people of the town to hear it, and
' so expose thy own weakness to thy disad-
' vantage, without benefit to thy neigh-
' bours? Consider it carefully; my heart
' yearns to the professors of truth in this
' town, and it seems to me that my business
' at present was only with them; and as I
' cannot have an opportunity, according to

' my

' my freedom and desire, I shall hold myself
' excused.' He answered, If nothing but a
meeting with friends will do, we must send
them word to come together as soon as
they can. I told him that would now by
no means do; for he was at present so chafed
in his mind, that he could not hear to much
advantage. He then asked me what end
would be answered by my coming there. I
told him, to detect such heady, unsound
members as he was, that thought it dishonourable for a few friends to meet together
to worship God, though their number was
more than two or three, to whom the promise was. He said, Then what will become
of the meeting? I let him know he must
look to that, who had without orders headily appointed it, and so left him, and went
to Mildenhall, where a friend told me, that
he being at the meeting aforesaid when publick notice was given, that it was on this
wise, ' Friends and neighbours, please to
' take notice, that a friend from America
' desires a publick meeting here on Wed-
' nesday next, at six o'clock in the even-
' ing,' which circumstance I did not know
when I was at his house. On the whole I
had inward peace in my observations and
conduct to this man, and many friends rejoiced; for several had been overborne by
him, to their grief: and I was since informed, that he somewhat laid the matter
to heart, and was often heard to say, that

he would not serve any friend so again. After which we had many meetings in this county, and passing into Cambridgeshire, had eight meetings therein: and I thought the life of religion was low in general, though there are a few tender friends in several places. We then went to divers meetings in Huntingdonshire, Northamptonshire, Bedfordshire, and Hertfordshire, in which it was mostly my lot to point out to friends the danger they were in of losing the pure favour of truth, for want of humbly attending to the dictates thereof in their own hearts, which had already occasioned a dwarfishness among the professors in those parts. Several friends met us at Waltham-Abbey from London, with whom we went to that city, in order to attend the yearly-meeting, which began on the twenty-sixth, and ended on the sixth day of the week, the thirty-first of the third month, (1751) and in the several sittings thereof, both for publick worship and the transaction of the affairs of truth, was thought, by many, to be the most weighty and solid meeting that had been known for many years; which was cause of humble rejoicing and deep thankfulness to many friends, in that the Lord had vouchsafed his heavenly presence in wisdom and power, to the praise of his sacred name. Several friends staying in the city after the meeting was over, we had a large and satisfactory one on the seventh day of the week, and I tarried, attending divers meetings, until the sixth of the fourth month; then went to Chelmsford, and sat with friends in their morning and afternoon meetings on first day, and from thence to the yearly-meeting at Colchester; but being taken ill of a fever, I was prevented attending more than one sitting of that meeting; yet through mercy was resigned, and had peace. I staid their meeting in that town on the fifth day of the week, and the next day set forward with my brother, William Brown, John Griffith, and my companion, in order to attend Woodbridge yearly-meeting, which began on the seventeenth of the month; and although the fever had not left me, I was enabled to attend every sitting of it, which was a large and solid meeting throughout, and friends were refreshed together, praised be the Lord! whose mercy is great to his people. My companion, John Pemberton, went with my brother to some adjacent meetings, but I staid the week day meeting in this town, which was through divine favour satisfactory. We met again at the yearly-meeting at Norwich in a few days, which concluded to satisfaction, and friends were made truly thankful to the Lord for this additional favour. We spent a few days longer at this city, and attended their monthly-meeting; after which, having a desire to visit a few meetings in company with my brother, William Brown, where

ranterism

ranterism seemed to prevail, he having the like concern, we took a monthly-meeting at Wymondham, also the meetings at Matishall and Ellingham, in which we were concerned to use great plainness to clear ourselves, on account of that ranting spirit. Then went to Wareham, and had a precious meeting with the few friends of that place, and to a very large general meeting at Downham, many of other societies being there; and it became my concern to recite the words of our blessed Lord, John v. 39, 40. "Search the scriptures; for in them
" ye think ye have eternal life; and they
" are they which testify of me. And ye
" will not come to me, that ye might have
" life." From whence I had to shew them the danger of trusting to information and knowledge, whether by reading the scriptures, or hearing them preached, and neglecting to attend unto the inspeaking voice of Christ immediately in the heart, which is the only sure interpreter of the scriptures, leading those who attend to his instruction in the sure way to life eternal. Then parting with William Brown, we went to Wisbich, and Thornyfenn, in Cambridgeshire, and taking divers meetings in Lincolnshire, we passed into the East-riding of Yorkshire, in which we had twenty-four meetings, and taking eight in the county of Durham, we came to Shields, in Northumberland, Newcastle, and Alnwick Abbey, and reached Kelso,

Kelso, in Scotland, on the first of the seventh month, where we met Susanna Fothergill, on her return home. We attended the morning and afternoon meetings at Kelso, on first day. Alas! truth is here at a low ebb; and feeling my mind not to be clear of friends in this place, I desired to have a select meeting with them, which Susanna and her companion attended, and we had an opportunity of clearing ourselves of friends there, who had much fallen from the simplicity of the pure truth, into the modes, fashions, and customs of the world, in their dress, language, and manners; and truth owned our service with a degree of its Divine authority; blessed be the Lord, the God of Truth! We then went to a meeting at the house of John Christy, at Ormston, to which many people came, and behaved quietly, and the doctrine of truth opened pretty freely to them. From thence to a meeting at Edinburgh, in which I had a sense that silence was best, apprehending the people had been too much fed with words. After some time one stood up, and spake of the excellence of resignation in ministers to speak, or contentedly to be silent; to be any thing or nothing, as the Lord was pleased to order: but a secret distressing fear attended my mind, that he was not enough inwardly engaged to distinguish the order and motion of the Spirit of Truth, from the busy imagination and will of the creature,

ture, unsubjected to the Divine Spirit; and I found a concern to shew the nature of true resignation, and the low humble quiet that attended the minds of ministers, or hearers, who had come to the real knowledge of it; the desire of such as was turned unto the Lord only for heavenly instruction, and an inward evidence of the life and motion of truth; for want of which, true gospel ministry was sometimes obstructed, and the reason of silence not fully understood. After I sat down the same person again stood up, and in a flow of words, and a zealous tone, said, that weakness, or the want of experience, led people to mistake both their own and the condition of others. As he appeared to me to be actuated by a confident, ranting spirit, my mind was greatly exercised after the meeting. I remained at this place the two following days, being detained by rainy weather, and attended the meeting in the morning of first day, at which I sat silent; but the same person spake some time, in words very encouraging to the auditory, as if all was well with them, which tended to increase the exercise of my mind, having a very different sense of the state of the meeting. I again attended their meeting in the afternoon, when the same person seemed as if he intended soon to stand up; but feeling the testimony of truth strong against that forward ranting spirit, and the sense thereof being weighty upon me, I endeavoured

voured to keep under it in patience, and soon the concern of that person began to diminish, and he to be drowsy, after which I had a favourable open time to clear my mind of the exercise that had been upon me.

Next day we passed over the Frith, about seven miles broad, landed at Kinghorn, and rode to a town called Cowper, and the day following reached to the house of one who esteemed himself a friend, near Montrose, where we endeavoured to have a meeting, but he would not allow it, alledging, that it would do his people or servants no good, and as for himself, he thought he knew as much of the truth as we could inform him: and, indeed, he seemed so whole and self-righteous, I thought it would not avail to say much to him. We were informed by a person who accompanied us a few miles, that this man, in his younger years, had a publick testimony to bear for the truth, but had for a long time left it off (as he worded it) and now, his men servants must not approach him with their heads covered. "If the light in you become darkness, how great is that darkness." From hence we went to Ury, the seat of Robert Barclay, grandson to the Apologist, but had no meeting until we came to the Old Town, near a mile north of Aberdeen, which was, through the goodness of the Lord, somewhat strengthening. From thence went to
John

John Elmflie's, at Old-Meldrum, and on firft day morning attended Killmuck meeting, and in the evening one at Old-Meldrum, to which many people came, and, through Divine favour, thefe meetings were fatisfactory. The next day we had a felect meeting with friends, of whom there are feveral here, tender and valuable, and we parted in love: and going to Kingfwells had a meeting there with many friends and others, truth owning the fervice, which was caufe of humble rejoicing. Continuing at and near Aberdeen, we had a large meeting on firft day at Robert Barclay's. Although the defcendants and children of friends, who were as bright as ftars in their day, may value themfelves on the worthinefs of their parents, yet if they do not love and ferve the God of their fathers with a perfect heart and an upright mind, he will not own them with his heavenly prefence, but they will be as unfavoury falt.

We then fet forward on our return towards England, taking two meetings in our way to Glafgow, where, on firft day, we had alfo two, which were large, open, and fatisfactory, to which many tender inquiring people came, who behaved well, and in the evening of the fame day, had another with thofe called friends by themfelves, having a concern to lay before them the need they had to look to their ways and converfation, that they might be as lights and good examples

amples among the people in that place, who were seekers after the truth, and not give them occasion of stumbling through an evil conduct. Then passing to Carlisle, in Cumberland, Morehouse, Scoby, Solport, and Kirklington, in most of which meetings truth seemed to be professed, but too few had the life thereof in possession, which occasions hard dry meetings; we rode to Cornwood, in Northumberland, and lodged at the house of a man who had been for several years of a disorderly conduct, and much given to the excessive use of strong drink, until he had very much impaired his constitution; but it pleased the Lord to open his understanding, and make him acquainted with his blessed truth, whereby he was made free from that evil, and received strength to forsake his old companions. But his joining with friends was a great grief to his wife, who informed me, that through prejudice, for a time, she would rather he had continued his former course of living than to become a Quaker, until observing the sweetness of his temper, and the recovery of his health, in some degree, with a solid and sober conduct, she was reached, and made to believe in the power by which he had known such a victory, and joined herself in the same religious profession: they appeared to be steady friends. I would to God, that all tipplers and drunkards would turn to that great Prophet which is

in

in Israel, that they might by him be cleansed from that leprosy of sin! We had a comfortable meeting the next day in his house, with his neighbours and some friends: and on first day were at Allandale meeting, where are some solid friends, though others much tainted with a spirit of ranterism, which is a confident, self-righteous spirit, and very hard to be won upon. After having a meeting at Aldstinmoor, we passed to the meetings at Penrith, in Cumberland, Terril, and Strickland, which is in a corner of Westmoreland. It was with some difficulty we had the meeting at Terril, a man of that place saying, he thought it needless, or questioned whether it would be to advantage, as most of their members had been at Penrith meeting; but after the meeting he desired that I would not take it hard of him for endeavouring to discourage me, owning that he was mistaken. Whereupon I cautioned him to be more careful in future how he discouraged such who had come so many thousand miles to visit them. Having meetings at divers places in the week following, I travelled in great pain and anguish of mind, from a sense of the prevalence of a dark, deistical spirit over many of the professors of truth; of which concern the Lord was pleased to give me strength and understanding to clear myself, both in publick and private. There is no power but his that can enable his servants

to do his work, and is over all the powers of Satan. On the next firſt day we were at Holme meeting. In the forenoon I ſat ſilent. One of the ſtock of the old ranters was there, and very troubleſome, accuſing many friends, no doubt falſely; and in the afternoon meeting I had not much to ſay, believing that old ranting ſpirit is rather fed with words, and delights in contention, but found it my place to exhort friends to retire deeply inward in all their meetings, humbly waiting to be admitted into the heavenly preſence, to know their place of feeding to be out of the reach of ſuch ranting ſpirits: for if they ſuffered their own ſpirits to riſe or reſent their ill uſage, the meeting would be the more diſquieted. Our next meetings were at Allonby and Broughton; from whence I went home with our friend Chriſtopher Wilſon to his houſe at Grayſothen, and the next day attended the burial of a young man at Pardſhaw Hall, and the day following the burial of a young woman at the ſame place; both of which meetings were very large and ſolid, and I hope, through Divine goodneſs, profitable to many. The firſt day of the following week we were at two meetings at Whitehaven, in both which I had ſome ſervice, under the influence and owning of truth. We put up our horſes at a friend's houſe, who had been uſed to lodge publick friends, but I was not free to tarry there, being
burthened

burthened with his conduct in the manner of his entertainment, which was even to superfluity and grandeur, no way becoming the simplicity of truth. So, after shewing my diflike therewith, I went to the house of John Harris, at Highfield, his wife being with us, and rested there a day, the weather being exceeding rainy. Then going to the meetings at Cockermouth, Isell, and Grayfothen, we returned to Cockermouth, and had a meeting with friends by themfelves, that is, without giving publick notice, which was, through Divine favour, to good satisfaction. Resting another day with our friend John Harris, we went to meetings at Pardshaw Hall, and at Kefwick, at which last I was concerned to exhort the few friends there to keep up their week day meetings, having a fear they were slack on that account. We lodged at an inn, where we had the company of some of those friends, and in particular one who was a publick friend. Some of them said, if he would attend the week day meeting, they believed the rest of them would; which gave me occasion to observe to him, that he did not example well, and ought to be more careful, as he had a publick testimony to bear for truth. He replied, that he was obliged to be industrious to support his family; but at last confessed, that ' he did
' not like to set with so few friends, for
' none else would come on a week day, and
' it

'it was very dull and poor sitting; and he
'liked to sit in meetings where there were
'many assembled, for then he had some-
'thing to say; so life did arise, and all were
'comforted and edified." By which it appeared that he had greater satisfaction in preaching than in humble silent waiting to experience the worship which is performed in spirit and truth, to edification and comfort. I told him, that I feared he was too much a stranger to pure religion, and the nature of divine worship.

From thence we went to Hawkshead, in Lancashire, and had an evening meeting there in a friend's house, and next day were at the Hight meeting, and then at Swarthmore, where George Fox formerly lived, which had been famous for the prosperity of truth, but it is now at a low state there. We then went to Kendal, in Westmoreland, where we attended their two meetings on the first day of the week; and after taking some other meetings in the neighbourhood, returned to that town, in and about which we tarried several days, and visited more than twenty families, and attended ten publick meetings; many of which opportunities were made precious, through the goodness and great condescension of our Lord and Saviour. And in the school of our friend Thomas Rebanks I had an extraordinary meeting; where many young folks not of our society were reached by the power of truth,

truth, which was comfortably over all, praised be the Lord for ever! In the course of our visiting families here, during our silent sitting in one of them, my mind was much taken up in thinking of a watch, and the several wheels and movements thereof, until I was grieved at such trifling thoughts, as I esteemed them; when suddenly there appeared something instructing therein, and I had a freedom to say, the several parts thereof seemed to represent the excellent inward faculties and gifts bestowed on man, and that though the wheels, &c. of a watch were truly made, and placed in their proper order, there must be a main spring to give them motion; so the gifts and faculties of men must have their main spring and cause of motion to every good work, a zeal to the honour of the Lord their Creator, and a fervent holy desire to answer the end of their creation: and as there is a regulating spring to a watch, so also there should be the true knowledge of God and of themselves experienced in his light, to preserve from going too fast, knowing, by his heavenly instruction, that no wisdom, zeal, strength, or ability, will enable to do the Lord's work to his honour and the good of man, but that which God giveth: and in order that a watch may answer the end intended by its maker, there is a visible face, and hands, to discover the inward motion, thereby shewing time; so it is needful that a man should be a co-worker with the spirit and gift of grace in his inward part, that others, beholding the light thereof, might be taught to glorify God, and in his light so to number his days, and walk in his fear, as to die in his favour. As a zeal for the cause of truth, and a fear of falling short of duty, may at times prompt man to rush on too fast, it is needful that he should wait in humble reverence to feel the love of God, and the influence of that knowledge and wisdom which is from above, and experienced by those who are spiritual, that the end of all their labour may be in the spirit of meekness to restore those who are overtaken in error. And that men may ever dwell in that which gives ability to labour with success in the church of Christ, it is needful that their minds should be enclosed in the bosom of truth, in humble retirement, to be preserved from the various tumults, cumbers, cares, and temptations of the world, which would otherwise clog their minds, and deprive them of their true spiritual sense and motion: and so in a watch it is needful that all the inward parts, which are so curious, should be inclosed from damps, vapours, motes, and dust, otherwise it would thereby be deprived of its motion, and become useless for keeping time.

My intent in this relation is to shew the infinite condescension of him whose mercy is over all his works, to instruct the children

dren of men, each as it were in his own tongue, or language suitable to his understanding; the man being by trade a watchmaker, and seemed to be tenderly reached, and we parted in a degree of sweetness. It was the Lord's doing, and marvellous to me, praised be his holy name for ever!

Being clear of Kendal, we took leave of friends in much affection, and went to a general meeting at Brigflatts, in Yorkshire, and to visit our friend Alice Alderson, who had been on a religious visit in our country, with Margaret Cowpland, whom we had before seen at Kendal, where she lives. Alice was glad to see us, and we found her tender in spirit, and strong in her love to friends. After attending meetings at Ravonstonedale and Garsdale, we rode to our friend John Burton's, who, with his companion, William Backhouse, had also been in our country on a religious visit. We rejoiced to see him, and were comforted by his grave conversation and conduct. We then went to a meeting at Dent, which was large, and favoured by the overshadowing of truth in a good degree, in the loving kindness of our Lord, who is worthy of all praise for ever! Then taking several meetings in Lancashire, and tarrying two days with our friend William Backhouse, which was an acceptable rest to us, the weather being very cold, the ways bad, and we weary, we came to Lancaster, and had an opportunity

opportunity of visiting our friend Lydia Lancaster, who several years past had visited our country. Her faculties of mind and love to friends appeared fresh and strong. From thence, attending divers other meetings in that county, we went to our friend Samuel Fothergill's, at Warrington, where we continued from the second to the fourteenth of the first month (new-stile) 1752: he and Susanna his wife being tender and kindly affectionate, we were refreshed in their company; having several meetings in that town and at Penketh, some whereof were made precious by the ownings of truth. After many other meetings in this county and Yorkshire, we reached Richmond, and had a meeting with friends there; and next morning set forward with a guide for Masham, in order to attend a meeting there, of which friends had previous notice. The distance was near sixteen miles, the days short, and roads deep and miry. After we had rode five or six miles, I desired our guide to mend his pace, fearing we should be too late: a little further we came to a place where the roads parted, and he taking the left hand I became uneasy, and asked him if he perfectly knew the way; he said, he thought he did: I let him know my being in doubt about it, and desired him to enquire of a man we saw in a field at a distance, but he rode on yet faster; when I told him, that I was persuaded we had

had almoſt turned our backs on the way we ſhould go, at which he ſmiled. When we had gone about a mile, ſeeing a man by the way ſide at work, I aſked him if that was the way to Maſham; he replied, Nay; for you have left it, and muſt go back, unleſs your horſes can leap over ditches very well, you may then ſave a mile; and, pointing over a field, ſhewed us a moor, on the other ſide whereof our right road was. Our guide ſet forward, we followed with ſome difficulty over the ditches, and he rode on a gallop, and ſoon left us. My mind inclined me to vary from his courſe, and eſpying a gate, called to him, pointing to it, and proceeded thither, on which he turned and came up, but ſaid he believed we were wrong. I let him know that my mind was eaſy to go that way, and in a while we came into a road at a publick houſe, which he knew to be right: ſo we juſt reached the meeting in time, which, through divine favour, was profitable and edifying. I mention this paſſage with no other view than to encourage friends to be inward in their minds, and to regard the ſecret ſenſe which the pure ſpirit of truth ſometimes gives on particular occaſions: for want of an inward ſtillneſs, and attention thereunto, the way is often miſſed in more reſpects than one.

At Maſham we lodged at the houſe of John Kelden, who related to me ſomething that paſſed between a knight of the ſhire and

and one of his tenants, a member of our religious society, in manner following, viz.

Landlord. So, John, you are busy.

Tenant. Yes; my landlord loves to see his tenants busy.

Landlord. But, John, where was you, that you was not at your quarterly-meeting at York the other day? I saw most of your staunch friends there, but you I missed. †

Tenant. Why, thou knowest I have a curious landlord, who loves to see his tenants thrive, and pay their rent duly, and I had a good deal in hand that kept me at home.

Landlord. Kept you at home! You will neither thrive nor pay the better for neglecting your duty, John.

Tenant. Then I perceive my landlord was at quarterly-meeting. How didst thou like it?

Landlord. Like it! I was at one meeting, and saw what made my heart ache.

Tenant. What was that?

Landlord. Why, the dress of your young folks: the men with their wigs, and young women with their finery, in imitation of fashions. And I thought I would try another meeting: so next day I went again, and then I concluded there was little difference but the bare name between us, whom

---

† The assizes are held at York always at the time of the quarterly-meeting.

you

you call the world's people, and some of you; for you are imitating of us in the love and fashions of the world as fast as you can. So that I said in my heart, these people do want a Fox, a Penn, and a Barclay among them: so he turned from his tenant.

I thought it would be a pity that the true and solid remark of this great man should be lost, understanding that it was rather expressed in pity than derision.

From Masham we proceeded to visit many other meetings in this county, in the course whereof we called to see good old John Richardson, who was strong in spirit, though feeble in body, and nearly blind through age, being about eighty-seven. And finding a draught to visit friends once more at Scarborough, we were there on first day the fifteenth of the third month, and had peace in my own mind, having done what I thought was my duty. But, from a sense of the prevalence of pride, which had occasioned a great poverty, as to true religion, among the professors of truth in that place, I left them with an aching heart, and went on our journey, in order to attend the quarterly-meeting at York, taking meetings in our way at Pickering, Thornton in the Clay, and Hewby. The several sittings of this quarterly-meeting were in the main satisfactory; but not having time fully to clear myself, I did not leave York quite easy. After this, having meetings at Clifford, Leeds, Gilderfome,

Gilderfome, Bradford, Rawden, Afquith, Farfield, Keighley, Skipton, and Lotherfdale, we rode to Settle, and then to attend the quarterly-meeting at Lancafter, which began on the fifth day of the week with a meeting of minifters and elders, and was comfortable. Next day was the meeting for publick worfhip, and the difcipline, wherein we were made to rejoice together, and praife the name of the Lord, who is worthy for ever! We went home with our friend William Backhoufe, and fo to Kendal quarterly-meeting, which was fatisfactory, and very large; then fet out for the quarterly-meeting for Cumberland, held at Carlifle, which began with a meeting of minifters and elders: next day were held two publick meetings, and the day following a meeting for the difcipline, which ended in the afternoon with another for worfhip: and going home with Chriftopher Wilfon, we were at a good meeting at Pardfhaw Hall on firft day.

My mind had been for fome time drawn towards Ireland, and being defirous to lofe no time, we went to Whitehaven, feveral veffels being there nearly laden with coals for Dublin; but on viewing the fhips, accompanied by feveral friends from Grayfothen, I had no freedom to take a paffage in either of them, at which I was much ftraitened, and inwardly turning my mind, Ireland was hid from my view; and going to to the house of a friend, we sat a while still, and I had a freedom to let friends know that I had no prospect but that the vessels might go their voyage with safety, and did not decline a passage on that account; but feeling a full stop in my mind, had no freedom to proceed any where at present, save to return with our friends John and Hannah Harris to Highfield. We therefore returned with them, and attended Pardshaw Hall monthly-meeting, where I had freedom to propose that friends would enter on the service of visiting families. They informed me that some years before they had nominated friends for that service, but meeting with some discouragement, they had not performed it: and being about to turn over the book, to see who were then appointed, considering it was a long time since, they concluded it was better to proceed to a new choice, but seemed at a stand about naming friends then. I had a singular freedom to let them know, that although I was a stranger, I could point out some who I believed would answer the service, if they would submit to it. After a solid pause, a friend said, as our friend has the matter before him, I am free that he should choose for us; to which I replied, that being a stranger to their members, one might be chosen who was under some impediment, and therefore it would be safer for the meeting to choose; but perceiving they were at a loss,

loſs, I pointed out a few friends in great
fear, with a ſingle eye to the ſenſe which I
did believe truth gave me, and the clerk
took their names. A friend ſaid he believed
it was the truth which had made the choice.
I then mentioned, that if they could ſoon
enter upon the ſervice, I found a freedom to
accompany them therein, if friends had
unity therewith, which ſeveral expreſſed.
Some women friends being alſo named by
their meeting to join in it, before the ſervice was much proceeded in, a heavy concern came upon me, from a ſecret ſenſe I
had that one of them was under the cenſure
of ſome, by which I feared her ſervice
would be laid waſte, unleſs it could be removed; and although I had no intimation
of any thing of the kind from any perſon,
I became heavily exerciſed, and at length
requeſted a friend to invite the man and his
wife to dine with him, who I apprehended
were uneaſy with the woman, and I deſired
her and her huſband to come to the ſame
houſe in the afternoon, who accordingly
came. Thus the parties being met unex-
pectedly to each other, I was humbled under the weight attending my mind, and no
others being preſent, except the friend and
his wife at whoſe houſe we were, I ventured
to let them know the exerciſe I had been
under ſome days, from an apprehenſion of
a difference, or prejudice, ſubſiſting between
them, which, if not removed, would devour

vour like fire; by which I believed they were already much affected; but as I had not received information, more or less, I might be mistaken, and did not desire they should say any thing on the subject before me, but honestly confer on it between themselves first, and if it was so, remove the cause; and if nothing was amiss, then to let me know, that I might be warned to be more cautious in future. Upon which I left them, and walked by myself about an hour, when the man of the house called me in, and they told me that I was not mistaken, for that there had been an hardness subsisting for some time, which they hoped was now done away. But when, in the course of our visit, we came to the house of the friends who had been uneasy, I felt it as fresh as before, and told them I did believe they were not easy that the friend should go on in the service. To which one of them answered, If she judges herself to be clear, and others are easy, I have no objection. Whereupon I asked what others were meant; the man replied, Her husband and relations. And as the matter rested upon me, it appeared that endeavours ought to be used for reconciliation before we could with satisfaction proceed on our visit; and, believing that the Lord had secretly engaged me, I hoped he would accompany, and bless the labour, for the restoration of peace; which in a few days he was pleased
to

to accomplish, and then we proceeded more chearfully; and I think I may say that the Lord was with us, to the praise of his great eternal name, who is worthy for ever!

We visited the families of friends in Whitehaven, Broughton, Cockermouth, Pardshaw Hall, Eaglesfield, and Graysothen, and others remote, and had several profitable publick meetings in those towns, and places adjacent. Having spent about seven weeks within the verge of Pardshaw Hall monthly-meeting, and finding my mind clear, we went to Whitehaven, and took passage in the ship Globe, James Grason master, for Ireland, on the eighth of the sixth month, (1752) N. S. and parting with our dear friends in much love, set sail about the fifth hour in the evening, and landed at Dublin on the eleventh of the same month, and were kindly received at the house of Samuel Judd; as I was going to which, this secret hint was presented to my mind, ' Live re-
' tired, and be not suddenly acquainted with
' any man.' After dinner our kind landlord said, I do not well in that I have not informed friends of your arrival: they will blame me. I answered, Let us first know that we are here; we are just come from sea, and are weary: for we had a troublesome passage by contrary winds and heavy rains, John Pemberton, my companion, having been very sea-sick, and myself a little so. The next day we attended Sycamore-Alley

Alley meeting, where we had the company of Sufanna Hatton, who had been in America with Ruth Courtney. We were at eight meetings in Dublin, alfo at a monthly-meeting, and a quarterly-meeting for their young people; in which I was deeply concerned, under confideration of the prevalence of pride and the world's fafhions, which was declared to them in the love of truth: and the Lord was pleafed to favour feveral of the meetings by his heavenly prefence, to the praife of his holy name.

Leaving this city, we went towards the North. At Drogheda there is a meeting-houfe belonging to friends, but they are there fo declined, we could not have a meeting to fatisfaction. We therefore went on to a meeting with a few friends at Rathfriland, in the county of Down, then to Moyallon, where the meeting was comfortable; and on firft day had two meetings at Lurgan, in the county of Armagh, in which place pride and a worldly fpirit much prevails. Then taking meetings at Newton, Lifburn, Hillfborough, and Ballinderry, in the county of Antrim, the laft of which was a large good meeting, we had one at Antrim, where the favour of truth feems much loft by the few profeffors there. We then paffed on to the Grange meeting, which was very dull, through the prevalence of a worldly dark fpirit; and from thence to a meeting at Ballynacree, and fo to Colerain, where

where we had a satisfactory opportunity with some of the town's people, who came to the meeting out of curiosity: but I felt no freedom to express the sense I had of the state of friends then; and as the meeting broke up, I stepped to a young woman, a friend, who lived near the meeting-house, and desired her to step forward, and turn the few friends in there, as she knew them, and let the others go by, which she readily performed. When we were all sat down round the room, it soon felt to me that if I delivered my concern in general terms, the intended end would not be answered: being in pain for their good, and close matters spoken might be taken by such to whom least belonged, and being greatly humbled, I was desirous to be rightly instructed (not knowing their names) to speak to them separately. The Lord, who never fails those who humbly trust in him, shewed me where and with whom to begin, and so to the next, and mine eye being fixed on the person to whom I directed my speech, each knew what was delivered to them in particular; and I hope the opportunity was beneficial, for I had great peace. When the friends were gone, I asked the young woman, who seemed in some surprize, what ailed her; she said, that several were very exactly told their condition, and she feared they would judge her for an informer. I told her, she need not matter that, as she knew
herself

herself innocent. I mention this occurrence as a remarkable kindness from the merciful Lord to the children of men, for their help and instruction, and that his servants may be encouraged to wait upon him for instruction to discharge their duty as faithful stewards in his sight, who knows the secrets of all hearts, and taught his servant in old time to know the wife of Jeroboam, though she feigned herself to be another woman. Blessed and magnified be his holy name, who is over all, worthy for ever, and ever!

Then taking meetings at Tobberhead, Charlemont, and Ballyhagan, we attended the men's meeting at Lurgan, having a great desire to sit with friends there in the management of their discipline, which was adjourned to this time at my request. It began with a meeting for worship, men and women being generally together; at the conclusion of which, the men went into the room where the meeting for business was usually held, when, after sitting some time in silence, a leading friend said, 'This 'is only an adjourned meeting,' and bid the clerk enter it, and they might adjourn to the usual time to do their business, when it would be more select. And the meeting sitting a while without proceeding any way, I asked them what was meant by the words, 'more select,' and further said, if any persons were present that had not a right to sit there, they should withdraw, they knew their

their own members: if they meant the friend who came with us, he was a neighbouring friend, and an elder; and as for myself, I esteemed myself a proper member of their meeting, as I came to visit them with the concurrence of my brethren at home, and had certificates from them, wherein I was recommended to friends in Europe, and elsewhere; and if I did any thing among them worthy of censure, I should submit to their dealing, and therefore desired them to go on with their business; for I had come thither with a concern to see how the affairs of the church went on. So without more debate, or much reply, they proceeded; and, to my surprize, things of disorder had lain several years without proper dealing with various offenders; such as drinkers of healths, some that had been at cockfightings and races, and one or more marriages out of the order of truth: which gave me an opportunity to clear myself fully of the concern that had for some days lain with weight on my mind, which I believe was acceptable to some secretly pained friends, however contrary to some others. So that I left the place with a peaceful mind, and thankful to the Lord, who had given me an innocent boldness to assert my right of membership: for I believe if we had not been there, the meeting would have been thought select.

We

We then went to Ulster Province-meeting at Ballyhagan, which held two days. The elders and other concerned friends here inquire into the state of things among their members in the province, and it was in the main a satisfactory meeting. From hence we went southward, taking meetings at Castleshane, Coothill, Ballihais, and Old Castle, and to Ballimurry, in Connaught, having a meeting in a barn at Gailey with a few friends, it being the only one kept up in that province, except at Athlone, which we likewise attended, and came to James Clibborn's, at the Moat of Granoge, where we also had a meeting; although I had travelled every day for more than a week with a fever on me, and had eaten little, occasioned, as I thought, by a cold taken by laying in damp beds, and was now very unwell, but sat the first day meeting. Next day my illness became very violent, so that friends thought I should lay my body there, and sent for an apothecary, who let me blood, which somewhat allayed the fever, and I fell into a sleep, when I began to bleed again, which brought me very weak, that I was awakened at midnight with great drops of sweat on my face, and sickness; and calling my companion, who watched with me, we found that I had bled much, the orifice in my arm being very large, and not carefully bound up. My kind landlord and his wife, being anxious about me, had prevailed with the apothecary to lodge in the houſe, who being called to me, on his coming, I defired him to peel a bladder, and apply a thin piece of it, about as broad as a halfpenny, on the wound. He aſked for what; I told him he would ſee: and when it was applied, I requeſted him to hold his finger on the piece over the orifice, ſo as to ſtop the blood, until the plaiſter dried and ſtuck, which it ſoon did, and it bled no more: he ſaid that he had not ſeen the like. I mention this for the ſake of others; for the bladder ſticks as the blood under it dies, and will ſtop the bleeding of almoſt any wound. Next morning a graduate phyſician of the town came to viſit me, and feeling my pulſe, I aſked him what he thought of me. He making no anſwer, I ſaid, be not afraid to tell me, for I am not afraid to hear. He replied, ' that ' is happy for you;' by which I ſuppoſed he thought I ſhould not recover. He viewed my ſpittle, and ſaid I was in a deep conſumption, and propoſed my taking a vomit. I told him that I had not taken one many years: beſides, as he judged my lungs were inflamed, a moderate purge was better; at which he replied, with an air of banter, ' You are an odd patient: come, you ſhall ' be phyſician, and I will be apothecary.' I took him at his word, and he ſent me a purge, which gave me ſome relief. He viſited me daily for a week, and could hardly believe

believe I should recover, though I told him I believed that I should. He still judged my cough to be consumptive, and at length told me, if I did recover, to go home as soon as I could; for that the Lord was more merciful than to require such an one as I was to travel as I did; and that I had already acted as a madman, to travel so long time with that fever before I lay by. I asked him, if he was master of a vessel at sea, which had sprung a leak that could not be stopped, what he would do. He replied, endeavour to make to the next port, for a dry dock, to unlade, and search out the leak. Why, doctor, said I, this is just my case: I saw no place to lay by until I came hither; at which he laughed, and wished me well. I think I never was reduced to so weak a state in so short a time, which might be occasioned by my great loss of blood; but the Lord was pleased to heal me, that I gathered strength to admiration, and on first day sat the meeting, which was comfortable, and continuing to recover, though not fit to travel, I tarried until fourth day, and attended their monthly-meeting; and understanding they had been endeavouring to visit families, but were backward in beginning, I told friends that I had a freedom to accompany them in the work for a few days, for their encouragement, and we accordingly went with them to a few places to good satisfaction; and friends received strength to go on with the service. Then taking an affectionate leave of our kind landlord, James Clibborn, and his wife, who is granddaughter to Robert Barclay, the apologist, we went to meetings at Birr, Kilconnermoor, Cashell, Killcommon, Clonmell, Youghall, and so to Cork on the first day of the week, where we also attended the men's meeting for discipline, and visited the women's meeting, which were both to some good satisfaction. Then going to Bandon, we returned to an appointed meeting at Cork, for parents and their children; and having strength given me to clear myself, it was, I hope, profitable to many, being a large meeting. We then went to Malo, and had a seasonable opportunity with a family of friends. Thence to the province-meeting for Munster, held at Limerick, the publick and select sittings of which, and for the discipline, ended comfortably. And after attending the week-day meeting, we went to a meeting at Ross, and returned to Limerick, and being unwell with a cold, we tarried their meetings on first day, which were large and satisfactory, and in the evening had one with a sick friend. Being clear, and taking three meetings in our way, we proceeded to Leinster province-meeting, at Mountmelick, which began on the sixth day of the week with a meeting of ministers, the next day for worship and the discipline, and on first day morning was a large and precious

precious meeting. In the afternoon the town's people came in, and it was a good satisfactory meeting, though not so large, friends being mostly gone home. We had a meeting next day at Tullamoor, and returning to Mountmelick, had a satisfactory one with the children in the school of James Gough. After the week-day meeting in this town, we went to Ballicarrol, Ballinakil and Cooperhill, having a meeting at each; then to Catherlough monthly-meeting on first day, and the next day to Athy; then to Ballitore, which was, through Divine goodness attending, made profitable: and we had also a satisfactory meeting with the scholars in Abraham Shackleton's school. After a meeting at Newton, we went to Samuel Watson's, at Kilconner, whose wife (late Abigail Bowles) had been on a religious visit in America several years past. She was now near her end, but sensible, and in a good frame of spirit, and greatly rejoiced to see us, and we were mutually comforted in a sense of the Lord's presence, for which his holy name was praised. After a meeting here, and another at Catherlough, we went to Waterford, and sat with friends in their morning, afternoon, and evening meetings on the first day; in all which, having cleared myself honestly, my spirit mourned under a sense of formality among the people, and a deadness to the pure inward life of religion. Then taking meetings at Ross, Lambstown,

town, Wexford, Randals-mills, or Castle-sow, Cooladine, and several other places, we came to Wicklow, at which meeting many soldiers attended, who behaved well, and truth owned the service in a good degree. I have observed where the soldiers came into our meetings, they were an awe to the rabble, and loose people, who are sometimes apt to be rude. From hence we went to Dublin, in order to attend the national half-year's-meeting, and were kindly received by our old landlord, Samuel Judd, and his family.

Leinster province-meeting began on second day, the sixth of the eleventh month, both for worship and discipline, and on third day the national meeting, which held four days: the several sittings thereof being in general attended with a sense of Divine goodness; and the testimony of truth ran strong against hypocrisy, covetousness, libertinism, and pride among the professors thereof, but in a consolatory stream to the humble and contrite children of the family; in a thankful sense whereof the name of the Lord was praised, who is worthy for ever and ever! We tarried a few days longer with friends in Dublin, and then went to meetings at Baltibois, Timahoe, Rathagon, and Edenderry, and a religious sitting at John Pim's family at Nurney. Then returning to Edenderry, attended their monthly-meeting, where having a concern to visit some families of friends,

friends, we went to moſt of them in that town, and to the houſe of a widow in the country, where we had a good opportunity with her and her children. I aſked the friend who accompanied us, whether there was any other friend's houſe to which we had not been. He ſaid he thought not; but my mind had a draught to ſome houſe, and I pointed toward it. He then ſaid he believed he knew where. So we went to the place, and the family being called together, I enquired whether there was not another belonging to the houſe, and was told there was. As ſoon as he came in, I knew it was the man whom my mind was concerned to viſit; and ſomething I had to expreſs reached and tendered him very much; he being exceeding wild and faſhionable, and did not love to attend religious meetings, but truth now reached him. On the firſt day following I ſaw him at Edenderry meeting, where the viſitation ſeemed to be renewed to him. I afterwards heard that he continued to be ſober and thoughtful, and I was thankful to the Lord that he was pleaſed to condeſcend in mercy to gather the outcaſt of Iſrael. Being clear of this place, I returned to Dublin; and having a concern on my mind to viſit the families of ſome who made profeſſion of the truth, but were diſorderly in their conduct, we began that ſervice, being accompanied by ſeveral friends, and the Lord was pleaſed to own the work.

During

During our stay we were careful to attend all the meetings in this city for worship and discipline; one of which was a quarterly-meeting for the youth, in which many were tendered by the love of God, through Jesus Christ, our Lord and Saviour. We visited about sixty families, in most whereof the Lord was pleased to favour with authority to set the testimony of truth over the heads of the corrupt, disorderly professors, and to influence with understanding to divide the word and counsel of truth to the different states of those we visited: in an humble sense whereof, let my soul obey and adore him, who is alone worthy for ever!

As I apprehended the women's meeting to be slack of doing their part of duty, as true helps in the exercise of the discipline, and a proper care over the flock and family of the Lord, a weighty concern attended me to express in writing my sense of what was the proper business belonging to women's meetings, which I shewed to the men friends, and had their concurrence to lay it before the women's meeting, in order for their encouragement and practice in the wisdom of truth, and it was afterwards sent to the women's meetings throughout the nation.

The vessel in which we came to Ireland being ready to sail, and the master desirous of our company to return with him, I felt so clear and easy that I intended to go; but when

when he sent us word to come on board, I was more inclined to stay that day, and went to meeting, being first day, and he sailed; but meeting with contrary winds and dark weather, was obliged to put back into Dublin harbour, after about a week's fatigue. My being withheld from embarking I thought was a remarkable kindness and favour from my great and good Master; praised be his name! We had afterwards several good meetings, in some of which it became my concern to recommend silence by example; of which they stood in much need. And on the twenty-third of the first month (1753) after having travelled in Ireland thirteen hundred and fifteen miles, and had one hundred and thirty-four meetings, besides many family visits, feeling my mind to be quite clear, we went on board a ship of Whitehaven, Allen Wilson master, having in much love taken leave of our friends; and after a short, but stormy rough passage of about twenty-three hours, arrived at Whitehaven, with hearts humbly thankful to the Lord who had preserved us: the master saying, that he had not known the like for twelve years, although he had sailed tween the two ports very constantly. Next day after our arrival, our friend John Harris, of Highfield, with whom we had left our horses, brought them to us, and we went home with him, and visited the meetings in the neighbourhood, several of which, particularly the last, at Pardshaw Hall,

were

were large and precious opportunities. And I thought I could perceive that my former painful labours among them had been blessed, for which I was truly thankful to the holy head of the church and master of the assemblies of his people. From thence we went to Lorton-hall, and had an evening meeting with the people of the town, to which came the priest, and most of his hearers; and although the craft and conduct of the hirelings were much set forth, all was quiet, and it ended well.

From thence we went to Kendal, and staying a general meeting there, proceeded to divers others in Yorkshire, and Lancashire, and to one we had appointed at Coln, where are no members of our society; and though a poor dark town in respect to religion, the people behaved soberly, and many were tendered by the gentle, yet powerful reaches of heavenly goodness; and I may say, that in riding through some towns in England, where no friend dwelt, I felt a secret salutation of love to the inhabitants, though as a seed yet ungathered; but my present business in general was to the children of the family, that when it shall please the Lord to open the eyes of others to behold Zion, no stumbling-block might appear to offend the beholders, or dim her heavenly beauty.

From hence passing to Halifax, we had a large open meeting there, and divers others
in

in Yorkshire, until we came to our friend John Haslam's, at Hansworth-Woodhouse; then to Sheffield, where we visited some families to our satisfaction; and after attending two meetings in Derbyshire, returned to John Haslam's, and again to Sheffield, and sat their morning meeting on first day, and in the afternoon attended the burial of Ellen Atwick, a friend of good repute, to which many people came, and I had a favourable opportunity. Being then clear, I went to Blythe, in Nottinghamshire, and had a meeting, and several in other towns this week, and reached Rawcliff, in Yorkshire, on first day. On the night before I had a dream, which much affected me. 'I
' thought I heard a kind of melody and
' singing at my left hand, whereupon I said,
' What do ye rejoice at? Which continu-
' ing, I said, Your singing is somewhat like
' David's rejoicing before the ark, but I see
' it not: and I heard a voice on my right,
' saying, the ark is in the land of the Phi-
' listines, where it was taken through the
' wickedness of the priests and sins of the
' people; who removed the ark from Shi-
' loh, to strengthen them in battle.' Whereupon I awoke, and was under some exercise for a time, concluding it was ominous, but saw no further, until we went to meeting in the forenoon, where I soon heard a kind of tuneful sighing, which kept increasing; and turning my head, to discover
from

from whence it came, found it to be at my left hand. After a while a person stood up, and spake a few sentences of extraordinary enjoyments which were to be felt. My mind was pained, and after he sat down I stood up, and said, What are ye doing? and what do you feel to occasion this rejoicing? and should have proceeded to have told them my thoughts, but instantly my dream came into my mind, and so with little addition sat down very sorrowful. After the meeting I went to dinner, but could not eat much, or be chearful. At the afternoon meeting we had the same tune, until my spirit was afflicted; but labouring to know that quiet which is not easily disturbed, I received strength in a loving frame of mind to inform them, that I feared they were mistaken in their states and conditions, for that death reigned, and it was rather a time of mourning: and as truth arose in some good degree, that floating formal sea became dried up. And in the evening having the company of the chief singer among them, I had a singular freedom simply to relate my dream to him, with a desire that he might examine whether the ark enclosing the pure testimony was preserved safe amongst them; which shut up further conversation. In a few days after, an intimate friend asked me how I fared there; I repeated to him my dream, and he told me it was very significant, for that a withering had taken place in in that meeting, and that person had several children that were married to such that did not profess with us; and being treated with as a parent, he said it might be a means of increasing the meeting, if those they had married came to meeting with them, and discouraged friends from dealing with them, lest it should prevent them.

Then taking a meeting at Selby, we proceeded to the quarterly-meeting at York, which continued two days, and was a good meeting. Here we met my brother, William Brown, to our mutual comfort, after a separation of nineteen months. We soon parted again, he going towards Lancaster, and we to several meetings in Yorkshire, and some in Lincolnshire. In some places I observed the form to remain, and life to be wanting, and in others the professors of truth are too generally declined from both. True life gives birth to a true form, but the mere form will never produce the life of truth. From hence we went to Retford and Mansfield, in Nottinghamshire, and at the last town had two meetings, one of which was with friends by themselves; for it did not always appear convenient to deliver too publickly those things which tended to the reproof of some disorderly walkers in the family, lest it should rather harden than restore and heal; especially where their conduct did not occasion open reproach. Then taking a meeting at Broughton, we went to
Notting-

Nottingham, and had three meetings there on firſt day, and the next at Oxham, with a few friends, who were glad thereof, being ſometimes miſſed by travellers. The day following we had an appointed meeting at Nottingham, to ſatisfaction. In this place they are troubled with ſome ranters, who force themſelves into meetings for diſcipline. Friends were exhorted to keep up the teſtimony of truth in the meek humble ſpirit thereof, in which its dominion will ſtand for ever. We then ſpent ſome time in viſiting many meetings in Leiceſterſhire, taking one at Oakham, in Rutlandſhire, where ſome innocent friends live; and I think it is the only meeting of friends in that county. At Boſwell-ſtreet we had a meeting with ſome who had been lately convinced, but had not yet known a true eſtabliſhment in humbly waiting for the power of truth, to give a ſolid growth in pure religion. The ſame evening we had a meeting at Coventry, to good ſatisfaction; and the week following came to Dudley, in Worceſterſhire, where we lodged at James Payton's, whoſe ſiſter Catharine was preparing to go on a religious viſit to America. Staying the meeting on firſt day in Dudley, we went to divers others in this county and Warwickſhire, and came to Eaden, in Northamptonſhire, at which meeting many people came, ſome of whom were very unruly; but the power of truth prevailing, it ended quietly;

praiſed

praised be the Lord, who is all-sufficient for his own work! Visiting several other meetings in this county, at one of them, held in an evening at Chipping-Norton, there were many tender young people, to whom I felt a salutation in the love of truth; but before I thought it safe for me to stand up, a young man, not much like a friend, stood up, and began to exhort them to be faithful in discharging whatsoever the Lord required of them, and how eminently he would be with, and qualify them for his work; as though they were all appointed to enter upon some extraordinary service. At which my mind was much grieved; for I thought it would be more suitable for them deeply to retire, and wait for the virtue of truth, and sap of life, to experience a growth in grace and the knowledge of God, that they might be prepared to work out their own salvation. To expect a young tree to produce abundance of fruit, before the branches are come forth and spread with strength to bear it, is not reasonable. The words 'sit down' passed through my mind for some time, and at length I spoke them so as for him to hear, which I perceived by a small stop he made. But going on again, I said, Prithee, friend, sit down, which he did; but I felt that my saying surprized the people, and perhaps offended some, and that it would be in vain to deliver what was on my mind; so expressing a few sentences only,

only, I sat down, and the meeting ended. I was informed by a friend at our lodgings, that he was one lately come from the Methodists, which I before apprehended by his appearance. On going to bed, I was much concerned lest it should hurt him, and deeply sought to know whether I had not spoken to him in a selfish spirit, because he had taken the time of the meeting appointed on my account; and feeling love towards him, I prayed in spirit that the Lord would be pleased to preserve him from harm thereby, and that if I had done wrong, I might be made sensible of rebuke for my future instruction; when in great calmness I understood that it would not hurt him, so I went into a quiet sleep. After a meeting next day at Sibbard, a woman friend, who was at the meeting the evening before, desired me to send by her a message, or write to the young man, for she was fearful he would go beside himself. I told her, that when I spake to him I thought myself right, and knew what I was about; but now I could not see what to do at present, and to act by her direction was dangerous; so we parted, and in about a week after a friend let me know that there was no danger of his receiving hurt, but hoped he would be benefited.

From hence, taking a few meetings on our way, we arrived at London on the seventh of the sixth month, and next day attended

attended Gracechurch-street meeting, and in the following week the yearly-meeting, which was comfortable and solid; divers weighty matters being therein proposed for consideration from several of the counties, which centred rather to benefit, though in the management of the affairs, there appeared in some a disposition to oppose what they thought to be new, notwithstanding the same things appeared very expedient to others, who, from their prospect thereof, might urge their sentiments rather too strongly. A prospect of the Lord's servants, truly disciplined, armed and qualified for his work, and of such who equip, arm, and arrange themselves, and move by their own direction, was presented to my view in a dream one night, during the time of this meeting. 'I thought I beheld two armies
' set in array against each other, one of
' them well armed with swords and muskets,
' the other had no formal weapons for their
' defence, but a charge given them by their
' general to keep their ranks, and gently to
' march directly forward, as he should lead,
' no man reaching forth his own hand to
' defend himself. They joined in battle,
' and when one of the unarmed soldiers was
' borne hard upon by his opponent, he
' reached forth his hand at arm's length,
' when a sword took off one of his fingers,
' and the blood sprinkled on several of his
' fellow soldiers; whereupon, knowing the
' orders

'orders given, I cried out, If that hand 'had not been so stretched out, this wound 'would not have been received;' and so I awakened; and on the morrow was fully convinced, that in transacting the affairs of truth, the honour of God should be our only view, with a single eye to his direction, (and self made of no reputation) which will be a shield against all reflections and personal censures. For it so happened, that a valuable zealous friend, being strongly reflected on, as being a prejudiced party, and being a little warmed thereby, made an overhasty, and perhaps too warm a reply, which is apt to stir up warmth in those who depend on no other guard than their own armour, and with their own strength use a selfish weapon. By this unguarded reply, the friend brought a reproof on himself and some others, that were united in the cause of truth. The victory belongs to the Lamb for ever, who when he was spit upon and reviled, did not again revile.

After staying in London, and attending the Peel-meeting on first day, and the meeting of ministers and elders on second day morning, we went to Chelmsford, and rested a day or two with our friend John Griffith, attended their week-day meeting, and a general meeting at Kelvedon, and proceeded to the yearly-meeting at Colchester, which held three days, and was a time of divine favour. Then going to Ipswich,

wich, and to a monthly-meeting at Woodbridge, we there continued on first day, and on the next began their yearly-meeting, which held until the fourth day of the week, in all eight sittings, some whereof were large and very good. No praise to him that willeth, or to him that runneth, but to the Lord alone, that sheweth mercy. And there being a marriage at the meeting on fifth day, I had an open time, wherein I had to set forth, that as man in the beginning was taken from the earth or clay, by the hand of the Lord, and a life breathed into him different from the earth, by which he became a living soul, and stood in the image and liberty of his Creator; but falling from the heavenly image, and liberty therein, through transgression, is now of the earth, earthly in his love and liberty; so he must now be separated from the earthly low estate which stands in the transgression and death, by the regenerating word of power; and transformed by the renewing of his mind, will, and affections, and placing them on heavenly objects. For as the potter separateth the clay from the other earth, and tempers it by itself, before he formeth and maketh a vessel thereof, so must man, by the operation of the heavenly hand, be tempered, wrought, prepared, and thereby freed from his own stubborn will, and made submissive to the heavenly will, that he may not be marred on the wheel,

wheel, but bear the turning of the heavenly hand, until he be formed a vessel to honour. But if the will of man does not become subject, but stands in rebellion, the Lord, who said, "My spirit shall not al-"ways strive with man," hath power over the clay, to reject that which will not be wrought into a vessel for honour, and suffer it to be marred in its own stubborn will. And when an earthly potter hath formed a vessel for use, he carefully setteth it aside, until it be prepared to bear a further operation, to harden and glaze it for the use for which it is made. If man should put even water into an earthen vessel, formed for that use, before it is hardened and prepared by fire, he would both mar the vessel, and expose that which was put therein. Let not such, therefore, who have known the heavenly hand of power so to prepare them, that they are willing to be whatsoever the Lord should make of them, marvel if the Lord should be pleased to set them by a while for the trial of their faith. If the earthly potter's vessel should crack in drying, it would be marred; so if these vessels of the Heavenly Potter keep not the word of his patience in this their drying season, to prepare them for the operation of the heavenly fire and furnace, in which the Lord will sanctify and fit his vessels for the use of his holy sanctuary, they will also be marred;

marred; but otherwife they will come forth veffels to honour in his houfe, &c.

I thought this was a remarkably good meeting, the praife thereof belongs to the Lord alone. We had alfo a felect meeting with friends, and vifited feveral families in the town to fatisfaction, truth owning us together; and after a good opportunity at a friend's houfe in the country, on our way, we went to Norwich, and attended their meetings on firft day; the yearly-meeting began the next, and ended on fourth day, after feven fittings, generally large and fatiffactory, through the overfhadowing of divine goodnefs. I continued in this city feveral days after, vifiting families, and fteadily attending their meetings, and had fome open fatisfactory opportunities. My way now opening for Holland, we went to Yarmouth, feveral friends accompanying us, and on the twenty-fixth of the feventh month embarked on board the fhip Three Brothers, Richard Smith mafter, my companion, John Pemberton, being willing to continue with me.

On the firft day of the week following we landed at Rotterdam, and lodged at an inn. Next morning, feeling my mind drawn forward, we went in a ftage-waggon to Turgow, and from thence in the tract-fkute in the evening to Amfterdam, the metropolis of South Holland, and were conducted to friends meeting-houfe at the Three-hooks,

hooks, in Princes-street, in which Michael Laars and his sister lived, and were kindly received, and rested the next day.

I found a concern to visit the families of friends in this city, in which service we spent most of the week to our satisfaction, John Vanderwarf, jun. being interpreter. We also attended their week-day meeting, in which Peter Linders was interpreter. On first day following the meeting in the morning was pretty large, and many people came to that in the afternoon, some of whom behaved rudely; but truth came over, and they were stilled, and seemed to depart satisfied. We continued here until their week-day meeting again, which many not of our society attended, and it was to general satisfaction. I then felt my mind drawn towards North Holland, and taking passage in the track-skute, passed through several towns, and arrived at the city of Hoorn, where we were met by our friend Cort Hendricks, who took us in his waggon to his house at Twisk, in North Holland, the same night; being accounted eighteen miles from Amsterstam to Hoorn by water, and from thence to Twisk by land six miles. Here also finding the like concern, we visited the families of friends, and had a meeting with them in the evening together. Next day we went to Abbey Kirk, a village, about two miles distant, where about five or six families of friends live, whom we visited also. The

friends

friends in general seemed to receive our visits kindly, except one family, where I was concerned to speak of, and open that saying of our dear Lord, " Except your " righteousness exceed the righteousness of " the Scribes and Pharisees," &c. for I was much burdened under a sense of a self-righteous, whole, exalted spirit. And in opening that passage, was also led to speak of the parable of the Pharisee and Publican, who went up into the temple to pray, which probably touched the heads of that family; and I felt a strong opposition in them, and perceived the passage was not pleasing to our interpreter. I could not shake off my burden, yet was preserved quiet in my mind, having honestly done my part, and so returned to Twisk, where the meeting was held for both villages, and which on first day morning was pretty large, friends being generally there; but our interpreter had most of the time, so that he was too much spent to interpret much for me. Several not professing with us attended in the afternoon, and I had a satisfactory time with them early in the meeting, when an awful sense of truth seemed to be over us, after which our interpreter had something further to say. I have often lamented the increase of words, and a repetition of former experiences, without the renewing of life; which disposition seems

to

to prevail in too many, to the burdening
sensible members in our society.

As we sat this evening at a friend's house
at Twisk, two elderly women came in, professors of truth, but very talkative. I had
seen them several times before, and as often
been burdened with them, and now had
something in particular to speak, but feared
that such plain dealing would be too strong
for our interpreter, who appeared to be very
sociable with them. Therefore I delivered
my mind, without singling them out, several others being present. These women took
it to themselves, but not in such a disposition as I desired, being disturbed; and following us to our lodgings, made their complaint to our interpreter, bidding him ask
me, if I took them to be such persons as I
had described: if so, they desired to know
what I had to accuse them with. At first it
put me to a stand, but being still, I soon
thought it was providential, that they thus
gave me an opportunity to clear myself of
the burden I had borne on their account,
and told them, that to enter into particular
charges was not my business; but was free
to let them know that I had been in pain
on their account from the first time I saw
them, and that if I had a true sense of their
states, they were not such as they ought to
be, but had lost the favour of what they
professed to enjoy, and could so freely talk
of, ' and told one of them that I took her

' to

' to be dark, and ignorant of her own
' state; and the other, that she was too
' light and chaffy in her spirit; and that
' they both wanted the true clothing of
' the Lord's children, which is humility
' of heart, and reverence of spirit; which
' would season all their conversation and
' conduct, that they would not be stumbling
' blocks to their neighbours, as I feared
' they were. I also told them, that I be-
' lieved when I spake as I did at the friend's
' house, it belonged to them, in which I
' was now confirmed; for had they been
' sincere-hearted, they would have born it
' without flinching; but now they had
' shewn that their sore places were touched,
' and I dared not to lessen the weight of
' what was then said, but desired them to
' receive and ponder it well; for I was sure
' it was delivered in love, and believed it
' to be a visitation to them in their old
' age.' Which being interpreted to them, they spake something to the interpreter, which I did not understand. Then one of them said, she had yet love in her heart for me. I told her, that I had nothing but good will towards her, and so they went away.

After which the interpreter told me, he had known these women many years; that I had a true sense of them, and he had delivered my words honestly, and hoped they would do them good.

We

We next had a meeting with friends of Twisk by themselves, in a private house, in which we were favoured with the favour of truth; the sincere-hearted being refreshed, and the disorderly warned to be more careful.

After taking some refreshment, we hasted to attend another meeting appointed for us at Abbey-Kirk in the afternoon, which was held in the same house where I felt the opposition before mentioned. I soon was sensible of some matter in my mind to divide to the people; first to a low, afflicted state, and things opened pretty clear, and were interpreted readily; but proceeding to the other states, I felt the current obstructed, and the force of my sentences evaded, and had a sense that the minds of the friends of that house were shut up against what I had to deliver, so I forbore going on, and the interpreter soon began, and continued to speak near an hour. When he had done, I felt a great weight on my mind, and desired him to interpret a few sentences for me. He did not seem very free, saying, ' Let it ' be short, then.' The substance was, ' that ' I had come in love to see them, and was ' in no way prepossessed or informed con-
' cerning any person or case among them;
' yet found they were shut up against what
' I had to deliver: nevertheless, I could
' not be easy without letting them know,
' that I did believe, unless they humbled
' them-

'themselves, and were stripped from that
'self-righteous wholeness, wherewith they
'had clothed themselves, they never would
'grow in the life of true religion, but
'would be as stumbling-blocks to the sin-
'cere-hearted among them;' so I went out
of the house, and returned to our lodging,
not having freedom to stay there longer.
Our interpreter, who tarried with them after we were gone, told me that they judged
a certain friend, who had been in Holland
some time before, and spoken very closely
to them, had informed me concerning them;
and I thought the interpreter also favoured
that sentiment, which made me not to wonder at the opposition I had felt both in him
and them. Whereupon I told him, that
until that time I never knew that the friend,
whom they thus judged, had been there,
and that I had never heard of their names,
nor the name of the town, until I came
with him, and desired him to give it in
charge to a friend of Twisk, who was present with us, to let those friends know from
me, what I then said of my innocency.

Feeling myself now pretty easy respecting
that place, we returned towards Amsterdam,
accompanied by two friends, to Hoorn,
where no friends now live, though formerly
there were, and sometimes meetings have
been held there. And I had some thoughts
of having one, but, being under discouragement, had almost concluded to proceed on
our

our way; but in walking through the city to the skute, which was to set off for Amsterdam in a few minutes, I felt my mind affected with a sense that my great and good Master was near, and desired with earnest breathings to know his will: and if he would be pleased to be with me, I was willing to do the same, as he should require and enable me. I then felt such a stream of love towards the inhabitants, that I was convinced there was a visitation to them, as though the Lord would in his own time gather a people there. As yet I had not disclosed my mind to any one, although I felt a draught back; when, seeing a young man in the street, I desired the interpreter to ask him if he thought we could have a meeting in that town; to which he readily answered, that he believed we might, and, taking hold of my baggage, said, if we would please to return to his house, he would endeavour to procure a place, and acquaint the people; which he very punctually, and with great speed performed. And we met about four in the afternoon, at the house of Cornelius Olyslager, and had a good opportunity, with a tender, friendly people, several of whom were reached and tendered by the virtue and favour of truth, which spread freely: for which the Giver of all good was reverently praised, who is worthy for ever. The people departed in much love, and we returned to the young man's house,

house, where we were affectionately entertained that night. We should have been glad to have conversed with the people, but could not understand their language, yet had a sense that they were satisfied with the meeting.

Being accompanied by this kind young man, Dirk Meschaert, our landlord, to the track-skute, we took leave, with tears on each side, and arriving at Amsterdam, we sat with friends that afternoon in their week-day meeting, to satisfaction; having travelled in North Holland about seventy-four miles, by boat and waggon. We then visited the remainder of friends families in this city, and were comforted therein; the Lord being pleased to own our labour, and I pray it may be blessed to them. On first day morning we had a large solid meeting, at which were several strangers, particularly two young men, Italians, supposed to be princes, who behaved well; also many of the citizens, who had never been at a friends meeting before. The afternoon meeting was also large; but some of the lower sort, who came to gaze out of curiosity, behaved rudely; yet it ended better than I expected. There seemed to be an openness in many to hear the testimony and principle of truth declared; but it is a dull way to speak by an imperfect interpreter.

On the twenty-second of the eighth month, was held what they call their yearly-meeting,

meeting, which was attended by several not of our society; but it has little more than the name of a yearly-meeting, the discipline of truth being much lost.

Feeling some concern still to continue on my mind towards the friends at Abbey-Kirk, where I was sensible of the opposition before hinted, I had freedom to write them a letter; but on considering that the friend and his wife to whom I wrote were persons of note, I was fearful that their resentment might hurt some others; and having a tender concern towards the sincere-hearted, it was with me to prepare the way by writing an epistle to friends of the meeting at Twisk, to which those of Abbey-Kirk do also belong; both which I got a friend of Amsterdam to translate. That to the meeting I sent immediately, that it might be read on a first day, and directed the other to be sent soon after.

That to friends at Twisk was as follows:

'Dear Friends,

'THE honest and sincere hearted
  'amongst you, I salute in Gospel
'love: and as I do believe there is a small
'remnant that are desirous to know and
'witness the peace of God in your hearts,
'and a sure hope of receiving the answer of
'well done at the conclusion of your time
'in this world, mind the instructions of
                                    'the

' the Spirit of Chrift Jefus in your own
' hearts; for it is that which leads into all
' truth: it fhews unto man of what fort
' the thoughts of his heart are, and it wit-
' neffeth againft every bad word and action.
' It was the Spirit of Truth that taught
' the children of God in all ages. It was
' by this Spirit of Truth that our worthy
' elders were led from the lo-here's and lo-
' there's which are in the world: it efta-
' blifhed them on the true foundation, viz.
' the revelation or teaching of the Spirit of
' God in their own hearts. By this they
' were upheld under fore afflictions, and
' outward fufferings, from the powers of
' the earth. By this they were preferved in
' the unity of the fpirit, in the bond of
' peace.

' Dear friends, beware of letting out your
' minds after the doctrines and teachings of
' men, who have not the word of Life
' committed to them, to preach in the love
' and power of truth: for if ye do, ye
' will be unftable and wavering; and a wa-
' vering man is as a wave of the fea, toffed
' to and fro with every contrary wind of
' doctrine. Neither look you too much to
' the example one of another, but wait to
' receive in yourfelves, a fenfe of what ye
' ought to do, and to join with, and what
' ye ought to be feparated from; then will
' ye be able to judge what you hear and fee,
' becaufe you have the fpirit of truth in

' your

' your own hearts; for that is the true rule,
' judge, and guide, which leads into all
' truth.

' Since I was with you, I have often
' thought, that you will never grow strong
' in the truth, nor teach the principles
' thereof one to another, until you be obe-
' dient thereunto in your own hearts, and
' act and behave in all things according to
' the pure witness thereof in your own
' selves. This makes living, sound, steady
' members, zealous both of love and good
' works, in themselves, and amongst their
' brethren and sisters.

' Dear friends, be careful to meet toge-
' ther, and admonish those that fall short
' of their duty herein. And when you are
' assembled, wait on the Lord with a mind
' turned inward; and if ye do wait in faith
' and patience, the Lord will be found of
' you, and reveal himself in the midst of
' you, to your comfort and consolation.

' With sincere desires that every good
' thought, and secret enquiry after the
' knowledge of God, in each of your hearts,
' may be strengthened and blessed, do I re-
' main your affectionate friend,

' JOHN CHURCHMAN.'

' Amsterdam, 23d of the
' 8th month, 1753.'

A copy of my letter to the friend and his wife here follows.

" My

' My Friends,

' I Have had an exercise on my mind ever
' since I came first into your house, to
' visit your family, which was on the ele-
' venth instant. I came an entire stranger,
' free from any information from man con-
' cerning you; but as soon as I came into
' the house, I felt the innocent life of
' truth, and pure seed of the kingdom, op-
' pressed in you.

' Our dear Lord said, " Learn of me,
" for I am meek and low of heart." ' His
' Spirit in us, if we take heed thereto, will
' teach us to be meek and low in heart. At
' this day his teaching is the same, and will
' remain to be so to all his followers for
' ever. O may you be humble, for it is
' the humble that the Lord doth teach of
' his ways; and the meek he guides in
' judgment: but the whole and self-righ-
' teous, who are wise in their own eyes, and
' prudent in their own conceit, the Lord
' will hide the mysteries of his pure wis-
' dom from these; but to the babes, who
' are truly changed, and born from above;
' and those sucklings, who are weaned from
' the breasts of the world, and its wisdom,
' and are leaning on the breast of Christ,
' their beloved, desiring the sincere milk of
' his word, that they may grow thereby;
' unto these the Lord will reveal true know-
' ledge,

'ledge, and wisdom from above: and that
wisdom is pure, peaceable, gentle, and
easy to be intreated; and those that have
the same in possession, they have the sea-
soning virtue of truth: they have salt in
themselves, and are therefore preserved in
peace and unity with the pure truth, and
also one with another. Such professors,
who inwardly know, and receive the most
holy faith, they know the same to work
in them by love, to the purifying of their
hearts. These are Jews inward, circum-
cised in heart, true Israelites indeed, in
whom there is no guile: and their righteousness exceeds that of the Scribes and
Pharisees.'

'I heartily wish that you may (in your
old age) be concerned to know the life of
pure religion; a sense of the want thereof
in your family, burthened my life whilst
I was in your house, which was the reason
why I could not be free to eat and drink
with you.

'In order to discharge myself towards
you, have I written these few lines, desiring that you may examine yourselves,
and see if there be not a cause,—and in
the love of truth, which leads us to deal
plainly one with another,

'I remain your real friend and well-wisher,

'JOHN CHURCHMAN.'

'Amsterdam, 23d of the
8th month, 1753.'

We continued with friends in this city, and attended their two meetings on first day, and in the evening had an opportunity with several to satisfaction; for our love rather increased. Next morning, feeling my mind clear of friends in Holland, I was easy to return towards England, and, accompanied by several to the skute, we took leave, and went to Turgow by water, from thence by waggon to Rotterdam, in all about forty-two miles. There are no members of our society left in this city. We went to see the meeting-house, and had some thoughts of having a meeting, but being the time of a great fair, which occasioned a concourse of rude people, there was no prospect of having one to advantage.

John Vanderwaarf, junior, came with us to Rotterdam, with whom we parted in much love early on fourth day morning, the twenty-ninth of the eighth month, and went on board the same ship which brought us hither; it having made a voyage to England and back since. We sailed with a fair wind down the Maese to the Briell before noon, when it becoming contrary, we lay at anchor until first day morning, then proceeding, we passed over the dangerous sands, and so to sea, and arrived at Yarmouth about one the next day, and had a meeting with friends the same evening.

In this journey to Holland, we travelled by sea and land about five hundred miles.

From Yarmouth we went in a chaise to Norwich, where friends were rejoiced to see us, and we were thankful for our safe return. And being concerned to spend some more time among them in this city, we visited a few families, and attended their monthly-meeting, also their two meetings on first day, which were dull and heavy. The minds of the people being too much outward, I found it my place to recommend silence by example more than by words, in both those meetings.

Next day, in company with other friends, I went to visit Hannah Lucas, a schoolmistress, who was newly convinced. She was in a low state of mind. Our visit was to mutual satisfaction, being comforted together.

At their week-day meeting on third day, I had a seasonable time to discharge my mind towards friends in that city, in which I was led to deal plainly with them. They are a loving people to strangers and each other, but there is a want of weightiness of spirit, and of a proper care in the exercise of the discipline of the church.

Before my going to Holland, I was at the shop of a barber in this city several times, to be shaved: the second time I was there, I had to wait a while for my turn, he having no assistant; and when others were gone out, he told me he was sorry I had to wait, and hoped he should have my custom:

custom: and that if I would come on Saturdays and Wednesdays, in the forenoon, I need not wait; but in the afternoon others came. I asked him what days in the week those were which he called Saturdays and Wednesdays: he seemed to wonder at my ignorance, but knew not how to tell me otherwise. I said, I do not read in the scriptures of any days so named: he replied, That is true. For what reason, then, said I, dost thou call them so? Because it is a common custom, said he. Suppose, then, said I, that we lived in a heathen country, among infidels, who worshipped idols, should we follow their customs, because common? He replied, By no means. I then said, if I have understood rightly, the heathens gave the days of the week those names. I never heard that before, said he; pray for what reason? I answered, they worshipped the sun on the first day of the week, and named it after their idol, Sunday; the moon on the second day of the week, so came Monday; and the other days after other idols, for they had many gods. Third day they called Tuesday, after their idol Tuisco; and after the idol Woden, fourth day they called Wednesday; and fifth day, after their idol Thor, they called Thursday; from Friga, Friday; and after Saturn they called the seventh day, Saturday. And as I believe in the only true God, and Jesus Christ, whom he hath sent, and expect eternal

nal life by no other name or power, I dare not, for confcience fake, own the gods of the heathen, or name a day after them; but choofe the names which the days were called by when the Moft High performed his feveral works of creation, viz. firft, fecond, third, and fo on, which is fcriptural, moft plain, and eafily underftood.

He feemed fomewhat affected with the information, and I defired him to enquire into the matter for himfelf, and not to think that I defigned to impofe upon him. The next time of my going to his fhop, he fhewed me fome papers, whereon he had began to learn algebra, and afked me how I liked it. I faid, it might be ufeful to fome, but that I could take up grubbing, or follow the plough, without ftudying algebra; as he might alfo fhave a man, &c. without it. Befides, I found it a more profitable and delightful ftudy, to be quietly employed in learning the law of the Lord written in mine own heart, fo that I might walk before him acceptably.

On my return from Holland to Norwich, a man ran to me in the ftreet, putting a paper into my hand, and immediately left me, whom I foon found to be this barber. The letter contained an innocent, child-like acknowledgment to me for my freedom with him, as is before mentioned, in language rather too much fhewing his value for me as an inftrument. And believing him to be

reached

reached by the love of truth, and in measure convinced of the principle thereof, I thought it beſt to leave him in the Lord's hands for further inſtruction, to learn by the immediate teachings of the Holy Spirit, that his love might be centered on the true beloved of ſouls; for want whereof many are hurt, looking outward, and growing in head knowledge, ſeeking the eſteem and friendſhip of men, from whom we are to ceaſe; his breath and life being ſtopped at the Lord's command.

I mention this paſſage with a view to ſtir up my friends of the ſame holy profeſſion, to let their language in words be the real language of truth to all men, in purity of ſpirit, and not to name the days of the week or months after the heatheniſh idolatrous cuſtoms, ſaying for excuſe, that they to whom they ſpeak do beſt underſtand them, and it ſaves them any further explanation; which excuſe is far from proceeding from a diſpoſition apt to teach, and letting the light of truth ſhine as they ought. " Neither do men," ſaid our bleſſed Inſtructor, " light a candle, and put it under " a buſhel, but on a candleſtick, and it " giveth light to all that are in the houſe," Matt. v. 21. Nor doth the Lord enlighten his candle, that is, the ſpirit of man, with the pure knowledge of truth, that we ſhould cover it, either with an eaſeful diſpoſition, to ſave ourſelves trouble, or hide

the

the work thereof under the covering bushel of worldly saving care, after the gain and treasure of this world; but that it may stand on the candlestick, and thereby crown those who are thus favoured with the holy light, that as a city set on an hill they cannot be hid.

The corrupt language of you to a single person, and calling the months and days by heathen names, are esteemed by some to be little things; but if a faithful testimony in these little things was blessed in the instance before mentioned, even to the raising an earnest enquiry after the saving knowledge of God and his blessed Son, whom to know is eternal life; perhaps such who baulk their testimony to the pure talent of truth given them to profit withal, may one day have their portion appointed with the wicked and slothful servant; see Matt. xxv. 24, 25, &c.

After the last mentioned meeting I found my mind easy to leave Norwich, and went with Richard Brewster and wife to Wymondham that evening, and next day to Edmondsbury; where, feeling an engagement of mind, we staid eight days, attending their several meetings, and monthly-meeting, which is composed of five particular meetings; where, under a sense of a forward formal ministry, my soul mourned, and was clothed with sorrow. The next day we had a precious meeting, and the same

same evening another with the ministers and solid friends, in which it became my concern to set forth the care they ought to exercise over each other, and how necessary it was to deal plainly with those that did not keep their places. Truth owned us together, and I believe the opportunity will be remembered.

My mind being drawn towards Wales, my companion, John Pemberton, who had been with me three years, having travelled together in much love and unity, inclining to go towards London, we parted in the same love; and I, accompanied by my kind friend Richard Brewster, went to Henry Gray's, at Godmanchester, in Huntingdonshire; and the next day to Wellingborough, in Northamptonshire, and were at their two meetings on first day, the twenty-third of the ninth month, which were heavy, for want of more faithful inward labourers. That evening I had also a sitting with a sick friend.

Next morning my friend Richard Brewster returned homewards; and several friends coming to take leave of me, I had an opportunity to remark to them the reason that their meetings were so dull and cloudy; for I thought I clearly saw there was a neglect among them of putting the discipline in practice, where disorders were evident; and that this neglect had caused them to suffer, which would still continue and increase,

until

until they set the testimony of truth over the heads of such who, by disorderly walking, had brought a reproach thereon. The friends were affected, and acknowledged they believed it to be the case amongst them. We parted in tenderness, and I proceeded on my journey, with an income of solid peace, and, after riding thirty-seven miles, reached Banbury, in Oxfordshire, and the next day Eatington, in Warwickshire, where I met with my friends Richard Partridge and Mary Weston, of London, and we were truly glad to see each other, spending the day together, and had a meeting with friends in the evening, to our mutual comfort. We went in company to Warwick and Coventry, and at the meeting at the last place, which was comfortable, I thought I sensibly felt the benefit of the painful labour I had been exercised in when there before. Richard Partridge returning to London, Mary Weston went with me to the quarterly-meeting at Leicester, which began with a meeting of ministers and elders, and one for worship and discipline was held the same day: the service in which lay heavy upon me, and truth favoured, the power thereof being felt, to the comfort of many. And I wish that season may not be forgotten by the members of that meeting. On the first day following I went to a general meeting at Badgeley, and had an evening meeting at Daniel Lythal's, at Polesworth, who hath a large

large family of hopeful tender children. I next went to Allen England's, at Tamworth, and had a satisfactory opportunity in his family, to which I had felt a drawing in my mind for some time; but did not know that it would fall so in the way to the quarterly-meeting at Stafford, which I attended, and there met my friend Joshua Tofft, in company with whom I returned to Rudgeley, and next day had a meeting at the widow Morris's, and another that evening at Uttoxeter: from thence to Leek, and, after a favoured meeting, went home with Joshua to Harugate, where, after resting one day, had another meeting at Leek, and an opportunity with some friends at Joshua Strangman's, wherewith I had a degree of peace.

Accompanied by Joshua Tofft, I went to a general meeting at Eaton, in Cheshire; then to Macclesfield, Stockport, Morley, and Farnly, the last of which was a good meeting. There my friend Samuel Fothergill met me, and we went to a meeting at Sutton. The next day Susanna Fothergill, and her brother Alexander, came to see me, and we had a comfortable time together at Thomas Hough's, being owned by truth. I was next at a laborious meeting at Newton, though it ended well; and after it I met again with Joshua Tofft, at Edgebury, and had a meeting the next day at Middlewich, then at Nantwich, and Chester; from
whence

whence rode to John Bellows, at Stretton. My travelling and labours through Cheshire was in a particular close manner, though there are some solid friends in that county.

Passing to Shrewsbury, in Shropshire, I was at a meeting on first day at Colebrookdale, and had some close work; but truth seemed to give victory: and in the evening, at Abraham Darby's house, had an opportunity, in which the testimony of truth prevailed, to the tendering some high and lofty young people; whose faults were told them in the power of the searcher of hearts, for which the sincere were truly thankful.

Next day returning to Shrewsbury, I went to visit Benjamin Thomas and Richard Bellows, who had been confined in prison about four years and a half for their conscientious refusal to pay tithes; and we had a comfortable season together in the jail, seeking the living presence of the Lord, which makes his people free, even in prisons.

The day following had a meeting in this town, and one in the evening, at the house of John Young, both which afforded some peace; but the life of truth is at a low state in Shropshire, and the professors with us few in number.

I then passed into North Wales, to Charles Lloyd's, at Dolobran, in Montgomeryshire, John Young being with me, and had a meeting there: at this place there was formerly a large a large meeting, but it is now much declined. From thence we went to Tyddenigarrig, in Merionethshire, and had a meeting with a few sincere friends at the house of Lewis Owen. After which I proceeded on my visit to the other meetings in this county: first at Llwindu, in the family of Humphry Owen, which was a comfortable time, though no other friends live in this place. Then at the house of John Goodwin, in Eskirgoch, in Montgomeryshire, where were several tender friends; but the living are scarcely able to bear the weight of those professors, who, although they know the truth, do not abide therein, and so are as withered branches cast forth. Next was a pretty large and satisfactory meeting at Talcoyd, in Radnorshire; then at Cwm, and Gluerindrew, and on a first day at Penbank, where are many professors, though but few solid friends. After which at Penplace and Caermarthen, which last meeting was much to my satisfaction, the few friends here being of the better sort. From hence to Haverfordwest, with friends by themselves mostly; and staying their meetings on first day, that in the afternoon was open and satisfactory, as to other professors, who came in: but pride and worldly-mindedness hath much hurt the members of our society, though there are a few tender friends. In the evening I had another opportunity with friends, and was enabled to relieve my mind among

among them with a degree of thankfulness. Next meeting was at James Town, and in the evening of the day following at Larn, with the people of the town, who behaved civilly, but seemed barren as to religion, in a right sense. There is but one in this town in unity with friends, and he seemed near his end, whom I visited. After crossing a ferry near a mile broad, not without great danger, being driven on shore, and the wind very high, the boat was likely to fill with water, that I was obliged to go over a marsh to Caermarthen, being thankful for the deliverance, where I had a publick meeting with the town's people, to a good degree of satisfaction; and next morning met with my brother, William Brown, at Swanzey, and we were made joyful in the company of each other. Here we had two meetings, and another with friends selected, in which he got some relief. After his leaving me here, having a concern on my mind, I visited the families of friends, though not without fear; but felt the help and strength of my great and good Master, who furnished me with power and skill to discharge my duty, both to the lukewarm, and the corrupt disorderly professors, without wounding his own children, some of whom there are in this town. I staid their meeting on fourth day, which season being divinely favoured, I pray may not be forgotten; the power which alone can enable to tread on scorpions

or

or serpents, and preserve from the force of deadly poison, being over all. The honour, praise, and glory, be ascribed to the Lord, who is worthy for ever!

Next day I rested, and, in a degree of humble thankfulness, made these remarks.

I continued many days longer in this town, in which time had divers meetings, some whereof were very satisfactory, many of the town's people attending; and the good hand of the Lord was stretched forth towards them, for which I was truly thankful. After spending sixteen days among them, I went to Llantrissent, and the next day had a meeting at Treveryg; then one at Hillary, with a tender enquiring people; also at Cardiff, with a seeking people, who had separated themselves from the publick worship, and met together in silence: this opportunity was an instructive season to them. On the first day following I was at Pontypool, where at two meetings I had many close things to deliver, observing want of order among them. In the evening had an opportunity with some of the friends most active in the discipline, and endeavoured to discharge myself: and on third day a large and pretty open meeting. Being detained by a great snow, I had another meeting with friends of the foremost rank on sixth day, in which I cleared my mind of a great burden, which I had borne on account of a formal ministry among them.

My next meeting was at Shire-Newton, which was pretty large, though dull; the favour of truth being much loft among friends here: yet I was favoured with ftrength to difcharge myfelf. And, in the feeling fenfe of peace, went that night to the paffage over the Severn, and next day to Briftol, my friend and kind landlord, James Griffitts, bearing me company from his own houfe at Swanzey.

On third day I attended their meeting in Briftol, but fat in filence, and was very heavy hearted, under a fenfe of a forward fpirit, which would prompt to anfwer the expectations of the people, and is apt to prevail on fome who feem to be called to the work of the miniftry; but truth only bleffeth its own motion.

I continued in and near this city about four weeks, attending their feveral meetings, but did not feel relief from the burden I was under; and on the fifteenth of the firft month, (1754) hearing that my brother, William Brown, was at Ann Young's, at Urcot, I went there to fee him, and we were comforted in each other's company; and next being their meeting day, we attended it to our refrefhment. From whence we returned together to Briftol, where we tarried until the twenty-fixth, in which time I had feveral open meetings, which fet me at liberty to leave that city; when we again parted, and I took meetings at Ulverftone, Thorn-

Thornbury, Sodbury, Didmerton, Tedbury, and two at Nailsworth, and another there in the evening, when I had an opportunity to the ease of my mind, heavily oppressed on account of the formal professors of truth, to the comfort of the faithful, which caused thankfulness.

From thence, calling to visit the widow Fowler, who was in affliction, I went to meetings at Painswick, Gloucester, Ross, in Herefordshire, Almerly, Leominster, and Sifton, where I visited the wives of the two friends before mentioned, who are imprisoned at Shrewsbury for their testimony against tithes. Then returning to Leominster, attended the monthly-meeting there, in which truth owned us; and, taking a meeting at Bromsgrove, went to Worcester, and on first day was at two comfortable meetings, and another on third day; and the next day attended the quarterly-meeting, which was a precious time, wherein friends were comforted. And finding a concern on my mind, I went into the women's meeting, wherein the power of truth accompanied, which is the crown of our religious meetings. Here is a tender seed, especially amongst the female sex, which will thrive, if this Divine power is kept unto.

Being now clear of this city, I departed with peace to meetings at Tewksbury, Cheltenham, and again to Nailsworth, where I was at two meetings, which though hard, I had an evidence that the Lord had not forsaken his seeking people. After attending a conference with several friends endeavouring to compose a difference, which ended to satisfaction, I proceeded to the quarterly-meeting for Gloucestershire, held at Tedbury, where I again met with my brother, William Brown; Divine goodness, and a degree of the authority of truth attending in the time of worship, and in transacting the affairs of the church.

Next day my brother went to Bath, and I to Cirencester, where I had a hard and dull meeting, the professors of truth having too much departed from the favour thereof. At another in the evening I had an evidence of having discharged my duty. Then proceeded to meetings at Farringdon, in Berkshire, Letchlade, Burford, in Oxfordshire, Milton, Stow in Gloucestershire, Chipping-Norton, Charlbury, Witney, Abingdon, Warborrow, North End, and from thence to High Wycomb, where, the weather being very cold, I tarried six days, visiting several families of sick friends; and the last publick meeting being in the evening, many of the town's people attended, and it was a solid opportunity. From thence I went to Amersham, though with difficulty, on account of the snow, and on first day had a meeting at Chesham; then to Hempstead, and had there a meeting, which was much enlarged

enlarged by the scholars of Thomas Squires's school, several of whom were affected. Then having a good opportunity with friends at Alban's, I went to London, where I remained seven weeks and three days, visiting the meetings, and felt much of the weight and burden of the service before me there; and, in the opening and authority of truth, I had to speak to the present state of our society, not only to the instruction of the seeking children, and comforting of the mourners, but also by way of rebuke to the disorderly, and close warning to the rebellious.

During my continuance here I felt my mind drawn towards Wiltshire, and thought of attending the quarterly-meeting there, but on the day on which I expected to set forward, I found a stop in my mind, though not relieved from a solid concern, which engaged me to enquire secretly what I should do; for notwithstanding this concern to Wiltshire, my burden respecting London seemed rather to increase; but as I kept quiet, I found my heart warmed in love, and my mind opened, and influenced to write an epistle to that quarterly-meeting, which with thankfulness I then esteemed a great favour from my great and good Master, being in a poor state of health, the weather unfavourable, and the journey long. So, in the opening of truth, I wrote as followeth:

‘ To

' To Friends in Wiltshire.'

'HAVING had strong desires in my
' mind for your welfare in the truth,
' I purposed to have attended your quarterly-
' meeting, but being let at this time, and
' not knowing that I shall ever have an op-
' portunity to see you, I feel a freedom to
' visit you with a few lines in the opening
' and love of truth, which flows to you-
' ward.

' Dear friends, male and female, old and
' young, as many of you as are desirous to
' be called the children of God, and fol-
' lowers of Christ Jesus, be humble, that
' you may be taught of him; for it is the
' humble that he teaches of his ways. And
' be ye meek and low in heart, that you
' may serve him in your generation, and one
' another in his pure fear; so you will know
' him for your rest, and his peace your quiet
' habitation.

' My soul hath mourned, and is in some
' degree covered therewith at this time,
' under a sense that the love of the world,
' and its pleasures and earthly delights,
' abound in too many, (which is iniquity)
' and because thereof the love of many to-
' wards God waxeth cold; and for want of
' witnessing the love of God in a pure heart,
' the mind becomes at ease, lukewarm, and
' indifferent about the things which belong

' to

'to our peace and future happiness: and so
'fathers and mothers, masters and mistres-
'ses, become dull, if not dead, to that
'holy concern, which should ever excite
'them, both by example and precept, to
'instruct and train up their children and
'servants in all godliness of life and con-
'versation.

'O dear friends! search your hearts, and
'diligently enquire whether something hath
'not subtilly crept in, and stolen away your
'affections from God, and the deep atten-
'tion of your minds from the instructions
'of his holy spirit of truth: and if this
'becomes your concern, I fully believe that
'the Lord will bless you with enlightened
'minds to see, and willing hearts to give
'up all to the fire and sword of his Word
'and Spirit, that your hearts may be purged,
'and made tabernacles and temples in
'which he would take delight to dwell:
'for if the soul is chaste in love to God,
'and the eye of the mind single to the in-
'struction of the spirit of truth, the whole
'body will be full of light. It is herein
'that the children of God are preserved safe
'in their own secret steps before the Lord,
'and free from giving occasion of stumbling
'to others.

'I am fully persuaded there is a remnant
'amongst you, who feelingly know that the
'living sense of the presence and power of
'God, in your meetings both for worship

'and discipline, is not plentifully enjoyed,
'but is at a low ebb: and it is in my mind
'to let you know what has appeared to me
'to be as one great reason, viz. there are
'many professors of the truth amongst you,
'who delight to be accounted of as friends
'in esteem in the society; who have a
'smooth and fawning behaviour, and flat-
'tering tongues, and do seek the love and
'friendship of such who are friends of
'truth, for their own honour and credit,
'and the reputation of self. Dear friends,
'of such beware, for their friendship is
'poison, and their intimate fellowship, if
'cleaved unto, is benumbing, even to in-
'sensibility. And for want of a clear dis-
'covery of that spirit, some of the tender
'and sincere-hearted among you have suf-
'fered.

'In whomsoever earthly-mindedness pre-
'vails, or the love of the world, and its
'friendship, there is a secret giving way to,
'and a gradual reconciliation with, its sor-
'did practices; and the eye that once saw
'in the true light, becomes closed or dim-
'med, if not wholly blinded by the god
'of this world.

'Liberty is then taken by parents, and
'indulgence is given to their children;
'which occasions pain and distress of heart
'to those who have not lost their sight and
'feeling. But some, for fear of being re-
'buked and disesteemed by such who have
'a sense

' a sense of them, will court their affections;
' with which bait they have been taken,
' and so have been afraid to speak their
' minds plainly, lest they should offend, or
' drive them further from the society: con-
' cluding there is a tender thing in them,
' because they seem to love friends. And
' so many who might have made great pro-
' gress have lost ground, for want of speak-
' ing truth to their neighbours. And thus
' the infection of pride, libertinism, and
' earthly-mindedness, has spread and pre-
' vailed, even to the hurt of some families,
' that were once exceedingly grieved there-
' with.

' Wherefore, my dear friends, fear God
' with a perfect heart, and in his light watch
' over your own selves and your families;
' so shall your hearts be warmly influenced,
' and filled with holy zeal and love to God
' and his truth, in which you will be bold
' to act in your meetings for discipline; and
' in the power of God, which is the autho-
' rity of the church, you will be able to
' judge those who walk disorderly; and,
' being faithful therein, you will remove
' the stumbling-blocks, and roll away the
' reproach which is imputed to the church.

' Then would the Lord feed such his
' faithful labourers with his heavenly bread,
' and honour them with his life-giving pre-
' sence; and whether the disorderly would
' hear or forbear, the Lord would be the
                                    ' shield

'shield and exceeding great reward of his
'people, and fill their hearts with praise to
'his name, who is worthy for ever and
'ever!
             'JOHN CHURCHMAN.'
'London, the 4th of the
  '4th month, 1754.'

'Let this be read in your men's and wo-
'men's meetings.'

I have before hinted, that in my travelling to the meetings in Wiltshire, and attending the quarterly-meeting in the seventh
month, Old Stile, 1750, I was straitened to
clear myself towards them, which occasioned
me to leave them in pain of mind; but
now, having sent them this epistle, I was
made easy, believing they would read it,
and send copies thereof to their several
monthly-meetings, which would be likely
to be heard by more friends, than if my
concern had been delivered in the quarterly-
meeting only. Inclosing it to an innocent
friend at Chippenham, I desired him to deliver it to the said meeting, which I afterwards understood he did, and that friends
had answered my request.

Now feeling my mind easy to leave London for a while, I went to Esher, in Surry;
was the next day at a large meeting at
Kingston on Thames, which was pretty open
as to doctrine; the people seemed attentive,
                                       and

and several much tendered. There are but few friends here.

I then visited divers other meetings in Hampshire and Berkshire, being made thankful to the great Author of all good, who had been with me in the journey, under my indisposition of body. Coming to London, I met with many friends, from different parts of the nation, in order to attend the yearly-meeting, which began on the second day of the sixth month, and continued ten days, being a very large, and in the main a solid meeting. Many weighty affairs relating to our religious society were therein considered; it was then also agreed that in future this meeting should begin with a meeting of ministers and elders, on the seventh day of the week, at the third hour in the afternoon, that enquiry might be made into the state of the ministry in general, which I hope may be attended with good service hereafter.

On the eleventh of the sixth month, and third day of the week, after the parting meeting, I went from London to Margaret's, in Hertfordshire; next day attended a yearly-meeting in Hertford, which was very large.

The next day I accompanied several friends who were appointed to visit a monthly-meeting, the members of which paid tithes, and contended for liberty so to do without censure. We had a conference with them,

them, in which the testimony of truth being set over them for that time, they were taken and confounded in their own arguments.

After this I attended a general or yearly-meeting at Baldock, which was very large and satisfactory. Returning next morning to London, I was truly thankful that I had been enabled to attend these three meetings, enjoying great peace in my labours there, which lay heavy upon me. My gracious and good Master gave me wisdom, boldness, and strength, to clear myself in the love and power of truth, to the tendering of many hearts: may I ever remember his mercies to me, and be enabled to bless and praise his holy name, who is worthy for ever!

Continuing in and near London about ten days, I then went to a large satisfactory meeting at Rochester, in Kent, where were several clergymen, who behaved well. Next morning had a meeting at the house of Thomas Crisp, with a few friends, and divers others. Then going to my friend William Patterson's, at Canterbury, I was at their meeting in that town, and the day following had one in the Isle of Thanet, where there are a few friendly people. The meeting next day at Dover was pretty open. On first day I was at two meetings at Folkstone, which were dull and heavy, though there are many friends in that place, amongst whom

whom I was favoured with strength to ease my mind.

I then visited the meetings at Mersham, Ashford, Tenterden, (to which friends of Colebrook came) Gardnerstreet, Lewes, Brighthelmstone, Ifield, Horsham, Shipley, Arundel, and Chichester; when finding a concern to visit the families of friends in this city, I spent two days in the service, and had some close exercise, though a good degree of peace. I also attended their two meetings on first day, which were heavy and laborious: for though here are some tender people, yet the spirit of the world has brought a blast on several professors.

From hence I went to Gosport, in Hampshire, where we had a meeting, also one in the evening at Portsmouth, John Griffith and Jeremiah Waring being with me; then going to Southampton, went in a boat to Cowes, in the Isle of Wight, and the day after had a good meeting at Newport, likewise one in the evening with the town's people. After another opportunity with friends, returned to Cowes, where I had another with a few of our brethren: so went back to Southampton. And on first day, the twenty-first of the seventh month, attended two meetings at Poole, in Dorsetshire, which were dull and laborious: a worldly libertine spirit has brought a blast on many. Next day we had a meeting with a few friends at Weymouth; then at Bridport: truth seems at a low ebb in Dorsetshire. The next meeting was at Ringwood, in Hampshire, which was dull: where the life of truth is not abode in, people will wither. The same evening we had a meeting to pretty good satisfaction at Fordingbridge; then one at Alton, at which place we had another very satisfactory meeting, on first day; and that evening at Godalming. The next day had a meeting at Capel, in Surry, and in the evening at Darking; on the day following at Ryegate, and in the evening at Croydon. From whence on fourth day morning, the thirty-first of the seventh month, coming again to London, for the last time, I spent eight days more with friends in that city.

On my coming here from Alban's, on the nineteenth of the third month before mentioned, I felt great fear to possess my mind, having at sundry times before spent about thirteen weeks in that city, mostly under a close exercise of spirit, without an openness to say much, in publick or private, to obtain relief: so that to go thither again appeared to me like entering into a cloud, although I was secretly bound in spirit to proceed. But attending all the meetings as they came in course, I felt a gradual openness and strength to declare those things, which before had been sealed up; being now made

made sensible that every opening or vision, which the Lord is pleased to manifest to his servants, are not for immediate utterance: but the Lord, who gives judgment, should be carefully waited upon, who only can shew, by the manifestation of his heavenly light, the time when, and by the gentle putting forth of his arm of power, abilitates in the opening of his spirit, which giveth tongue and utterance to speak the word of truth, in the demonstration of the spirit and power; that openeth a door of entrance in the hearts of them who hear. Our dear Lord said, " For it is not ye that speak, but " the Spirit of your Father, which speaketh " in you," Matt. x. 20.

Now as my service opened and strength increased, I was invited by some to their houses to dine, who before looked on me with indifference, but now said they should be glad to see me there, to be more acquainted; but as I felt, on my first arrival in this city, a secret prohibition from going much from house to house, without inward leave, so now the same restraint continued with me, lest by going to such places, I might somewhat contradict by example the precepts which truth had directed me to deliver in publick; to wit, a life of self-denial and temperance in eating and drinking, with a steady inward attention to the teachings of the spirit of grace, in order to know an establishment of heart thereby, as being the certain duty of every follower of Christ Jesus our Lord.

Thus I think I have seen that there is great need to be exceedingly careful, when the Lord is pleased to reach unto and convict disorderly walkers by instrumental means, that we do not lessen the weight of divine reproof, by being familiar with such, as if all was well: for they are apt to be fond of the instrument through whom they have been reached; and if by their fondling they gain the esteem of such a friend, it seems to heal them before their wounds are searched to the bottom: so that I rather chose retirement, and to live as private as I well could. Now I also saw that if I had sought many acquaintance, and thereby beheld the conduct and behaviour of some in their families, my way would not have been so open as it now was.

In many meetings the love and power of truth was felt by the humble dependent children, whose eyes were fixed on their heavenly Helper; and at some of the last in London I had, with an innocent boldness, to appeal to friends to bear witness of the manner in which I had spent my time in that city. That I had not sought to be popular, nor endeavoured to gain the praise of any, or the friendship of those who were not the real friends of truth; keeping in a good

good degree under the innocency and simplicity thereof; yet with a near affection I felt my spirit united to the children of the heavenly family amongst them; but had never sought to steal their love from the great Parent to whom they did belong; my prayer and heart's desire having been, that their abode might be in the truth, and their affections placed on God, and the whole delight of their hearts to meditate in his holy law. That if through me, as an instrument, they had received any benefit, the praise belonged to the Lord, the only supreme good: and if in future they did but love, fear, and serve him, it was little to me whether they ever remembered that I had been amongst them. Nevertheless, a participation of the love of God, by the members of the true church, has taught them to know the communion of saints, and the deeply engraven unity of the one spirit, which makes them as epistles written in one another's hearts, which time or distance can never erase.

Having spent first and last in London about twenty-three weeks, on the ninth day of the eighth month, and sixth of the week, after a solid meeting at Gracechurch-street, I felt myself at liberty to set my face homewards. The same ship in which I came over, and the same captain, Stephen Mesnard, being now ready to go for Philadelphia,

delphia, I went that night to Gravesend, accompanied by about twelve friends; the next morning we went on board the ship, where we had a precious uniting time, and then returned on shore to dine: after which my friend Samuel Fothergill and myself, taking leave of our friends, went on board again, and passed down the Thames to Margate Bay, near the Isle of Thanet. On first day, the eleventh, we went to the Downs, by Deal: though very much indisposed in body, I enjoyed such quietude of mind, that I was borne up, and preserved from repining. Samuel Fothergill, before mentioned, came over with me, on a religious visit to friends in America; and during our passage great nearness was between us. We held meetings constantly on the first and fifth days of the week, and landed near Wilmington, in Newcastle county, on Delaware, on the twenty-fourth of the ninth month, (1754) in the forenoon.

My brother, William Brown, with our friend Joshua Dixon, from the county of Durham, in Great Britain, who was coming over also on a religious visit to friends in these colonies, having embarked in another ship, which sailed some time before us, arrived likewise the same day, and, quite unexpected to each other, we met in this town, to our mutual joy and satisfaction. From whence, after dining, they,
with

with Samuel Fothergill, proceeded up to Philadelphia, and I went home that evening, where I found a kind reception.

In this visit I was absent from home four years and twelve days, having travelled by land about nine thousand one hundred miles, and attended about one thousand meetings, besides those in London and Dublin, (in which cities I spent near half a year) and visited all the families of friends in North and South Holland.

CHAP. V.

His attending the quarterly-meetings at Philadelphia and Concord—The yearly-meeting at Philadelphia, and quarterly-meeting at Shrewsbury, in New-Jersey.—An account of an exercise attending his mind relating to war, and the publick commotions.—A conference of several friends thereon, with their address to the assembly of Pennsylvania on the subject, and an epistle to friends in that province in the year 1755.—His attendance of the general spring-meeting in Philadelphia in 1756, and some account of the calamities of the Indian war in Pennsylvania.—An account of the yearly-meeting in Philadelphia the same year.—A relation of a visit of Peter Gardner to friends in Scotland.—A brief account of an Indian treaty at Easton in 1757.—Some sentences expressed in two of his publick testimonies.

OUR yearly-meeting for worship at Nottingham was held in the week after I landed, and I was greatly rejoiced to see many of my friends and acquaintance there.

In the eleventh month following I went up to the quarterly-meeting in Philadelphia, and returned to ours at Concord, where also was Samuel Fothergill. It was a very large meeting,

meeting, in which he was divinely opened in speaking to the state of friends in his publick ministry, and serviceable in the discipline. He also attended our general meeting in the same month at London-grove, which was also large and profitable; then went towards Lancaster, on his way to the southern provinces.

I spent this winter mostly at and near home, at times attending some neighbouring meetings, until towards the spring, I took a small journey to seven or eight others.

During my late travels in Europe, beholding the declension of many of the professors of truth from the ancient simplicity, in habit and deportment, I sometimes was ready to cry out, and say, O Pennsylvania! may thine inhabitants be for ever strangers to the vanities of the world; and the professors of truth keep their garments clean from the spots thereof, pride, and superfluity of every kind! But now, with sorrow of heart, I thought I beheld many of the youth of our society taking their flight as into the air, where the snares of the prince of the power thereof are laid to catch them; some of whom being already so much ensnared, to their unspeakable hurt, I knew them not, otherwise than by their natural features, and a family resemblance, their demeanor and habit being so exceedingly altered in a little more than four years; yet, to my comfort, I saw a few, who, by walk-

walking in the light, had escaped the wiles of Satan, and were growing in the truth.

In the fourth month (1755) I attended the general annual-meeting at Duck-creek, also meetings at Little-creek and George's-creek; the last of which was more open than I expected, several of other societies being there, who behaved orderly. After which I spent most of the summer at home, diligently attending our meetings for worship and discipline; and had to observe, that the general part of the members of our meeting were for some time remarkable in their care to come together near the hour appointed, and we had some precious opportunities, many of which were held in silence; wherein I often saw it to be a time of renewed visitation to many, which, if not carefully improved, would not be continued very long, but that a more trying season would overtake us, (of which I was sometimes led to speak, as truth opened) wherein the door of outward ministry would be more closed up, which would prove the religion of the professors of truth, and manifest what they attended meetings for, whether to wait upon God, for the spiritual bread, or on man, for outward ministry.

In the ninth month I attended our yearly-meeting in Philadelphia, which was large and solid, wherein many weighty matters coming under consideration, were concluded to satisfaction, that many friends parted in a feel-a feeling sense of the overshadowing of the heavenly wing, with reverent thankfulness of heart.

In the tenth month I attended Shrewsbury quarterly-meeting, in East-Jersey, at which also were our friends John Evans and Joseph White; it was large, the sittings thereof being favoured with a degree of the Divine presence. We also attended the monthly-meeting there, and had some service: friends were encouraged to deal with such who were disorderly in conduct, there having been some slackness among them in that respect.

As the sound of war and publick commotions had now entered the borders of these heretofore peaceful provinces, some solid thoughts attended my mind at Shrewsbury, respecting the nature of giving money for the king's use, knowing the same to be intended for the carrying on of war. John Evans accompanying me homewards, we took three meetings in our way, the last being at Evesham; at which place I told him, that I felt an engagement of mind to go to Philadelphia, and he consented to go with me. When we came to the city, the assembly of Pennsylvania being sitting, we understood that a committee of the house was appointed to prepare a bill, for granting a sum of money for the king's use, to be issued in paper bills of credit, to be called in and sunk at a stated time, by a tax on the inhabitants; on which account several friends were under a close exercise of mind, some of whom being providentially together, and conferring on the subject, concluded it was expedient to request a conference with those members of the House who were of our religious profession: on applying to the speaker, who was one himself, we obtained an opportunity of conversing with them. After which, we believed that an address to the assembly would be necessary; but we then being only few in number, consulted with several weighty friends thereon. At length upwards of twenty met together, who, after solidly considering the matter before us, were all of opinion, that an address to the assembly would be proper and necessary: whereupon one was drawn up, which being considered, agreed to, and signed by all of us, we went together to the House, and presenting it to the speaker, it was read while we were present. A copy whereof here follows, viz.

' To the Representatives of the Freemen of
' the Province of Pennsylvania, in Ge-
' neral Assembly met.'

' The Address of some of the People called
' Quakers in the said Province, on Behalf
' of themselves and others.

'THE consideration of the measures
' ' which have been lately pursued,
' and are now proposed, having been weigh-
' tily

'tily impressed on our minds, we appre-
'hend that we should fall short of our duty
'to you, to ourselves, and to our brethren
'in religious fellowship, if we did not in
'this manner inform you, that although we
'shall at all times heartily and freely con-
'tribute, according to our circumstances,
'either by the payment of taxes, or in
'such other manner as may be judged ne-
'cessary towards the exigencies of govern-
'ment; and sincerely desire that due care
'may be taken, and proper funds provided,
'for raising money to cultivate our friend-
'ship with our Indian neighbours, and to
'support such of our fellow subjects who
'are or may be in distress, and for such
'other like benevolent purposes; yet, as
'the raising sums of money, and putting
'them into the hands of committees, who
'may apply them to purposes inconsistent
'with the peaceable testimony we profess,
'and have borne to the world, appears to us,
'in its consequences, to be destructive of
'our religious liberties; we apprehend
'many among us, will be under the neces-
'sity of suffering, rather than consenting
'thereto, by the payment of a tax for such
'purposes: and thus the fundamental part
'of our constitution may be essentially af-
'fected, and that free enjoyment of liberty
'of conscience, for the sake of which our
'forefathers left their native country, and
                                    ' settled

'settled in this, then a wilderness, by degrees
'be violated.

'We sincerely assure you, we have no
'temporal motives for thus addressing you:
'and could we have preserved peace in our
'minds, and with each other, we should
'have declined it; being unwilling to give
'you unnecessary trouble, and deeply sensi-
'ble of your difficulty in discharging the
'trust committed to you irreproachable in
'these perilous times; which hath engaged
'our fervent desires, that the immediate
'instructions of Supreme wisdom may in-
'fluence your minds; and that, being pre-
'served in a steady attention thereto, you
'may be enabled to secure peace and tran-
'quillity to yourselves, and those you re-
'present, by pursuing measures consistent
'with our peaceable principles: and then
'we trust we may continue humbly to con-
'fide in the protection of that Almighty
'Power, whose providence has heretofore
'been as walls and bulwarks round about
'us.'

'Philadelphia, 11th month 7th, 1755.'

A bill was, however, brought in by the committee of the assembly, and a law enacted for granting a large sum of money proposed to be sunk, or called in by a general tax.

When this service before related was over, which I apprehended it my duty to be concerned

cerned in, I returned home; but a close exercise remained on me, as well as on the minds of divers other friends, on account of the law now passed. And as care had been taken to apprize the assembly of the solid sentiments of friends thereon, that we apprehended our charter respecting liberty of conscience would thereby be affected, therefore a large committee of the yearly-meeting, which had been appointed to visit the quarterly and monthly-meetings, met at Philadelphia, in the twelfth month, had a conference thereon, together with another committee, nominated to correspond with the meeting for sufferings in London; and, after several solid opportunities of waiting on the Lord, to be rightly instructed, in which being favoured with a renewed sense of the ownings of truth, many friends thought they could not be clear, as faithful watchmen, without communicating to their brethren, their mind and judgment concerning the payment of such a tax. For which purpose an epistle was prepared, considered, agreed to, and signed by twenty-one friends: copies thereof were concluded to be communicated to the monthly-meetings, being as follows, viz.

' An

'An Epistle of tender Love and Caution to Friends in Pennsylvania.

'Dear and well-beloved Friends,

'WE salute you in a fresh and renewed sense of our Heavenly Father's love, which hath graciously overshadowed us in several weighty and solid conferences we have had together, with many other friends, upon the present situation of the affairs of the society in this province; and in that love, we find our spirits engaged to acquaint you, that under a solid exercise of mind to seek for council and direction, from the High Priest of our profession, who is the Prince of Peace; we believe he hath renewedly favoured us with strong and lively evidences, that in his due and appointed time, the day which hath dawned in these latter ages, foretold by the prophet, wherein swords should be beaten into plough-shares, and spears into pruning-hooks, shall gloriously rise higher and higher; and the spirit of the gospel, which teaches to love enemies, prevail to that degree, that the art of war shall be no more learned. And that it is his determination to exalt this blessed day, in this our age, if in the depth of humility we receive his instructions and obey his voice. And being painfully apprehensive, that

'the large sum granted by the late act of
'assembly for the king's use, is principally
'intended for purposes inconsistent with
'our peaceable testimony; we therefore
'think, as we cannot be concerned in wars
'and fightings, so neither ought we to con-
'tribute thereto, by paying the tax directed
'by the said act, though suffering be the
'consequence of our refusal, which we
'hope to be enabled to bear with patience.
'And though some part of the money to
'be raised by the said act, is said to be for
'such benevolent purposes, as supporting
'our friendship with our Indian neighbours,
'and relieving the distresses of our fellow
'subjects, who have suffered in the present
'calamities, for whom our hearts are deeply
'pained, and we affectionately, and with
'bowels of tenderness, sympathize with
'them therein; and we could most chear-
'fully contribute to those purposes, if they
'were not so mixed, that we cannot, in the
'manner proposed, shew our hearty con-
'currence therewith, without at the same
'time assenting to, or allowing ourselves in
'practices, which we apprehend contrary
'to the testimony which the Lord hath
'given us to bear, for his name and truth's
'sake.

'And having the health and prosperity of
'the society at heart, we earnestly exhort
'friends to wait for the appearing of the
'true light, and stand in the council of
'God,

'God, that we may know him to be the
' Rock of Salvation, and place of our
' refuge for ever. And beware of the spi-
' rit of the world, that is unstable, and
' often draws into dark and timorous rea-
' sonings; lest the god thereof should be
' suffered to blind the eye of the mind; and
' such, not knowing the sure Foundation,
' the Rock of Ages, may partake of the
' terrors and fears, that are not known to
' the inhabitants of that place, where the
' sheep and lambs of Christ ever had a
' quiet habitation; which a remnant have
' to say, to the praise of his name, they have
' been blessed with a measure of, in this day
' of distress.

' And as our fidelity to the present go-
' vernment, and our willingly paying all
' taxes for purposes which do not interfere
' with our consciences, may justly exempt
' us from the imputation of disloyalty; so
' we earnestly desire that all, who, by a deep
' and quiet seeking for direction from the
' Holy Spirit, are or shall be convinced that
' he calls us as a people to this testimony,
' may dwell under the guidance of the same
' Divine Spirit, and manifest, by the meek-
' ness and humility of their conversation,
' that they are really under that influence;
' and therein may know true fortitude and
' patience to bear that, and every other
' testimony committed to them, faithfully
' and uniformly. And that all friends may
' know

'know their spirits cloathed and covered
'with true charity, the bond of Christian
'fellowship, wherein we again tenderly sa-
'lute you, and remain your friends and
'brethren.'

'Philadelphia, 12th month 16th, 1755.'

In the year 1756, I attended our general spring-meeting in Philadelphia, at which we had the company of our dear friends Samuel Fothergill and Catharine Payton, from Great Britain, and her companion Mary Peasley, from Ireland, and it was a solemn edifying meeting.

The Indians having burned several houses on the frontiers of this province, also at Gnadenhutten, in Northampton county, and murdered and scalped some of the inhabitants, at the time of this meeting two or three of the dead bodies were brought to Philadelphia in a waggon, with an intent, as was supposed, to animate the people to unite in preparations of war, to take vengeance on the Indians, and destroy them. They were carried along several of the streets, many people following, cursing the Indians, also the Quakers, because they would not join in war for destruction of the Indians. The sight of the dead bodies, and the outcry of the people, were very afflicting and shocking to me. Standing at the door of a friend's house as they passed along, my mind was

was humbled, and turned much inward, when I was made secretly to cry, 'What will become of Pennsylvania?' for it felt to me, that many did not consider, that the sins of the inhabitants, pride, profane swearing, drunkenness, with other wickedness, were the cause, that the Lord had suffered this calamity and scourge to come upon them. The weight of my exercise increasing as I walked along the street, at length it was said in my soul, 'This land is polluted with blood, and in the day of inquisition for blood, it will not only be required at the frontiers and borders, but even in this place, where these bodies are now seen.' I said within myself, 'How can this be; since this has been a land of peace, and as yet not much concerned in war?' but, as it were in a moment, mine eyes turned to the case of the poor enslaved negroes. And however light a matter they who have been concerned with them may look upon the purchasing, selling, or keeping those oppressed people in slavery, it then appeared plain to me, that such were partakers in iniquity, encouragers of war, and the shedding of innocent blood; which is often the case, where those unhappy people are or have been captivated and brought away for slaves. The same day I went to Pine-street meeting, under an exercising mournful state of mind, and thought I could be willing to sit among the people undiscovered.

I at-

I attended our quarterly-meeting at Concord in the fifth month, and in a few days after went to the yearly-meeting at West-River, in Maryland, which was large, and in a good degree satisfactory; then going to meetings at Herring-Creek, and the Clifts, returned the following first day to West-River, where I had a good opportunity to clear myself towards friends of that place; being concerned on account of several of the elders, who did not conduct so exemplary as they ought before the youth, and left them relieved in my mind. From thence I returned home, taking several meetings in my way.

In the ninth month I was at our yearly-meeting for Pennsylvania and New-Jersey, held this year at Burlington, which was large and edifying; many weighty matters being in much brotherly love resulted to satisfaction: our friend Thomas Gawthrop, from Great Britain, was there. In the time thereof our worthy friend and brother John Evans, of Gwynnedd, departing this life, Thomas and I went to attend the burial; on which solemn occasion he had a seasonable opportunity to remind a large gathering of people of their latter end, and I thought it was a solid time.

Being one of the committee appointed by the yearly-meeting to visit the quarterly and monthly-meetings, I was careful in attending on that service, as way was opened, in company with other friends; as likewise our meeting for sufferings, this year established, which is held monthly in Philadelphia, frequently taking meetings in my way going and returning.

In the spring of the year 1757, I also attended our general meeting for ministers and elders, held at Philadelphia.

Having often remembered a remarkable account given me when in England by our ancient worthy friend John Richardson, which, as it made some impression on my mind, I committed to writing, and now reviving, think it is worthy to be preserved, being nearly as follows, though I was not particular in regard to the time of the occurrence, viz.

' Peter Gardner, a friend, who lived in
' Essex, had a concern to visit friends in
' Scotland; but being low in circumstances,
' and having a wife and several children,
' was under discouragement about it. The
' Lord in mercy condescended to remove
' his doubts, by letting him know he would
' be with him; and though he had no
' horse to ride, and was but a weakly man,
' yet he would give him strength to perform
' the journey, and sustain him so that he
' should not want for what was sufficient.
' And having faith, he laid his concern be-
' fore the monthly-meeting he belonged to,
' with innocent weight. And friends con-
' curring with him therein, he took his
                                    ' journey

'journey along the east side of the nation,
' through Norfolk, Lincolnshire, and York-
' shire; and coming to a week-day meeting
' at Bridlington, where John Richardson
' then dwelt, he lodged at his house. In
' the evening, the doors being shut, Peter
' asked him if any friend lived that way;
' (pointing with his finger) John told him
' he pointed towards the sea, which was
' not far from thence. He said he believed
' he must go and see somebody that way in
' the morning. John asked him if he should
' go with him; he said he believed it would
' not be best, and so went to bed.

' In the morning, when John's wife had
' prepared breakfast, he thought he would
' go and see if the friend was well, but
' found the bed empty, and that he was
' gone, at which John Richardson won-
' dered; but soon after Peter came in, to
' whom John said, Thou hast taken a morn-
' ing walk, come to breakfast. And before
' they had done eating, a friend from the
' quay or harbour (the way that Peter Gard-
' ner pointed to over-night) came in, and
' said, " I wonder at thee, John, to send
" this man with such a message to my
" house," and related as follows, viz. that
' he came to him as he was standing at the
' Fishmarket-place, looking on the sea, to
' observe the wind; that he asked him if he
' would walk into his house; to which Pe-
' ter answered that he came for that pur-
' pose;

'pose; (this was in the twilight of the
' morning) that when he went into the
' house, he enquired whether his wife was
' well; to which the man answered that
' she was sick in bed, and invited him to
' go in and see her: he said he came so to
' do. Then being conducted into the cham-
' ber where the sick woman was, he sat
' down by her; and after a short time, told
' her, the will and resignation of her mind
' was accepted instead of the deed, and that
' she was excused from the journey which
' had been before her, and should die in
' peace with God and man. Then turning
' to the man (her husband) he said, " Thy
" wife had a concern to visit the churches
" in another country beyond the sea, but
" thou wouldst not give her leave; so she
" shall be taken from thee: and behold the
" Lord's hand is against thee, and thou shalt
" be blasted in whatsoever thou doest, and
" reduced to want thy bread." So the man
' seemed angry with John Richardson, who
' said to him, " Be still, and weigh the
" matter; for I knew not of the friend's
" going to thy house, but thought he was
" in bed, and did not inform him about
" thee nor thy wife:" at which he went
' away. So Peter pursued his journey to-
' wards Scotland, John Richardson and an-
' other friend going with him to Scarbo-
' rough on horseback: (for he would not
' let them go on foot with him) he kept

' be-

' before them full as faft as they chofe to
' ride; and when they had gone about half
' way, he gained ground on them, and John
' faid he was filled with admiration, for he
' feemed to go with more flight and eafe,
' he thought, than ever he had feen any
' man before. And riding faft to overtake
' him, he thought he beheld a fmall white
' cloud as it were encompaffing his head.
' When he overtook him, John faid to him,
' Thou doeft travel very faft; Peter replied,
' My Mafter told me before I left home,
' that he would give me hind's feet, and he
' hath performed his promife to me.

' When they came in fight of Scarbo-
' rough, Peter faid, take me to a friend's
' houfe, if there is any there; John replied,
' I will take thee to the place where I lodge,
' and if thou art not eafy there, I will go
' until we find a place, if it may be. So
' John Richardfon took him to his lodg-
' ings; and juft as they entered the door,
' they heard fome one go up ftairs, and anon
' the woman friend of the houfe coming
' down with a neighbour of hers, invited
' them to fit down. And in a fhort time
' Peter faith, Here is light and darknefs,
' good and bad in this houfe. The woman,
' after fhe had got them fome refrefhment,
' came and afked John, "Who haft thou
'' brought here?" "A man of God," he
' replied. Having a meeting at Scarborough
' the next day, John Richardfon ftaid with
                                        ' him,

'him, and said he had good service. He
'also went with him to several friends
'houses there, and he frequently spake his
'sense of the state of the families. But as
'they were near entering one house, Peter
'stopped, and said, "My Master is not there,
"I will not go in," so they turned away.

'Next morning, at parting, John Ri-
'chardson asked him how he was prepared
'for money; telling him his journey was
'long. To whom Peter answered, I have
'enough; my Master told me I should not
'want: and now, a bit of bread, and some
'water from a brook, refreshes me as much
'as a set meal at a table. But John insisted
'to see how much money he had, which
'was but two half-crowns; upon which
'John took a handful of small pieces out
'of his pocket, and forced Peter to take
'them, telling him, it was as free to him
'as his own; for so the Lord had put it
'into his heart. Thus they parted, John
'and the other friend returning home.

'In about two weeks afterwards, the
'man's wife (before mentioned) died, as
'Peter had foretold. At that time, the
'same man had three ships at sea; his son
'was master of one, a second son was on
'board another, and in their voyages they
'were all wrecked, or foundered, and their
'cargoes chiefly lost; his two sons, and se-
'veral of the hands, being drowned. The
'man soon after broke, and could not pay

'his

'his debts, but came to want bread before
'he died, though he had been in good cir-
'cumstances, if not very rich.

'John Richardson further said, that af-
'ter some time he heard Peter Gardner was
'dead in Cumberland, on his return from
'Scotland, and being attached to him in
'near affection, he went to enquire how he
'ended.

'John Bowstead, a noted friend near
'Carlisle, gave him an account that Peter
'had been through Scotland, and came to
'Carlisle, and the small pox being there,
'he took the infection very suddenly, and
'lay ill with it. So John Bowstead went
'just as the pock was coming out on him,
'and took him to his house; they never
'came out kindly, but swelled him very
'much, so that he was blind, and died
'about the seventh day; was quite sensible
'to the last, and knew the states of those
'who came to see him. He had enough to
'pay his funeral charges.'

On the twelfth of the seventh month this year I left home, in order to attend a treaty to be held between the Indians and our government, at Easton, in Northampton county, and proceeded to Philadelphia, where I was present at several conferences with friends; the governor having declared his dislike to their attendance at that treaty, or their distinguishing themselves by giving the Indians any presents. The result was, that as mutual tokens of the revival of ancient friendship had passed between them and the Indians, with a view to promote a general peace, it would be of bad consequence now to neglect or decline attending on this important occasion; though it was judged necessary for friends to act with great caution. We therefore set forward, and, taking a meeting at Gwynnedd in the way, reached Easton on fourth day, the twenty-first of the month, the governor being got there about two hours before us; but did not enter on business that day.

Many friends from Philadelphia, and other parts, being here collected, we held a meeting on fifth day, which was low and dull, things appearing very dark. In the afternoon the Indians, with Teedyuscung, their king, or chief man, went to the governor, and signified the sincerity of their intentions to promote the good work of peace; when he delivered several strings and belts of wampum, in order to certify the full power and authority given to Teedyuscung for that purpose; who also desired, that as things had heretofore been misunderstood or forgotten, he might have the liberty to choose a clerk, to take the minutes of the transactions at this treaty on behalf of the Indians, which was put off by the governor at that time.

Next morning Teedyuscung renewed the same request, but was again put by: then the

the Indians began to be very uneasy, from an apprehension, that some people from the Jersey side of the river were likely to rise, with a design to destroy them; but on going to converse with them, and giving them some pipes and tobacco, which they were told was a present from friends, they became more quiet, and seemingly pacified: this day and the next there was little business done.

On first day, the 24th of the month, friends held a publick meeting in the Treaty-booth, to pretty good satisfaction, to which a great number of people came, two friends having acceptable service therein. In the afternoon friends met again, but there seemed so great a cloud over the meeting, by reason of a raw careless spirit prevailing over the minds of the people, as though there was no God, notwithstanding his judgments are so conspicuous, especially in these parts of the country, that life did not arise in this meeting. About sunset this evening, we heard that the Mohawk Indians had requested to have a fire made to dance round, which the governor allowed, as he had the evening before to the Delawares; with both which we were very uneasy, as the tendency thereof was to make the Indians drunk; but no endeavours of ours could prevent it.

On second day morning the governor agreed to allow the Indian king to choose himself a clerk,

a clerk, which he did, and about one o'clock that day the treaty was first opened in publick; when Teedyuscung was desired fully to inform, with an open heart, wherein he apprehended the Indians had been defrauded by the Proprietaries, to which he answered that he would to-morrow; but they must first clean up the blood, (as he expressed it) and bury the dead bodies. Next day being again met, the king said, ' that, according
' to his word, he had now met some of
' the several nations to do what they could
' for settling peace; but now in the first
' place he had seen and considered the black
' cloud that hung over the land, the blood
' and bodies of the people who had suf-
' fered,' and then said, ' I have gathered up
' the stained leaves, the blood and dead bo-
' dies, and looked round about, when all
' seemed terrible, that I could find no place
' to hide them; but looking up, I saw the
' great and good Spirit above. Let us hear-
' tily join in prayer to him, that he may
' give us power to bury all these things out
' of our sight; that neither the evil spirit,
' nor any wicked person, may ever be able
' to raise them; that we may love like bre-
' thren, and the sun may shine clear upon
' us; that we, our wives, our young men
' and children, may rejoice in a lasting
' peace; that we may eat the fruits of the
' earth, and they may do us good; so that
' we may enjoy peace in the day time, and
' at

'at night lay down and sleep in it.' Gave a belt of seventeen rows of wampum.

By another belt he told the governor, that he took him by one hand, and the five nations of Indians and their allies took him by the other; 'therefore,' said he, 'let us
' all stand as one man, with one heart and
' one mind, and join in this good work of
' peace. When we intend to lift or remove
' a great weight, we must be strong; if all
' do not exert themselves, we can never do
' it; but if all heartily join, it is easy to
' remove it. Our forefathers did not pro-
' ceed right when they met together; they
' looked at the earth and things present,
' which will soon pass out of our sight, but
' did not look forward to the good of pos-
' terity: let us set out right, and do better
' than they did, that a peace may be settled
' which may last to our children.'

He next acquainted the governor, that one of the messengers who had gone on a late message to the Indians afar off, (meaning Moses Tatamy's son) was shot on his return by one of our young men, and lay in a dangerous condition: and by a string of wampum insisted, that if he died, the other should be tried by our law, and suffer death also; and that some of their people should be present, to be able to inform the other nations of Indians of the justice done. He also revived the ancient agreement, that if any of them should commit the like offence,

fence, the criminal should be delivered up to be tried according to our laws, and suffer death in the same manner.

On fourth day there was no publick treaty; things seemed in much confusion, and very dull, but friends kept quiet. The next day I found myself much indisposed, and therefore thought it best to leave Easton before the treaty ended; but before I left it friends had a solemn opportunity together; at which time I thought I saw, that the working of the dark revengeful spirit, which opposed the measures of peace, was one reason why friends were so baptized into distress and suffering; of which I made some mention to friends, and that if they kept quiet, the clouds, as to them, would somewhat break away: Daniel Stanton had a solemn time in supplication. After this meeting, taking leave of friends, I rode to Richland, and though my distemper increased, and I was very ill, I pursued my journey the next day, and the day following reached Philadelphia; where I was carefully attended through a time of tedious and close affliction. My dear wife coming to me in my illness, was also taken with the same disorder, that we were not able to move homewards until the twenty-third of the eighth month, but, through the goodness of kind Providence in supporting us, got to our own habitation the next day in the evening; when, after about a week's stay, I set

I set out again, to attend the meeting for sufferings in Philadelphia, and, though very weak, got there. After tarrying part of three days in town, I went forward, in order to attend the monthly-meetings in Bucks county, of which I had a view while I lay sick, when it appeared to me, the way to recover my strength was to be faithful to every discovery of duty; accordingly, in company with several other friends appointed by the yearly-meeting, I visited the several monthly-meetings in that county, in some of which a good degree of the Divine presence being felt, was cause of thankfulness; though at one of them we had some remarkable close work, both in the time of worship and discipline.

Returning to Philadelphia, I perceived myself much recovered. I spent five days there, attending meetings as they came in course, and then went to Newtown meeting, in Chester county, which was small, there being an evident slackness of attending weekday meetings. From thence I went to Uwchlan, to the marriage of William Trimble and Phebe Thomas, which was a good meeting; where I met my dear wife, on her way to the yearly-meeting at Philadelphia: and, after attending a meeting at Merion, we went into the city the next evening. Our friends Thomas Gawthrop, Samuel Spavold, William Reckitt, and others, from Great Britain; also Thomas Nicholson,
from

from North Carolina, were at this yearly-meeting, which was large and satisfactory, holding from the seventeenth to the twenty-third of the ninth month, 1757.

Here I may note, that before I left home to attend the late Indian treaty at Easton, in my sleep I thought I was riding eastward, in the twilight, and saw a light before me towards sun-rising, which did not appear to be a common light, but soon observed the appearance of something therein, whereat the beast that I rode was much affrighted, and would have ran from it, which I knew would be in vain; for I took it to be an angel, whose motion was as swift as thought, so rather stopped, and reined in my beast towards it. It was encompassed with a brightness like a rainbow, with a large loose garment of the same colour down to the feet. It rather seemed to move even along than to walk, and then stood still in the midst of many curious stacks of corn. It was of a human form, about seven feet high, (as I thought) and, smiling on me, asked where I was going; I said Towards yonder building, which I thought was an elegant one, directly before me: it seemed to approve my way, and vanished upwards. Then I awakened, and had particularly to remember the complexion of this angelick apparition, which was not much different from one of the Indians, clean washed from his grease. Remembering my dream very fresh,
when

when I had seen the Indians at the treaty, and had heard some matters remarkably spoken by some particulars of them, I was made to believe it was not unreasonable to conclude, that the Lord was in them by his good Spirit, and that all colours were equal to him, who gave life and being to all mankind. We should therefore be careful to examine deeper than the outward appearance, with a tender regard to station and education, if we desire to be preserved from error in judgment.

The following sentences being delivered in two of his publick testimonies, were soon after committed to writing by a friend who was present, and appearing worthy to be further preserved, are now communicated, viz.

In a first day meeting at East Nottingham, the nineteenth of the twelfth month, 1756, he expressed nearly as follows:

' I felt my mind in this meeting remark-
' ably drawn from outward observation, and
' was commanded to center in deep and
' awful silence, wherein there was such a
' flowing of good will to mankind, as is
' scarcely to be uttered by tongue; but thus
' centering with diligent attention, I thought
' I felt

'I felt a strong power of darkness and stu-
'pid ignorance, seemingly combined to
'make war against this solemn attention of
'mind; yet, after patiently waiting some
'time, to my comfort, I felt a secret vic-
'tory, and the darkness vanished: then a
'voice was uttered in me, attended (I
'thought) with Divine authority, thus: "I
"will bow the inhabitants of the earth,
"and particularly of this land, and I will
"make them fear and reverence me, either
"in mercy or in judgment." 'Hereupon a
'prospect immediately opened to my view,
'of a day of calamity and sore distress,
'which was approaching, and in which the
'careless and stupid professors, who are easy,
'and not concerned to properly worship
'and adore the Almighty, and have not la-
'boured to witness their foundation to be
'laid on him the immoveable rock, will be
'greatly surprised with fearfulness: and on
'the behalf of such, a piercing cry and la-
'mentation ran through me, thus: "Alas,
"for the day! Alas, for the day! Woe is
"me!" (several times repeated) and a voice,
'which seemed to be connected with the
'foregoing, said further; "yet once more,
"saith the Lord, I shake not the earth only,
"but also heaven: not only the situation of
"those that know not any place of safety
"or refuge; that which is outward and
"earthly; but also those who assume a
"higher place, and in their specious ap-
"pearances

"pearances amongst men, do value them-
"selves on their assumed goodness, and
"would fain be accounted of the highest
"rank, and even place themselves amongst
"the saints, and are by some accounted as
"stars in the firmament; yet in the day of
"my power, wherein I will shake the hea-
"vens and the earth, those stars shall fall
"to the ground."
'In the opening, something within me
'was ready to say, "Amen, so be it; O
"Lord Almighty, cut short thy work in the
"earth, in order that thou mayest put an
"end to sin, and finish transgression; that
"thy fear, and the knowledge of thee, may
"cover the earth, as the waters cover the
"sea." 'Wherefore, my friends, the fer-
'vent desire of my soul is, that all present
'may with diligence labour to have your
'minds truly centered and humbled before
'God, to know a being fixed on that foun-
'dation which only standeth sure; that in
'a time of outward distress, which, per-
'haps, may come in your day, ye may find
'a place of safety and refuge.' All which,
with more to the like effect, was delivered
in great humility and brokenness.

At a week-day meeting at the same place, the seventeenth of the second month, 1757, several persons by unseasonable coming in had interrupted the quiet of the meeting, he gave a suitable caution in that respect, in gentle, winning terms, reminding those met of the awfulness and solemnity which should attend us when we approach the presence of him who is most holy; and in what reverence, fear and care, we ought to come together, not forgetting the hour appointed; and then expressed nearly as follows:

'A certain sentence has been presented to the view of my mind, which seemed to contain a gentle engaging caution, and matter of instruction to me, attended with sweetness; which was, "Work while it is day." 'Friends, this is our day, wherein we ought to be diligent and industrious; in the light of the day we may see and understand how to work, and what to do, that at the conclusion we may obtain from the Master of the day, who dwelleth in light, the answer of "Well done;" for the night will come, wherein no man can work. We are now favoured with liberty, in this our day, to assemble together for worship unmolested; and my hearty desire is, that we may properly improve this mercy; for the time to some of us may come, before our day in this life is closed, wherein this privilege may in some measure be taken from us. Something in me would be ready to say, The Lord forbid that should be the case; but, by reason of the great declension which has overspread the church, I hardly dare to expect

'any

' any other! Oh may we therefore be care-
' ful to prize the mercy of God, and en-
' endeavour to gain an inheritance in the
' light, that when night overtakes, and
' darkness, as to the outward, may hang over
' us, we may be favoured to withdraw into
' the sure hiding-place, and know a quiet
' habitation!'

CHAP. VI.

Sundry visits to meetings in Pennsylvania and New-Jersey—Also in Maryland and Virginia.—His apprehensions of duty to proceed on a visit to Barbadoes, and resignation thereto, but at length became most easy to decline it.—The settlement of Uwchlan monthly-meeting, with his epistle to friends there.—Also some weighty expressions uttered in the time of his sickness in the year 1761.

HAVING some drawings in my mind to visit the meetings of friends in the counties of Philadelphia and Bucks; being also under an appointment of the yearly-meeting to join with some others in a visit to the monthly-meetings; in order to proceed on my service, I acquainted our monthly-meeting at Nottingham, with whose concurrence I left home on the third of the twelfth month, 1757, accompanied by a near relation, and attended Darby meeting on first day; wherein, though life and the power of truth seemed to be low, I thought the humble waiters were encouraged. We went to the evening meeting in Philadelphia; next morning attended the meeting of ministers and elders, and the day following a meeting at the Bank, also a meeting for sufferings, and on fourth day returned to Darby, to their monthly-meeting; where we found friends under a strait about disowning one among them who denied the divinity of our Lord and Saviour Jesus Christ, on whom they had bestowed much labour to convince him of his error: the meeting ended well, the company of of friends who attended it being acceptable and of service. We were next day at Haverford monthly-meeting, held at Radnor, where the lively exercise of the discipline appeared to be very low, yet I was glad I was there. During the time of the business, feeling a concern on my mind to appoint a meeting at Haverford, to be held the next day, I proposed it for concurrence, which being readily agreed to, we attended there accordingly, and had a large meeting, much to satisfaction; having great peace in observing the motion of truth respecting this appointment. On the following day, accompanied by my friend Hugh Evans, I visited some ancient friends, who, by reason of old age and indisposition, could not get out to meetings; wherein I was favoured with

with that peace which I have often experienced to attend the acceptable work of visiting the afflicted. On first day, after a satisfactory meeting at Merion, I went to the evening meeting in Philadelphia, in which truth favoured with a degree of openness, to the instruction and comfort of many. On third day afternoon, accompanied by my brother, William Brown, went forward to Richland monthly-meeting, held on the fifth day, where we had some close hard work; which generally happens, when a lifeless formal spirit hath the prevalence in managing the affairs of the church, for want of feeling after and waiting for the true authority, even the power of God; yet we were glad that we were there. From thence my brother returned home, the rest of us going to an appointed meeting at Plumstead, which, though the weather was severely cold, was large and comfortable, in the sense whereof we were thankful to the Author of all good. The meeting next day at Buckingham was small, but satisfactory. I have often observed, that the severity of the weather is not a sufficient excuse for the Lord's panting children to neglect publick worship, which is a duty incumbent on us, and due to his glorious name. At Wrightstown meeting the next day the Master of our assemblies was pleased to appear in an eminent manner, to the comfort of the poor, instruction of the enquirers, rebuke

buke of the backsliders, and edification of many: for which the sacrifice of thanksgiving and praise was offered to him, who alone is worthy for ever. After this meeting, I felt the value of that peace which by the humble is better felt than expressed. We had next a good meeting at Makefield, at which were many seeking tender young people; then attended the Falls preparative meeting, which was satisfactory, a comfortable degree of unity subsisting among friends. Our next meeting was at Bristol, in which, after a dark distressing time in silence, what I had to communicate was introduced by a question, thus: 'Are you 'found in faith and practice?' And I was led to set forth, 'that to profess and acknow-
'ledge even sacred truths, without a life of
'self-denial, with an answerable honest con-
'duct, was no way sufficient; that being a
'dead faith, which produceth not good
'works in him who saith he believeth;
'shewing what stumbling-blocks the no-
'minal professors are, who by their exam-
'ple plainly manifest, that they are not
'possessors of what they profess to have,
'and are the greatest enemies the truth
'hath; which I was doubtful was the case
'with some among them.' I had peace in this plain dealing. Our next was a laborious meeting at Byberry, yet yielded a degree of the same peace. A friend afterwards told me that the state of the meeting was clearly
spoken

spoken to; which I relate not for any praise to man, but that it was an additional confirmation of the Lord's sufficiency to his own work; and when we are weak, foolish, or contemptible in our own esteem, his strength appears, and his wisdom inspires with true knowledge, whereby he magnifieth himself. We went home with our friend James Thornton, and next day to Horsham, where was a large and good meeting; after which we had a comfortable time in the family of John Cadwalader. Next day we attended the monthly-meeting at Abington, in company with Samuel Eastburn and Joseph White. We found things low here, because of a want of that strength in which stands the authority of the church. It is only the pure wisdom from above that preserves friends in peace, meekness, gentleness, and unanimity in the distribution of right justice and judgment in the church of Christ.

We were next day at Gwynedd monthly-meeting, which was a precious time, through the power of that sacred name, which is as ointment poured forth; the favour whereof continued through both worship and discipline, in which the faithful were mutually comforted. We from thence went to Ellen Evans's, and had an evening meeting, some of the neighbours coming in; several friends were much enlarged in counsel, and the opportunity ended in solemn prayer and thanksgiving.

We went from thence to Exeter monthly-meeting, which ended to satisfaction in the main; then home with our friend Ellis Hugh, where Joseph White and Samuel Eastburn left us, to return homewards. My companion and I proceeded to Reading, had a publick meeting in the Court-house, which I thought was pretty well, considering the company, many loose people attending; but truth seemed to come into dominion, and quieted them, that the meeting ended in a degree of awful sweetness.

On first day, being also the first of the new year, 1758, we were at Maiden Creek meeting, which, although a low time, afforded peace and comfort, from a prospect that there were, among the youth in particular, some true branches of the vine of life, who therefore could not be satisfied without the living sap from the holy root, and in the Lord's time would be favoured therewith, if there was a patient waiting for that springing season. We returned to Reading that evening, to a meeting held by appointment at a friend's house for the members of our society in that town, in the attendance of which I found peace. Crossing the river Schuylkill, we were next day at Robinson or the Forest meeting; after which I was much humbled in a sense of the great condescension and mercy of the Lord our God, who

was

was pleased to renew the reaches of his power to several, who had many years made profession of the pure truth, and yet dwelt in that which is impure, as drinking to excess, and other evils, some of whom I knew, but did not know that they were there till the meeting was over: the weak were strengthened, and the humble seekers encouraged, and great love flowed towards the youth. Returning again over Schuylkill, we went to that called Evans's meeting, which was very open for doctrine, several not of our society being present. The first sentences that appeared in my view were, " Many are called, but few are cho-" sen," attended with such weakness, and such a sense of my own foolishness, and inability for handling that subject, that I was afraid, because I had a secret apprehension that some would incline to make an advantage of those words, " but few are chosen," in applying them to strengthen themselves in the corrupt manner in which they hold election; but it appeared that the words, " all have not obeyed," was the reason why so few are chosen. My mouth was opened in fear, even to trembling, yet with a secret hope and confidence that the Lord would be mouth and wisdom, with desires that he would bind my attention to his own immediate instruction, that the language of his Spirit might be only uttered by me; and he was pleased to magnify his own truth in
the

the opening of these passages. I give this hint, that they who are concerned in the ministry may humbly trust in God, and not lean to their fears, knowledge, experience, or wisdom, in opening the mysteries of the gospel, but confide in the key of David, which when it opens none can shut. Next day we were at Providence or Perkiomin meeting, which though poor, and truth low, peace was afterwards measurably enjoyed, from an evidence of having been honest according to the ability given; and the day following, at Plymouth, faithful friends were comforted in the gracious condescension of our holy Head, who was pleased to favour with the aboundings of the life and love of truth. We then returned to Philadelphia, with thankful hearts for the evidence of peace.

My companion returning home, I went, in company with my brother, on first day morning to Frankfort, having felt an engagement for a considerable time to visit that meeting. A sense of the declension of friends in this place, both in respect to numbers and the life of religion, was cause of heaviness of heart; but having performed my visit in faithfulness, according to ability, returned with a degree of peace to the evening meeting in the city, which was comfortable, staying there until the fifth day of the week; in which time I attended the usual meetings, one with the negroes, much to to satisfaction, and also the meeting for sufferings. I got safe home on seventh day, the fourteenth of the first month, having travelled in this journey about four hundred and ten miles.

On the twenty-second of the second month I again left home, in order to attend the quarterly-meeting at Burlington, and some particular meetings in New-Jersey, as well on account of the yearly-meeting's appointment, as my own sense of duty, of which I had the approbation of our monthly-meeting, signified by a minute. In my way I attended the monthly-meeting in Philadelphia, with some degree of satisfaction. Then taking Chester or Adam's meeting in New-Jersey, reached Burlington on first day evening; the next day being the quarterly-meeting, at which, with William Horne, and my brother, William Brown, I had some service. After staying the youth's meeting, they left me, and I went to a meeting on fourth day at a school-house, where several friends met, also divers others, who, perhaps, had not been at any place of worship for some time, and were easy about religion; to whom it became my concern to shew how disagreeable and loathsome that state was, from Rev. iii. 15. " I " know thy works, that thou art neither " cold nor hot: so, then, because thou art " lukewarm, and neither cold nor hot, I " will spew thee out of my mouth." It
opened

opened to me, that a lukewarm condition, to hold a profession of religion, so as to take it ill not to be thought a Christian, but at the same time to remain easy, and not in earnest to experience the life, virtue, and power of Christianity; not so cold as to forget the name, nor so hot or zealous as to witness the life of true religion, was very displeasing to the Almighty. A good degree of power attended the opening, and in treating on that passage, with much love to such lukewarm professors, several were reached and tendered beyond expectation; but no praise to man, though he may will or run, but to God, who sheweth mercy.

At Chesterfield monthly-meeting, my friend John Woolman met me the next day; a raw company attending on account of a proposal or two for marriage, which, I suppose, they expected to be there presented; it was a time somewhat low and distressing. The advice of the yearly-meeting not being here enough observed, which is against allowing such who are not members of our society to sit in our meetings for discipline, unless they are nearly related to the parties concerned, of which that meeting was modestly reminded. I was also grieved that matters were introduced too much at the judgment or pleasure of individuals, by reason that they are not in the practice of holding preparative meetings; the service of which was particularly recommended to
their

their confideration. I had fome reward of peace in having attended this meeting. We were next at a meeting in Trenton with a few friends, whom the fpirit of the world (I thought) had much laid wafte. There feemed more opennefs towards a few of other focieties prefent, fome of whom were tendered by truth's teftimony, which feemed to reach the witnefs in them. At Bordentown meeting, next day, many were made thankful, the Divine prefence being felt among us. From hence John Woolman returned home, and John Sykes accompanied me to Upper Springfield, where the meeting was large, and, through the Lord's mercy, open and fatisfactory, the teftimony of truth flowing, in his love, towards the youth, many were tendered thereby, the faithful were encouraged, and the negligent warned. After which I went to Burlington, to attend that monthly-meeting, then to the burial of Margaret Butcher, at Mansfield; which was a laborious painful meeting, compofed of a mixed multitude, yet fomething of an evidence attended truth's teftimony, fo that the meeting ended with folidity. From thence I went to Peter Harvey's, and was thankful for the enjoyment of a peaceful quiet mind, though poor. Next day was at Old-Springfield meeting, which was flow and late in gathering, dull and heavy in fitting, as will be the cafe, when and wherefoever the life and power of religion is wanting,

wanting, or not carefully sought after and waited for, by those who profess it; which was observed to them in the love of truth, and in the simplicity and plainness thereof: so that I left this meeting with a heavy heart, not from a sense of any omission of duty on my part, but lest they should too soon forget what manner of persons they saw themselves to be in the light, that discovers and answers the witness, as face answers face in a glass. Then taking meetings at Mount Holly, Rancocus, and visiting the widow of Peter Andrews, I was at a large meeting at Evesham on first day following; but the expectations of the people being much outward, occasioned a painful deep waiting a considerable time, or at least I thought so; when at length I felt some pressure on my mind to stand up, which as I followed carefully, truth opened into the state of the meeting to my admiration, that I was enabled therein with an innocent boldness to attend thereto in speaking; which yielded me great peace after the meeting, and I was thankful for that opportunity. Next day I attended Haddonfield monthly-meeting, at which were Samuel Nottingham and William Horne, whose company was comfortable, and of advantage to the meeting. I then visited the meetings at Pilesgrove, Alloways Creek, Greenwich, Lower Alloways Creek, Salem, and one at Raccoon Creek, to which many sober people came, not professing with us; also a large,
and

and I believe to some a satisfactory meeting, at Woodberry, the state whereof opened pretty clearly, the humble being instructed; but I was sensible of an opposition here to some part of what I had to deliver to a self-righteous state; yet, through the mercy of our gracious Lord, I left this meeting with an evidence of peace, and an affectionate heart-yearning towards them. Then went to Haddonfield, to attend the quarterly-meeting for Gloucester and Salem counties, and from thence to the general spring-meeting at Philadelphia; after which I returned home, having been out five weeks and three days.

After this journey I did not go much abroad for more than a year, except to attend our quarterly-meeting, and the yearly and general spring-meeting at Philadelphia.

In the year 1759, I had some drawings in my mind to visit a few meetings in Maryland and Virginia, also the yearly-meeting at West-River; in which having the concurrence of our monthly-meeting, I left home on the twenty-eighth of the fifth month, and next day was at Gunpowder-meeting; then at Elkridge, with a few friends and divers not professing with us, amongst whom there was an openness to hear the testimony of truth declared; but for want of a steady walking in the professors thereof, it seems in a great measure laid waste. That night I lodged at the house of a kind a kind man, but have to remark, that natural affability in any one, unlefs it is fweetened by the baptifm of the fpirit of truth, is of little value. On fifth day I was at a new meeting-houfe, at Indian Spring, with a few friends, fome of whom, I fear, fcarcely know what they profefs. The next had a meeting at Samuel Plummer's houfe, at Patuxent, to fatisfaction: and on feventh day the yearly-meeting at Weft-River began, which held until fourth day following; which was in the main the moft open and fatisfactory meeting I was ever at in that place: I thought a difpofition rather prevailed among the younger fort, to attend to the difcipline more clofely than in times paft. Then taking a meeting at Sandy Spring, I proceeded to Fairfax, being about forty miles, where I had a comfortable meeting on firft day; for which the hearts of many were made thankful to the Author of all good: the fame day we had alfo a fatisfactory opportunity in Mahlon Janney's family, his mother being indifpofed; and the next day attended Monaquafy meeting in Maryland, where truth is at a low ebb, through the conduct of fome unfaithful profeffors. Our next was a precious meeting, with a few fincere friends, at Bufh-Creek: that evening I went to William Farquar's, having a meeting at Pipe Creek next day, which was pretty open and fatisfactory; and one the day following at Petapfco tapſco Foreſt, amongſt a withered people. Alas! to profeſs the truth, and not to poſſeſs it in ſanctification of ſpirit, makes little meetings feel deſolate. From thence I returned home to our monthly meeting, being abſent nineteen days, and rode near three hundred and fifty miles, Samuel England being my companion.

In this year I was alſo engaged with my friend John Woolman, in viſiting ſome active members of our ſociety, who held ſlaves, firſt in the city of Philadelphia, and in other places; alſo in New-Jerſey, in which ſervice we were enabled to go through ſome heavy labours, and were favoured with peace; divine love in a tender ſympathy prevailing at times, with a hope that theſe endeavours would not be in vain.

In the ſecond month 1760, I acquainted our monthly-meeting, that in order to proceed in performing the appointment of the yearly-meeting, having alſo a draught in my own mind, I had an inclination to viſit ſome meetings up the river Delaware, particularly the monthly-meeting of Kingwood, in New-Jerſey, with which, having the approbation of friends, I ſet out from home on the twenty-ſixth of the fifth month following, and reached the Bank-meeting in Philadelphia the next day. From thence proceeded to the quarterly-meeting for Bucks County, held at Buckingham, where, though things were low, the affairs of the church were transacted in a good degree of amity and peace. It was a large meeting, there being a great appearance of young people, some very hopeful, who in the love of truth were exhorted to come up in their places, by learning discipline of the author thereof, viz. the Spirit of Truth; and they were cautioned against that very unbecoming and hurtful practice, though too common, of going out after worship, and standing without in companies talking, when they should keep their places in the meeting, which should quietly and solidly proceed on the business coming before it: heavenly love was felt by the tender in spirit, which I hope will be remembered by many. The next day the general or youth's meeting was large, open, and satisfactory in the main; for which the name of the Lord was praised. Next day I spent in visiting a widow, also other aged and infirm friends; in the performance of which duty I had some satisfaction: and on first day was at Plumstead meeting, which was large, and very comfortable; the Divine presence being felt, the power of truth prevailed, to the tendering of many: but such favour being not of him that willeth or runneth, but of God, that sheweth mercy, to him belongeth the praise of all, who is worthy for ever! In the evening I attended a meeting at a school-house, near Samuel Eastburn's, in which I had some particular service, the states of many present

present being very clearly opened before them in the love of the gospel, which made deep impression on some who were much broken; and I believe it would be as dew on their hearts, if they would remain enough in the valley of humility.

I was the next day at Buckingham monthly-meeting, which in the time of business suffered much by the prevalence of a talkative noisy spirit, which mightily darkens counsel in those who give way to it, and leads into doubtful and trifling disputations; so that I left that meeting with pain of heart, in a sense that the time had been so lost, that several weighty matters could not be brought under consideration to advantage, which were therefore continued until the next month.

Wrightstown monthly-meeting on third day was more satisfactory, the spirit for discipline rather reviving, and I hope a desire, among the youth at least, for an improvement. It too frequently is the case, that some of the elderly sort are so bigotted to their old forms and customs, that they will scarcely trouble themselves to examine whether these customs are agreeable to the testimony of truth, or whether through inattention they have not swerved and fallen short in various matters, that now occasion a difficulty in the churches, which difficulties must be laboured under for a season by the baptized members, who, nevertheless,

theless, as they keep their places will grow stronger.

Accompanied by my friend Thomas Ross, I attended the Falls monthly-meeting, wherein I was comforted, from a sense that a tender people were among them, though they felt a time of dearth, whom the Lord would in his own time water as his peculiar heritage: but this comfort was heavily ballasted from a secret fear attending me, that there were among them some, who, like the heath in the desert, know not when good cometh; such who were easy in a dead form, and contented with a name, neglecting to wait for that transforming power, which would renew into the image and life of the Son of God; to whom, in the love and plainness of the gospel, I was constrained to clear myself. The meeting for discipline was pretty open, and ended in a good degree of sweetness. We went home with the wife of Joseph White, who was then on a religious visit to friends in Europe, and had a comfortable season in the family with the children; she appearing to be resigned in the absence of her husband, her spirit being sweetened with the truth in innocent quietude.

At Middletown monthly-meeting the next day truth seemed to be low, but we had some service in the discipline, that I came away with peace; and the day following, in company with Joshua Ely, went to Jacob Birdshal's,

Birdshal's, in Amwell township, New-Jersey, and had a meeting in his barn, which (being a wet time) was small: there are few here who profess with us, some of whom seem to have nothing more than the name. Next morning we called at the house of an old professor; he and his wife were both ancient, but full of talk. I felt a desire to visit them, and had a full time to clear myself, in a close and plain manner, though in love to them. After which, going to Kingwood, or Bethlehem, attended two meetings there on first day, when truth favoured in opening the states of the people in mercy to many; which may be of advantage, if rightly remembered. Then proceeding to the Drowned-lands, so called, had there a meeting with a few professors, who seemed too much withered: then taking another at Paulin's Kiln, to pretty good satisfaction, returned to Kingwood monthly-meeting, then held at Hardwick: several hopeful young people belong thereto; the meeting was comfortable, friends rejoicing in the company one of another, and in the Lord, for his merciful regard. Next day I returned to Bethlehem, and from thence to Gwynedd meeting on first day; after which I rode to Uwchlan, about twenty-eight miles, from thence home, where I found all well, having been absent three weeks, and rode about four hundred and sixteen miles in this journey.

Having a draught of love, and a motion therein, to visit the monthly and particular meetings within our own quarter, on the West side of Susquehanna river, with the concurrence of our monthly-meeting on that occasion, I sat out from home on the seventeenth of the tenth month, in company with my brother-in-law, James Brown, who likewise had the approbation of Goshen monthly-meeting for this purpose. We visited the meetings at Pipe Creek, Bush Creek, and Monaquasy, in Maryland, in the first of which the Lord was pleased to favour in opening the state of friends to the tendering the hearts of many; the other was satisfactory, and the last seemed to be a renewed visitation to a raw declining people, several of whom were tendered, through the gracious long-suffering of infinite goodness. We were next at the preparative meeting at Fairfax in Virginia; then at Goose Creek, wherein truth owned our service, to the comfort of the faithful. We then attended the meeting of ministers and elders, also the monthly-meeting at Fairfax, likewise the first-day meeting there, and one that evening in Francis Hague's house, whose wife was indisposed: several disorderly walkers being present, the Lord was pleased to open, and give ability to speak to their states in a measure of his heart tendering love, to the reaching the witness in some. After this returning to the widow Janny's, we had a precious

precious opportuity with her and children, to our mutual satisfaction.

Our next meeting was at Pott's, near the South-mountain, which was open for doctrine, several of other religious professions attending, who appeared loving, and well satisfied; then at Crooked-run, near the north branch of Shanandoa-river, in company with several other friends from Pennsylvania, some of us being a committee appointed by our quarterly-meeting, the friends living here having requested to have a meeting settled among them. The opportunity was to some satisfaction, there being some young people, who, I hope, will grow in the truth, though some of those who are elderly appear too superficial. From hence we went to Hopewell preparative meeting, also to a small meeting over the mountain near Jesse Pugh's; then we attended a select meeting at Hopewell, and at the same place on first day, which was large and solid, many therein being much tendered, to the praise of the Lord, whose mercy endureth for ever! In the evening we had also a satisfactory meeting at the widow Lupton's, near Winchester. Next day we were at Hopewell monthly-meeting, where we found considerable weakness, as to the practice of the discipline, on which account we had some labour, to the comfort of the well-minded. On our return we had meetings at Monallan, Huntington, War-

Warrington, and Newberry in York county, Pennsylvania, and a seasonable opportunity, with friends in York-town; from whence I proceeded home, with a thankful mind, having travelled about four hundred miles in this journey.

In the spring of the year 1761, having an engagement on my mind to visit Barbadoes, and some of the adjacent islands, I proposed the same to my brethren at home for their weighty consideration, before I asked for their certificate, who, after a time, expressed their unity therewith, and gave me a certificate, to which the quarterly-meeting signified their approbation. At our next yearly-meeting I laid my concern before the ministers and elders, when, for any thing that appeared, I had their unity and prayers. I came home intending to proceed before the winter set in, and attended our general meeting at Nottingham in the tenth month, but in a few days after was taken ill of a fever, which, with bodily pain, and exercise of mind, reduced me to a very low and weak state;* but the Lord was pleased to give me inward strength, influencing my mind with love to all men, and great love to the members of our religious society, the state whereof I saw in a clear manner; and I so far recovered as to attend our quarterly-meeting at London Grove, in the eleventh month,

---

* See page 285.

month, at which I had an opportunity to clear myself, to my humble admiration, and was inwardly comforted. Soon after which (my concern for going to Barbadoes continuing) I went to Philadelphia to enquire for a passage, when my friends informed me of five vessels, three of which were near ready to sail; but understanding that all of them were prepared with guns for defence, I felt a secret exercise on my mind, so that I could not go to see any of them, but kept quiet from sixth day evening until second day morning, when I went to the meeting of ministers and elders, where I had a singular freedom to let friends know, 'That I came to town in order
' to take my passage for Barbadoes, but found
' myself not at liberty to go in any of those
' vessels, because they carried arms for de-
' fence: for as my motive in going, was to
' publish "the glad tidings of the gospel,
" which teacheth love to all men," 'I could
' not go with those who were prepared to
' destroy men, whom Christ Jesus, our Lord
' and Master, laid down his life to save and
' deliver from that spirit in which wars and
' fightings stand.' I further added, 'If I
' had a concern to visit in gospel love those
' now living at Pittsburgh, or Fort Du-
' quesne, do you think it would become
' me to go with a band of soldiers, as if I
' wanted the arm of flesh to guard me?
' Would it not be more becoming to go
' with

'with a few simple unarmed men? I now
'tenderly desire your sympathy and advice.'
One honest friend said, 'Keep to the tender
'scruple in thy own mind, for it rejoices
'me to hear it;' and several said, 'they
'believed it would be best for me to mind
'my own freedom.' I then begged that
friends would consider weightily, whether it
was right for any professing with us to be
owners, or part owners, charterers, freight-
ers, or insurers of such vessels that a friend
could not be free to go passenger in on a
gospel message. And as I returned to my
lodgings, I felt so much peace of mind in
thus bearing my testimony, that I thought
if all my concern ended therein, it was worth
all my trouble, though at that time I did
not think it would, yet was quite easy to
return home, and wait until my way appeared more open. And as my concern went
off in this manner, I have been since led to
consider, that I could not have borne that
testimony so fully and feelingly, if I had
not been thus restrained. "The wisdom
" and judgments of the Lord are unsearch-
" able, and his ways past finding out, and
" happy are they who move at his com-
" mand, and stand stedfast in his counsel."

Our worthy friends John Stephenson,
Robert Proud, Hannah Harris, and Elizabeth Wilkinson, of Great Britain, being in
this country, on a religious visit, attended
our yearly-meeting in Philadelphia this year,
which

which was large, and favoured with humbling goodness, and in a sense of the Divine presence, that meeting ended very solidly. The services of these friends, I think, have been great amongst us in this land, both in their publick ministry, also in the discipline of the church, and the remembrance thereof is precious, I believe, to many, whom the Lord is preparing for his work.

After this I spent a considerable time at and near home, except attending the quarterly, yearly-meetings, and the general spring-meetings, as they came in course; in the mean time being careful to frequent the meeting I belonged to.

A new monthly-meeting being allowed to be established at Uwchlan, in Chester county, it arose in my mind to salute friends there with an epistle, a copy whereof I sent to their first meeting in the first month, 1763, being as follows:

' DEAR FRIENDS,

' IN the gentle springing up of gospel
' love and fellowship I salute you, my
' dear brethren and sisters, and hereby let
' you know, that it is my fervent desire and
' prayer, that you may individually attend
' to the gift of God in your own hearts,
' and therein wait for the arising of his pure
' life and power, that therein and thereby
' only, the affairs of the church may be
' transacted

'transacted to the honour of truth and your
' own peace and safety: for to speak in the
' church to the business and affairs of truth,
' by the will, wisdom, and power of man,
' (however knowing he thinks himself) will
' lead into it's own nature, and in the end
' minister strife and contention, and break
' the unity of the one spirit, wherein the
' peace of the church stands. Wherefore, I
' beseech you, beware thereof, and as I
' know there are among you such, whom
' the Lord by his Spirit, and the gentle
' operation of his power, is preparing for
' his own work, mind your calling, in deep
' humility, and holy attention of soul; for
' in your obedience only, will you be elected
' and chosen to the work whereunto he hath
' called you: so shall you be made skilful
' watchmen and watchwomen, placed on
' the walls of Zion to discover the approach
' of an enemy, in whatsoever subtle ap-
' pearance, and enabled to give warning
' thereof to others. May each of you stand
' upright in your own lots in the regenera-
' tion, waiting for the pouring forth of the
' Spirit, and anointing of the Holy Ghost,
' by the renewing whereof, a true qualifi-
' cation is given in the influence of the love
' of the Father, rightly to oversee the flock
' and family of our God, amongst whom
' there are some plants with you worthy of
' your care.

' I should

'I should have been glad to have sat with you, in your monthly-meeting, from the sense of that love which I now renewedly feel to spring and flow towards you, but cannot well leave home; I therefore, at this time, in the pure refreshing stream thereof, again salute you, and remain your friend and brother,

'JOHN CHURCHMAN.'

'East Nottingham,
'1st month 4th, 1763.'

In the time of his illness in the year 1761, as mentioned in page 280, he uttered divers weighty expressions, some of which were committed to writing by a friend who was present; and being well worthy to be further preserved, are here inserted, viz.

In this sickness he was reduced very low, and sometimes said it looked unlikely that he should recover: in the fore part thereof he often mentioned his being in great poverty of spirit, saying, that before he was taken ill, he felt such deep distress of mind, that he thought he was a cumber to the ground, and scarcely worthy to partake of the meanest necessaries of life, that even bread and water seemed too good for him.

On the fourth of the eleventh month, four friends being present, he spake in a very

very awful frame of mind nearly as follows:
'Such build on a sandy foundation who
'refuse paying that which is called the pro-
'vincial or king's tax, only because some
'others scruple paying it, whom they esteem,
'yet I have now clearly seen, as well as
'heretofore, that the testimony of truth,
'if deeply attended too, will not be found
'to unite with warlike measures: and that
'it will, in the Lord's time, be exalted
'above all opposition, and come to possess
'even the gates of it's enemies; though it
'may appear mean and contemptible in the
'eyes of some now-a-days, as the conduct
'of our primitive friends did, in divers re-
'spects in the world's view. And whosoever
'continues to trample upon or despise the
'tender scruples of their brethren, in re-
'lation to their clearness concerning war,
'will certainly find it a weight too heavy
'for them to bear.

'My testimony on this account, so far
'as I have borne it, yields me satisfaction
'at this time: and the painful steps I have
'taken, on sundry occasions, both in publick
'and private, to discharge my conscience
'in the sight of God, in giving faithful
'warnings to my brethren and conntrymen,
'both in a civil and religious capacity, af-
'ford me comfort in this distressing season.
'I have clearly seen, and the prospect at
'this time adds divine strength to my soul,
'that the God of Truth is determined, in
                                        'due

'due time, to exalt the mountain of his
' holiness above all the hills of an empty
' profession; and all such who shall be ad-
' mitted as clean inhabitants thereon, he
' wills them to be quite clean handed; and
' that they should become subject to the
' Lamb's nature in every respect, and not
' shake hands with that nature which would
' tear and devour, nor in any shape contri-
' bute to the price of blood.'

At another time he said, ' I have been
' led, in the present dispensation allotted
' me, to behold the situation of divers par-
' ticular friends, to whom I feel ardent af-
' fection, who seem to have given, or sold
' away, for this world's friendship, the tes-
' timony they should have borne for the
' Prince of Peace, who is the High Priest
' of our profession; and, for fear of break-
' ing an outside unity, which will surely
' come to be broken, that the true unity in
' the bond of peace may be exalted, have
' acted contrary to the former sight of their
' duty, and are thereby become halt, and
' dimsighted in several respects; such, though
' they still seem to desire it, cannot attain
' to the spotless beauty of truth, nor ap-
' proach to the top of the mountain: on
' whose account I am afraid that some of
' them will never recover their former
' strength, nor attain to that dignity the
' truth would have placed upon them, if
' they had been faithful: the situation of
' whom

'whom I have bewailed with anxiety of
'mind. I have been from my youth up
'accustomed to sorrow, and am a man ac-
'quainted with grief, and now remarkably:
'the lives of my brethren, and of all men,
'appear exceeding precious in my sight. It
'looks doubtful whether I shall ever see
'my friends met in a quarterly-meeting
'again, yet, if it be the will of Divine
'Providence, I much desire it; having here-
'tofore, through a timorous disposition, lest
'I should offend some, and for fear of the
'frowns of elder brethren, concealed some
'things I should have declared. And if I
'should now never more have a publick
'opportunity, I speak this in your hearing,
'to let it be known that I am still a well-
'wisher to all men, and that my integrity
'to the testimony of truth, against all con-
'nections with wars and fighting, is now
'full as strong, or stronger than ever.'

On second day morning, the ninth of the eleventh month, he said to this effect, viz.
'I have been led to see the necessity there
'is for friends to beware of the custom of
'drinking drams, or strong spirits mixed; I
'have for many years rarely taken any, ex-
'cept on particular occasions, and then but
'a very small quantity. It is my judgment,
'that the less any of us accustom ourselves
'to the use of those spirits, the better it
'would be for our constitutions in general.
'I believe it is not consistent with the will
'of

'of Divine Providence, that the course of
'nature should be obstructed and changed,
'and our animal spirits corrupted, through
'the unnatural warmth of spirituous li-
'quors.

'From my present sense and feeling of
'that regular temperance which is truly
'pleasing in the eyes of Heaven, I have
'mourned that the use of strong drink
'should become so prevalent amongst us,
'who make so high a profession; whose
'bodies should be temples of the Holy
'Ghost, and should not be defiled, or tainted
'with any degree of intemperance. In har-
'vest there is generally plenty of other re-
'freshment, which would keep the bodies
'of men as strong, and as capable to per-
'form hard labour: witness the health and
'strength of our forefathers in the first set-
'tlement of this country, when strong li-
'quors were very little used amongst them.

'Alas! how dimness has overtaken us,
'when we compare ourselves, and our prac-
'tices, with the temperance and moderation
'of our forefathers, and the early settlers
'of this province! how sumptuous now are
'the tables, how rich and costly the appa-
'rel, the diet, and the furniture, of many
'of our friends, even in the country; but
'more especially in the city! How is the
'simplicity and plainness of truth departed
'from, and pomp and splendid appearances
'taken their place! And how much cost

'and time might be spared from needless
'things, and applied to better uses, to the
'bettering of our country, and helping to
'turn away the judgment which hangs over
'us, in part occasioned by these things.

'I desire that my grandchildren may be
'brought up in a plain simple way, accus-
'tomed to industry, and some useful busi-
'ness in the creation; not aiming at great
'estates, nor following others in that way;
'but give them useful learning; and rather
'chuse husbandry, and a plain calling for
'them, in the country, than endeavour to
'promote them to ways of merchandize:
'for according to my observation from my
'youth up, the former is less dangerous,
'and less corrupting. I observed when I
'was in England, that some of the greatest
'and wisest men, in a religious sense, were
'brought up at the plough tail, or in some
'laborious occupation; where the mind is
'less liable to be diverted from an awful
'sense of the Creator, than in an easy idle
'education. How many great men there are,
'whom I could name, whose way of living
'is mean and homely, in this world's ac-
'count, so that they have little more than
'real necessity requires; and yet they are
'rich in the best sense.'

The next day, being asked how he was,
he said nearly as follows: 'I have slept
'sweetly, and seem much refreshed; and
'though I feel myself very weak in body,
'I am

'I am full of Divine confolation, having
' never before had fuch profpects of hea-
' venly things: it feems even as though my
' foul was united in chorus with glorified
' faints and angels, both fleeping and wak-
' ing. I now believe I fhall recover, and
' that this ficknefs did not happen to me
' altogether on my own account. My way
' to recover is to be induftrious and diligent
' in what I believe is required of me: I
' have many meffages to deliver, both in
' publick, and privately to divers friends,
' whom I have feen to have miffed their
' way, and have in a great meafure deprived
' themfelves of the beauty wherewith an
' humble abiding in the truth would have
' dignified them: and fome of my elder bre-
' thren, for whom I feel an uncommon
' nearnefs of affection, their lives never ap-
' peared to be more near to me, and I dare
' not conceal counfel from tnem, whether
' they will hear or forbear. Yea, I thought
' laft night, I had a clear profpect of the
' fituations of many within the verge of
' our quarterly-meeting; it feemed as though
' the inward ftates of particulars were opened
' to me in full view; the pure life, in the
' brightnefs of religion, never appeared to
' be more precious; an uncommon earneft-
' nefs attends my mind, for the recovery of
' the rebellious, hypocritical, and back-
' fliding profeffors of all ranks amongft us:
' and if I get to our quarterly-meeting,

' (which

' (which I believe I shall) and can have
' time allowed me when there, I have
' tidings, important tidings, as from a dy-
' ing man, to many particulars. I have seen
' the myftery of the three days, or the
' prophet's laying three days and three nights
' in the belly of the fish. A wicked and
' adulterous generation are now, as well as
' formerly, feeking for a fign to things
' fpoken clofely, but no fign fhall be given
' them, fave the fign of the prophet Jonah.
' Our Saviour's fufferings for mankind, and
' afterwards defcending into the bowels of
' the earth, prefigured that his followers
' muft, after his pattern, defcend into fpi-
' ritual baptifm, that they may rife again,
' freed from the dregs of nature, and from
' the corruptions of the creaturely paffions,
' before they can be qualified to fee, and
' fuitably to adminifter, to the ftates of
' others. I have likewife feen the myftery
' of Ezekiel's fufferings, and bearing the
' fins of the houfe of Ifrael for the fpace
' of 390 days, which being accomplifhed,
' he was commanded to turn on the other
' fide, and to bear the fins of Judah forty
' days, for the corruptions of that princely
' tribe, who fhould have been as way-marks
' to others. My ftate has been for feveral
' years paft, my deep baptifms, and painful
' fittings in our meetings, like bearing the
' rod of the wicked; in which difpenfation
' I have been fometimes ready to conclude
                                        ' with

' with Elijah, that the altars were thrown
' down, and the Lord's prophets slain, and
' I, a mean, worthless servant, left alone,
' and that my life was sought also. I have
' now seen the use of those dispensations to
' me, with the use of my late sickness,
' whereby I am reduced to great weakness
' of body; that I might be as a sign to
' this generation, and, as with the mouth
' of a dying man, utter tidings without fear
' of giving offence: tidings which I have
' heretofore concealed, through a timorous
' disposition. I have seen at this season that
' the Lord hath preserved a living number
' in Israel, who have not bowed the knee
' to Baal, or the god of this world; I have
' also seen the conditions of many who
' have worshipped strange gods; and the
' corruption even of some who have assumed
' the station of ministers in our society;
' how they are deceived so far as to believe
' a lye; have seen lying visions, and have
' caused the weak to stumble: they have
' been speaking peace to the people as in
' the Lord's name, when it was only a flash
' or divination of their own brain; which
' has tended to corruption and putrefaction
' in the churches. And I have seen how
' that many little ones have laid groaning,
' as under the burden and oppression of
' these things; whose day of redemption
' draweth near, when they shall be made
' by the Almighty, as bright stars in the
' firma-

'firmament of his power; and those who
'are corrupt, and settled on their lees, shall
'be punished. In this dispensation I have
'abundantly witnessed the incomes of that
'peace and love which passeth all under-
'standing; neither my tongue nor capacity
'are able to set forth the bowels of com-
'passion which I livingly feel to flow to-
'wards the whole bulk of mankind, and
'especially to my brethren in profession.
'Yea, it seems as though no affliction
'would be too great to endure for their
'sakes, if it might be a means to have some
'of them (whose situation I have now been
'led to behold as particulars) restored to
'their former greenness and spiritual health,
'from whence they have fallen, and dim-
'ness has overtaken them. And though
'my outward man seems almost wasted, my
'spirit is strong in the Lord, and, in the
'inexpressible strength of affection, I have
'found my spirit led from place to place
'over the country, to visit the souls in pri-
'son. Yea, I have beheld the dawning
'of that precious morning, wherein cor-
'ruption shall be swept away from the
'church, and righteousness and truth begin
'to flourish greatly. The day seems to me to
'be at hand; and what if I say, I have a
'degree of faith that some of the children
'now born may live to see it. Through
'innocent boldness, my face now seems to
'be as brass; and, in the openings of the
                                         'vision

'vision of life, I think I could utter gospel
' truths, and discover the mystery of ini-
' quity which I have seen, without fearing
' any mortal man. I may be raised to live
' a while longer, though to die now would
' be a welcome release to me: yea, I could
' not desire to live, but for the longings of
' soul, and pantings of heart, which I feel
' towards the precious seed in many whom
' I have now been led in spirit to visit. I
' have beheld their situation to be as lumps,
' taken or cut out from the bowels of their
' mother the earth, though much hidden
' from the view of mortals; and are tem-
' pering and fashioning by the Divine Pot-
' ter, in different shapes, for divers uses;
' and I have seen that the Potter's power is
' sufficient to pick out, and take away,
' every gravel and little pebble of nature.
' Many I have beheld in this situation, set
' by (as it were) out of sight to dry, until
' all the dampness and natural moisture is
' removed from them; not being yet fitted
' to undergo the operation of burning: but,
' when properly prepared, and thoroughly
' dried, many will be brought to the fire,
' burned, and glazed, so that they may re-
' tain the liquor or wine of the kingdom
' with a sweet taste, without any degree of
' taint, or nauseous smell.'

On the twelfth of the eleventh month, early in the morning, he spake to this purpose: 'I believe I must endeavour to go 'to our quarterly-meeting, (which began the fourteenth) although as to bodily strength I am very weak. There my mind is remarkably, sleeping and waking: there I hope to be relieved of some things which seem to remain like a fire in my bones. I dare not forbear; I know it is the way for me to recover my strength outwardly, and to be eased of that which is a heavy burden inwardly: I see I must go, and believe I shall recruit, and gain strength every day.' (Which was the case accordingly). He further said, ' My mind has, for several days, been attended with an uncommon sweetness, the like I never knew for so long together; with a succession of soul-melting prospects. I have freedom to relate what I had a sight of this morning before day, as I lay in a sweet slumber;' (which was nearly in these words, viz) ' I thought I saw Noah's ark floating on the deluge, or flood, with Noah and his family in it; and, looking earnestly at it, I beheld the window of the ark, and saw Noah put out the dove, and I beheld her flying to and fro for some time; but, finding no rest for the sole of her foot, I thought she returned, and I saw Noah's hand put forth to take her in again. After some time I thought I beheld her put forth a second time, and a raven with her; the dove fled as before for some time, and then I saw her return with a green olive leaf in her mouth,

' mouth, as a welcome token of the flood's
' being abated: I thought I saw alfo the
' raven fly, cawking, to and fro, but he did
' not return; and it came into my mind,
' this is a ravenous bird, and feeks only
' for prey to fatisfy its own ftomach, other-
' wife he might have returned to the ark
' with good tidings, or fome pleafant token,
' as well as the dove. Again, after a fhort
' fpace, I thought I beheld the mountain
' tops, and fome of the tree tops, begin-
' ning to appear above the waters, and that
' I could perceive the flood abate very faft;
' and as the waters fell away, I faw the
' trees began to bud, and a gradual green-
' nefs of new leaves came upon them; and
' I heard the voice of the turtle, and faw
' many fymptoms of a pleafant and happy
' feafon approaching, more than I can now
' relate: and the profpect thereof ravifhed
' my foul. I beheld the trees bloffoming, the
' fragrant vallies adorned with grafs, herbs,
' and pretty flowers, and the pleafant ftreams
' gufhing down towards the ocean. Indeed,
' all nature appeared to have a new drefs:
' the birds were hopping on the boughs of
' the trees, and chirping; each, in their
' own notes, warbled forth the praife of
' their Creator. And whilft I beheld thefe
' things, a faying of the prophet was
' brought frefh in my memory, and appli-
' cable, as I thought, to the view before
' me, viz. " The mountains and the hills
                                         " fhall

" shall break forth before you into singing,
" and all the trees of the field shall clap
" their hands. Instead of the thorn shall
" come up the fir-tree, and instead of the
" brier shall come up the myrtle-tree: and
" it shall be to the Lord for a name, for an
" everlasting sign, that shall not be cut off."
See Isaiah, lv. 12, 13.

'When I awoke, the prospect remained
' clear in my mind, and I had a sweet relish,
' which now continues with me; and the
' application of the vision seems to me in
' this manner: the flood which appeared to
' cover the face of the earth, is the corrup-
' tion and darkness which is so prevalent
' over the hearts of mankind; the ark re-
' presents a place of safe (though solitary)
' refuge, wherein the Almighty preserves
' his humble attentive people, who, like
' Noah, are aiming at perfection in their
' generation. The dove sets forth the in-
' nocent, harmless, and loving disposition,
' which attends the followers of the Lamb,
' who are always willing to bring good ti-
' dings, when such are to be had. The
' raven represents a contrary disposition,
' which reigns in the hearts of the children
' of disobedience, who chiefly aim at gra-
' tifying their own sensual appetites. The
' waters gradually abating, the trees appear-
' ing, and afterwards budding, the voice of
' the turtle, and the pleasant notes of the
'·birds, all seem clear to me, to presage the
' approach

'approach of that glorious morning, wherein corruption and iniquity shall begin to abate, and be swept away: and then every thing shall appear to have a new dress. I am fully confirmed in the belief, that that season will approach, which was foretold by the prophet, wherein the glory of the Lord shall cover the earth, as the waters cover the sea; and in a sense of these things, my soul is overcome. I feel the loving-kindness of the Lord Almighty, yet waiting for the return of backsliders with unspeakable mercy; and my soul, in a sense of it, seems bound stronger than ever, in the bonds of a gospel travail; which travail, I hope, will encrease, and spread amongst the faithful, for the enlargement of the church; that the nations may flock unto Sion; which shall become an eternal excellency, even the joy of the whole earth.'

Again he expressed his having a prospect of the morning, and said, 'The day-star is risen, which presages the approach of the morning: I have seen it in its lustre, and have a lively sense of that saying being again fulfilled in the new creation: (see Job xxxviii. 7.) "The morning stars sang together, and the sons of God shouted for joy." I have heard their sound intelligibly, and my heart is comforted therein. The potsherds of the earth may clash together for a season; but the

'the Lord in due time will bring about
'the reformation. The predictions of arch-
'bishop Usher (mentioned in the preface
'to Sewell's History) have come fresh in
'my memory, and nearly correspond with
'the sense I have, that a sharp and trying
'dispensation is to come upon the profes-
'sors of Christianity; wherein the honest
'and upright-hearted shall be hid, as under
'the hollow of the Lord's hand; when
'rents, divisions, and commotions, shall
'encrease among the earthly-minded, and
'one branch of a family be at strife with
'another, like the daughter-in-law against
'the mother-in-law, &c. and happy will
'it be for those who endeavour to stand
'ready for the approach of such a dispen-
'sation.'

CHAP. VII.

His visit to the quarterly-meeting at Salem, and the general meetings at Uwchlan and Goshen, in 1764.—His attendance of the yearly-meeting in Philadelphia, 1767—And the general meeting at Cæcil in Maryland.—The death of his wife.—His visit to divers meetings in Chester and Bucks Counties—To the yearly-meeting in Maryland—Also to several meetings in New-Jersey—And some others in York County, Pennsylvania—Also to Fairfax, &c. in Virginia.

IN the spring of the year 1764, I acquainted my friends that I had a desire to attend the quarterly-meeting at Salem, in New-Jersey; wherewith having their concurrence, on the seventeenth of the fifth month I left home, and went to Wilmington; and next day, in company with several friends, from thence by water, to our friend Joshua Thompson's, at the mouth of Salem-Creek. At the meeting of ministers and elders we were comforted together, through the goodness of the Lord. On first day there was a large gathering of a mixed multitude, and quiet, the Divine power being felt, and gospel truths preached; by the influence of the love whereof many hearts were tendered: though I thought the beauty and

and solemnity of the meeting was a little marred by an appearance that was continued too long. To begin in the life, and conclude in the power and life, is becoming a minister of the gospel.

On second day morning the meeting of ministers and elders was again held; it was a precious instructive season in the love of Christ, our holy Head, by which the humble were united. Afterwards we had a large meeting for publick worship, wherein the testimony of truth flowed freely; the call to the ministry, and qualification necessary to preach the gospel, being clearly set forth. In humble admiration I could renewedly acknowledge, ' Thou art, O Lord! strength
' in our weakness, mouth and wisdom, yea
' all things, to thy humble depending ser-
' vants, whose trust is on thee, waiting for
' thy putting forth in the way, and gently
' going before them, blessed be thy holy
' name for ever!' In transacting the affairs of the discipline a spirit of brotherly love prevailed. The youth's meeting at Pilesgrove was also large and edifying, the great Shepherd of Israel being pleased to stretch forth the crook of his love, for gathering of the straying youth from pursuing after lying vanities and worldly pleasures; ministering reproof to hypocrites and formal professors, yet comforting his children and humble dependent followers, to the praise of his own eternal name. The meeting of
minis-

ministers and elders sat again by adjournment, when we had an uniting parting season. I returned to my friend Joshua Thompson's, next day to a meeting at Wilmington, and in the evening home, being thankful that I had been enabled to perform this small journey.

After which, having a strong desire to attend the general meetings at Goshen and Uwchlan, on the eighth of the sixth month my dear wife and I left home, though I was very unwell with a cold, taken in my return from Salem, and a fever attending me every day. We attended Uwchlan meeting on first day, also one in the evening, at the house of our brother, Daniel Brown; which was dull and exercising, from a sense of the prevalence of a spirit which leads many into forgetfulness of God, after the vanities, love and pleasures of this perishing world. Next day the general meeting at Goshen was very large, and much disturbed by the going out and coming in of many, but, through Divine goodness, it came to a better settlement before it concluded; when solid friends, in a degree of the renewing of the Lord's comforting love, were refreshed in him and one another; a visitation being continued to the youth, the praise whereof belongs to the great Author of all good!

The general meeting at Uwchlan on the day following was also large, and measurably attended with the ownings of truth;
under

under the influence of which, admonition and counsel flowed freely to the youth, the Divine witness in several of whom was reached, and the name of the Lord praised, who is for ever worthy!

In these large meetings, as on all other such occasions, it is necessary, in order for a proper qualification to minister to the people, humbly to wait to know the inward life and baptizing virtue of the spirit and power of Jesus Christ, our all in all, without whose help we can never do his work to his praise, but, instead of gathering the flock, we shall minister to their scattering from the true place of feeding. After being at the preparative meeting at East-Calne, and a meeting at Uwchlan, we returned home, thankful to the Lord, who had mercifully supported us in this small journey; both of us being weakly, and indisposed in health.

In the ninth month, 1767, I attended our yearly-meeting in Philadelphia, which held a week; all the sittings whereof, both for worship and discipline, were, through the overshadowing of Divine favour, instructive to the humble waiters; and the testimony of truth, particularly against the unjust and unrighteous practice of slave-keeping, greatly prevailed: and friends were fully cautioned against bequeathing by will, as slaves to their posterity, the poor negroes, their fellow-creatures; it being an unlawful act

act in the sight of the great and righteous Parent of all mankind. This meeting concluded with a degree of awe and reverence, under the sweetening influence of the Father's love. I returned home to our general meeting at Nottingham, which was held on the fourth and fifth days of the tenth month.

After which, having a strong desire to attend the general meeting at Cæcil in Maryland, I sat out, in company with several other friends, and reached the first sitting of the meeting, which was small and dull. The publick meeting next day was very large, and attended with some satisfaction; those of other societies who were there were mostly pretty quiet. At the meeting of ministers and elders the want of solid elders being evident, the consideration thereof was proposed to the quarterly-meeting, which was held in the afternoon of the same day; when it was recommended to the monthly-meetings to observe the directions of the yearly-meeting, to chuse well qualified solid friends for that weighty station.

The meeting for publick worship was again large, being attended by many of other societies; and my brother, William Brown, was largely opened in doctrine, to the edification of the auditory: after which I had a short testimony, tending to close the foregoing. In the meeting for discipline I had occasion to lament, that there were too few who feelingly understood the weight of such meetings, or were clean handed to move therein, either to their own profit, or the help of their brethren; yet there are a few who seem to be under a preparation for the work, and I hope will grow in their gifts. On third day morning business began again, and ended full as well as I expected. I thought the Lord was mercifully pleased to open considerable instruction to such among them who had ears to hear, and hearts disposed to receive it. The meeting for worship held that afternoon was not so large as on the other two days; the service thereof lay weightily on me, and I had a full opportunity to relieve my mind towards the people, in opening to them the nature and ground of spiritual worship and true prayer, also the true call and qualification for gospel ministry: declaring what it was to " live of " the gospel," in opposition to a forced maintenance: truth favoured, and the people were solid, several being much reached; the meeting ending to satisfaction, with a sense of humble thanksgiving in many hearts to the Lord, whose mercies through Christ Jesus are, to his people, yea and amen for ever.

His wife being under many years affliction with a cancer on her head, which was now
so

so greatly encreased, as to require his daily affectionate attendance, confined him mostly at home until after her decease, which was on the seventh month, 1770. She was a steady exemplary friend; concerning whom the monthly-meeting of Nottingham give the following testimony:

'Our friend Margaret Churchman was
'born (of believing parents, William and
'Esther Brown, who lived at Chichester,
'in the county of Chester, in Pennsylvania)
'the thirteenth of the first month, 1706-7;
'her father removing with his family into
'Maryland, near Susquehanna, died before
'she was ten years old. In the twenty-
'third year of her age, she entered into a
'marriage state with John Churchman, of
'Nottingham, and being religiously inclined
'from her childhood, became a diligent
'seeker after that bread which nourishes
'the inward man, and thereby grew in re-
'ligion; and about the thirty-fourth year
'of her age, it pleased the Lord to put her
'forth in the ministry, in which she was
'frequently exercised to the comfort and
'edification of the churches where she vi-
'sited, in this and the southern provinces;
'being delivered in a degree of life, and
'gospel sweetness, in pertinent expres-
'sions, free from unbecoming gestures. She
'was an example in plainness, a diligent
'attender of meetings, and an humble
'waiter

'waiter therein; serviceable in meetings of
' business, having a good sense of discipline,
' with a becoming zeal to support the tes-
' timony of truth in its various branches;
' and useful in the weighty service of visit-
' ing families.

' In the latter part of her life she was for
' many years afflicted with a cancer on her
' head, which she bore with remarkable pa-
' tience, resignation, and innocent chearful-
' ness, attending meetings, to the admira-
' tion of many who knew her disease;
' which, notwithstanding various applica-
' tions, so encreased, that she became too
' weak to attend meetings some time before
' her decease; yet she retained her love to
' truth and friends to the last; and in the
' sixty-fourth year of her age, being a mi-
' nister about thirty years, she departed this
' life, on the twenty-eighth of the seventh
' month, 1770, and was buried on the thir-
' tieth, in friends burying-ground at East-
' Nottingham, attended by many friends and
' neighbours, at which time we had a solid
' satisfactory meeting.

' Given forth by our monthly-meeting held
   ' at East-Nottingham, the twenty-seventh
   ' of the seventh month, 1771, and signed
   ' on behalf thereof, by

' SAMUEL ENGLAND, } Clerks.'
' REBECCA TRIMBLE,

Having

Having an inclination to attend Chester quarterly-meetings, also some meetings within the verge thereof, with the concurrence of friends, I sat out on the first of the second month, 1771, attended New-Garden monthly-meeting next day, in which the love of our merciful Father was measurably felt, to the comfort of the humble in heart; and on first day at Birmingham; on the next had a meeting in the house of Richard Downing, at Miltown, with people of various sorts: the Lord was pleased to assist with wisdom and ability, in measure, to divide his word in reproof, counsel, admonition and caution, to the praise of his own name. On third day at Pikeland was a pretty full meeting, though a very cold day: truth was felt to be near us. A profitable opportunity was had also in the family of the widow Meredith; she, being weakly, did not get out to their meeting. Next day had a cold ride to Nantmell, where was a large full meeting, and, I believe, beneficial to many present, by the tendering goodness of the blessed Shepherd of spiritual Israel; the crook of whose heavenly love is still stretched forth to his sheep, who are not yet acquainted with the true fold of rest, and safe feeding-place: his own works praise him. Uwchlan monthly-meeting on the day following was a laborious season, yet, through Divine favour, made comfortable to the weary travellers; who had to rejoice together

gether in a participation of the confolation of Ifrael, and therein to worfhip his name, who is worthy for ever. Gofhen monthly-meeting was alfo laborious: when former experience is fed upon, or the love or honour of the world and flefhly eafe takes place, a fpirit grows up in the church which cannot judge for God and his truth; for the judgment is his, in whofe fear his children are made to rejoice, when his prefence is known, and his humbling goodnefs manifefted to his people. On firft day I was at Middletown meeting, in which there feemed to be a tender vifitation and call to the youth, to acquaint themfelves with the God of their fathers, his love being meafurably witneffed among us. The quarterly-meeting for Chefter, held at Concord, was folid and edifying, through the extending of the heavenly Father's love to the children of his family. From thence I went to Wilmington, vifited fome of my acquaintance, and had a comfortable fitting in the family of David Ferrifs, his fon Benjamin being ill of a confumption; I alfo attended the monthly-meeting, which, though a fearching time, was I believe to the comfort and edification of many: the uniting love of truth being experienced, refted on friends in the time of the bufinefs. After which I went to the monthly-meetings at Center and Bradford, and from thence to our quarterly-meeting at London-Grove; then returned

turned home, having great peace in performing this journey, and being favoured with ability, felt a degree of reverent thankfulness to the Lord, who is all things to his servants, who truly abide in nothingness of self; he is therefore worthy of all obedience and honour for ever.

On the twenty-first of the third month I left my habitation, in order to attend our general spring-meeting at Philadelphia; in my way called at Wilmington, and was at the burial of Benjamin Ferris before-mentioned. Our spring-meeting was to me very comfortable, in a sense of the living presence of the holy Head of the church, in which his true children were edified, and strengthened, and mutually comforted one in another; blessed be his name for ever!

At this meeting the brethren, both ministers and elders, apprehend it their duty, in the love of Christ, to appoint such who are willing to give up their names to attend the several large or general meetings, which come in course in the ensuing summer before our yearly-meeting; to which they are expected to give some account of the meetings so attended by them: and feeling a small draught in my mind to be at that at Duck-Creek, I gave in my name to attend it.

On my return from Philadelphia I sat with friends at their week-day meeting in Wilmington, which, through the continued goodness of the Lord, was in some measure a profitable season, I hope, to many. Here I felt a strong desire to see the friends together who are owners of the grist-mills lately built at and near Brandywine, and, upon notice thereof, they met the same afternoon, at the house of Daniel Byrnes; when I had an opportunity to discharge my mind in an affectionate manner of what had impressed it towards them, which they appeared to receive in a degree of the same love; and, as I believe it came from the Author of all good, who is alone worthy of praise, a blessing may attend that opportunity, if rightly remembered.

On the twenty-sixth of the fourth month, being accompanied by a friend and neighbour, I went to Duck-Creek, and was at the monthly-meeting there the next day, which was heavy, occasioned by the prevalence of a formal, lukewarm, worldly spirit, over many of the professors belonging thereto, but, through the long-suffering and continued mercy of God, there seemed to be a renewed awakening visitation to some. The meeting on first day was very large, the Lord being mercifully pleased to open the states and conditions of many, in a particular instrumental manner, and in a measure of his holy heart-tendering power, which reached the witness, divers were humbled, and the meeting ended with thanksgiving, prayer

prayer and praises to the Lord, who is worthy for ever!

On second day the meeting was not so large, occasioned by a fair being near; nevertheless, it was a season in which the doctrine and mysteries of the kingdom of Christ were largely set forth to the people, by the influence of the Spirit, and in the love and wisdom of the holy High Priest, who is all in all to his people.

We had also three select opportunities with the ministers and elders, among whom there was great apparent weakness; the reasons whereof were plainly made known to them, from the sense given in the love and fear of him, who will not own and unite with such as are defiled; which plainness we had a hope would be profitable.

Next day several of us were at George's-Creek, which meeting is much declined. Where the love of the world, and its alluring vanities, prevail on the professors of truth, their affections are drawn from God, they grow slack in attending meetings, and are a bad example one to another. It was a hard meeting, but, through the love of Christ, a measure of gospel anointing enabled to open to them their states, in great love and plainness, which seemed to affect some particulars; may it be remembered with reverence before him, who is the Author of all good, and praise-worthy for ever!

Soon

Soon after my return home, feeling my mind engaged to attend the quarterly-meeting in Bucks County, with a few other meetings in Philadelphia quarter, I set out on the twenty-sixth of the fifth month, accompanied by Samuel England, and on the third day of the week following was at the Bank-meeting in Philadelphia, which was comfortable; on fifth day at the quarterly-meeting at Buckingham, and next day at the general youth's meeting, which was large, and divinely favoured. Then visiting several indisposed friends, on first day I attended Plumstead meeting, and in that week the several monthly-meetings of Buckingham, Wrightstown, the Falls, and Middletown, also a publick meeting at Makefield; was on first day at Bristol, from whence I went with my friend James Thornton to their afternoon meeting at Byberry; had an appointed one at the same place next day; and in that week visited the several neighbouring meetings, one of which was a general youth's meeting at Horsham, large and instructive, wherein the love of our heavenly Father was felt by his truly depending children. Then taking meetings at Gwynedd, Providence, Richland, Oley, Exeter, Maiden Creek, Reading, and on first day at the Forest, I from thence rode to Uwchlan, and on second day had a meeting at Milltown, in the house of Robert Valentine; then proceeded home, having rode about three hundred

dred and seventy miles in this journey, in which I was favoured with my health, and held travelling beyond my expectation. At the gentle drawings of truth I left my habitation, having little prospect of much before me, but was preserved in a quiet resignation to the Divine will to do whatsoever should appear my duty, beseeching the Lord to enable me to watch against every appearance of self in the great and pure work of declaring the gospel to the people, and have great cause to be humbly thankful, that the Lord was pleased to own my service beyond expectation, to the exaltation of his own truth; blessed be his name for ever!

In the tenth month following I went to the yearly-meeting at Third-haven, in Maryland: the meetings for worship held three days, and each of them were very large, and many gospel truths were delivered in the love and power thereof, by which the witness of God was reached in the hearts of many of the people, and friends comforted and made thankful to the Lord, that he was pleased to own us with the overshadowing of his heavenly love. On fourth day morning the affairs of the discipline were finished, when we had a parting meeting, which, through Divine favour, was a precious time to many. I had never been at the yearly-meeting when held at this place before, and now witnessed my heart enlarged in the love of the gospel, to declare the same among the

the multitude of people who profeſs the Chriſtian name, and to remind them of their conduct and dreſs; how different it was from that of thoſe who formerly ſuffered martyrdom for their religion, as now profeſſed by the members of the church of England, ſo called, who own the reformers as their predeceſſors.

Feeling a draught of love in my mind towards ſome meetings at New-Jerſey, particularly at Egg-harbour, having the concurrence of my friends at home, I ſet out on ſecond day, the firſt of the ſixth month, 1772, and, taking in my way a meeting at Haddonfield, and another at the houſe of my friend Thomas Evans, which, through the preſence and power of the ſearcher of hearts, was made profitable to ſome there preſent, reached Little Egg-harbour on ſeventh day, and the next attended the yearly-meeting; in which the love of the goſpel was felt to flow towards a looſe, raw, uncivilized people, who appeared to attend there more out of curioſity, than a reverent thoughtfulneſs of worſhipping Almighty God. In the afternoon of the ſame day the continuance of Divine favour was remarkably evident towards the inhabitants, for which the Lord made the hearts of his ſenſible children thankful to himſelf, who is the Author of all good. The meeting on ſecond day was alſo very large, in which the true children of the family were comforted in Chriſt

Chrift Jefus, the Lord and holy Head of the church; by the anointing virtue of whofe precious name and power, they were made to rejoice in the company one of another. Here parting with many valuable beloved friends, I went over the bay, to the upper meeting on Great Egg-harbour fhore, which was large, confidering the notice. Here I was comforted in knowing for whofe name fake I was made willing to leave my company, and turn that way; the Lord being pleafed to own my fervice by the infpiration of a degree of his heavenly wifdom and love, to fpeak to the ftates of thofe that were prefent, bleffed be his name, who is worthy, for ever! I went home with my friend Jofeph Mapes; next day attended the lower meeting, which, through Divine favour, was a precious feafon; then paffed over to the Cape, and next morning was at a meeting at the upper houfe, where many not of our fociety attended, to whom the doctrine of the gofpel flowed, in defcribing the nature of pure and undefiled religion, and wherein it confifted: the people were ftill and quiet. In the afternoon of the fame day I had a meeting at the lower houfe, which is called eight miles down the Cape: this was an heart-tendering time, for which friends were made truly thankful. I thought it feemed like to be my laft vifit to thefe parts. From thence I went to Cohanfy, forty-five miles, to Mark Reeve's, where I refted rested the next day, being very weary, and almost overcome with hard travelling; on first day I was at Greenwich meeting, and in the afternoon at Alloways Creek, which was very large; many of other societies attending, the doctrine of truth flowed to them in a measure of the love thereof. Next day the meeting at Salem was held in the Courthouse, the meeting-house being taken down, and a new one building. On third day I was at the upper meeting near Alloways Creek, which, through Divine goodness, was an instructive time to some seekers: the passage treated upon was our Lord's description of the pharisee and publican who went up to the temple to pray; the great difference in the form of their addresses was opened in a clear manner, by the spirit of him who gave forth that parable, to my humble admiration, which was cause of reverent thankfulness; they who were sensible being encouraged, and the conceited formalists rebuked.

From hence I went to John Davis's, had a comfortable opportunity with some indisposed friends in his family; then taking meetings at Pilesgrove, Upper Greenwich, and Woodberry, was on first day morning at Haddonfield, and in the afternoon at Newtown, which last was laborious, though I believe, being blessed to several present, was thereby made profitable. That evening I went over to Philadelphia, weary in body, but

but chearful in mind, being sensible of a degree of thankfulness for the continued favour of my Lord and Master, who had been to me a quiet habitation and secret support in this journey. After staying two days, and on each attending meetings in the city, I took Wilmington-meeting on my way home; having travelled about three hundred and fifty miles, attended about twenty meetings, besides having several comfortable opportunities in families.

Being under an appointment with other friends of our quarterly-meeting, to visit friends of the monthly-meetings of Warrington and Fairfax, I set out on the seventh of the tenth month, and, taking a meeting with friends in York-town, we were at Warrington on first day; then visited the several meetings of Newberry, Huntingdon, and Monallen, in which truth owned our service in a good degree: our labour of love appearing to be kindly received, I hope may be useful. On the first day following five of us were at Pipe Creek meeting, then at Bush Creek, Monaquesy, Fairfax, Goose Creek, and Southfork, wherein the Lord was pleased, in his wonted goodness and mercy, to magnify his own name, who is praise-worthy for ever!

After a seasonable opportunity with friends, held in the house of Abel Janny, at parting with them, we returned to Fairfax meeting on first day, where, under the influence of the

the Divine presence, the testimony and doctrine of truth flowed freely to the people; in an humble sense whereof, praises ascended to his holy name, who is over all, worthy for ever!

Several of our company now returning homewards, three of us not being easy yet to return, two of us went to visit a friend who lay in a languishing condition, which I believe was serviceable, the love of our heavenly Father being in some degree felt among us. On third day we had a meeting at the Gap (so called) among a raw people, where Divine goodness measurably favoured the opportunity; on the day following we attended Fairfax preparative meeting; the two next days we visited some sick friends, and on seventh day were at the monthly-meeting, which was in the main satisfactory. On first day the meeting was thought to be the largest ever held at this place, and the gospel being preached in the love of it, to the tendering the hearts of many, the meeting ended in humble thanksgiving to the holy Author of all good. Next day, in company with several friends of Fairfax, I attended a meeting at Monaquesy, where some came who did not make religious profession with us; which was an instructive tendering season, through the Lord's goodness. After a meeting at Bush Creek, and another at Pipe Creek, I travelled to Gunpowder, and attended the quarterly-meeting for

for the Western shore of Maryland, likewise the general meeting for worship on first day, at which were several not of our society, whose hearts were reached by the love of truth. Next day I had a meeting at the Little Falls, and from thence returned home, whence, after staying three days, I went to our quarterly-meeting at London-Grove, the two last days of which afforded some comfort and satisfaction. On the fourteenth of the twelfth month I went to Wilmington, on which day Margaret, the wife of John Perry, was buried, after a short illness; I spent part of the evening in his afflicted family to satisfaction: staying in the town two days, I attended their monthly-meetings, and thought there was a want of more members deeply baptized for the work, which appears necessary in the church at that place. At this time Deborah, the daughter of David Ferriss, being in a consumptive declining state, and wasting fast, I visited her to my satisfaction; she, appearing to be in a resigned humble frame of spirit, was an exemplary young woman, whom I esteemed. Then going to Center and Hockesson meetings, I was at New-Garden on first day, which I thought, through Divine favour, an instructive profitable meeting to myself, and perhaps to some others: the subject which opened was the necessity of not leaning to, or following, any man, but of attending to the pure motion and secret influ-

influence of the Spirit of Truth manifested in the heart, in the meekness and purity of the wisdom from above; it was that by which the churches were gathered, and the members preserved in the unity of the one blessed Spirit, and perfect bond of peace and good order.

I next attended our preparative and monthly-meetings, after which was confined mostly at home for about a month by a fever, during which time my mind was often much humbled under a sense of the prevalence of a dull, lukewarm spirit, as to the life and power of truth; earthly-mindedness, and the cares and cumbers, concerning the things of this present life, having drawn the minds of many into death. I never more clearly saw the necessity there was for us, who profess the truth, singly to attend to the gentle instructions of the holy Spirit thereof, which only doth, and ever will, lead and guide into all truth, and preserveth from those errors and failings which are so abundantly evident among us, whereby our hands are weakened in respect to a careful exercise of the discipline of the church.

CHAP.

CHAP. VIII.

His attendance of the Western quarterly-meeting in the second month, 1773—The spring-meeting in Philadelphia—And the genera meeting at Duck-Creek—The quarterly-meeting at Shrewsbury—With several other meetings in New-Jersey—The spring-meeting in Philadelphia in 1774.—His last visit to New-York—And Long-Island.—His last attendance of the yearly-meeting in Philadelphia.—His being at the spring-meeting there in 1775.—And his last journey to sundry meetings on the Eastern-shore of Maryland.—His last illness, with some weighty expressions in that time.—His death and burial.

BEING somewhat recovered of my indisposition of body, I sat in our select meeting of ministers and elders on the first of the second month, 1773, in which I was comforted under a sense of our being owned in some degree by the visitation of Divine love; and afterwards attended our quarterly-meeting at London-Grove, each sitting whereof was favoured with a continuance of heavenly help, to the encouragement of the humble waiters. I returned home with thankfulness in my mind to the Lord, who had furnished me with strength in my weak state to sit with my friends, in which we ought to be good examples. I attended our own meeting on the fifth and firſt days following, and in the ſame week went to Wilmington, to the burial of Deborah Ferriſs, before-mentioned; after which, a ſolid and profitable meeting was held.

On the twenty-ſixth of the third month I ſet out from home, in order to attend our general ſpring-meeting at Philadelphia, but did not get there in time for the firſt ſitting thereof; ſuch of them as I did attend, I thought, were, in the main, times of Divine favour. On my return homeward I was at a ſmall meeting at Cheſter, alſo the general meeting at Wilmington, and ſoon after at the general meeting at Duck Creek, and their monthly-meeting preceding it. The meeting there on firſt day was large, and, though a mixed multitude attended, it was ſolid, through the overſhadowing of heavenly power; the Lord was pleaſed to open the myſteries of the kingdom, influencing my heart to preach the goſpel in the love thereof, to my humble admiration, and many were tendered; for which renewed viſitation and favour, a ſacrifice of thankſgiving aſcended from the hearts of his children, to the all powerful and merciful God, who is worthy for ever. The meeting on ſecond day was a time of conſolation to the heavy-hearted, inſtruction to the humble ſeekers, and a ſeaſon of ſtrengthening to the weak, bleſſed be the name of the Lord, for his mercies

mercies endure for ever. I was next at George's Creek meeting, in which friends were encouraged, and in some degree refreshed, divers not of our society attending: the doctrine of personal election and reprobation, as held by some, was refuted, and it was clearly pointed out wherein the election stood, viz. 'in Christ the seed, which 'cleaved unto, and chosen by man, for his 'true instructor and leader, by his light and 'witness in the heart, as a reprover for 'sin, and so followed and obeyed, man 'comes to know himself elected in him.' I went home with George Ford to Back Creek, and had an opportunity in his family, I hope to some profit.

Towards the fall of the year I had a draught in my mind to attend some meetings in the Jerseys, particularly the quarterly-meeting at Shrewsbury; of which having acquainted my brethren at home, and had their concurrence, after attending our yearly-meeting in Philadelphia, and returning from thence, I set out, in company with my friend Samuel England, on the twelfth of the tenth month, but was detained at Philadelphia by a fever, which held me several days; yet I so far recovered, as to proceed on our journey, taking on our way meetings at Mount Holly, at a schoolhouse, near Shreve's Mount, in Upper Springfield; in which I had a concern to warn the youth to beware of deism, and to shew the

ground and cause of falling into that error; also at Upper Freehold, and in a friend's house, near that called Robbins's meeting. There seems to be a visitation to the youth in that place, to which if they are faithful, that meeting may again encrease. We reached the meeting of ministers and elders at Shrewsbury, in which truth owned the lovers thereof. The publick meetings on the three following days were large, and thought to be the most quiet and satisfactory which had been known of late years there; the affairs of the discipline were, as I thought, pretty well conducted. Finding myself not clear of the members of our society at this place, I therefore proposed to several friends that they would favour me so much as to meet on their week-day meeting day, which I understood they usually had omitted in this week, requesting that they would acquaint their members with my desire of seeing them, their children, and families, together: I therefore waited until fifth day, when they generally met, which gave me an opportunity comfortably to clear myself towards friends here, to the encouragement of the sincere; being led to shew the active members the cause of dwarfishness, the love of the world, and its friendships, choaking the good seed, which should grow and bear rule: I was thankful for this opportunity, and left them with the enjoyment of a quiet mind. From hence we passed to Rahway, had a
meeting

meeting at Woodbridge, and another at Plainfield, in both which truth owned my service: I thought there was a tender visitation renewed to friends in those parts, in the sense whereof I was made thankful, and that I had been favoured with strength to pay them a visit in the love of my great and good Master; may I ever walk answerable to his manifold favours, who is praiseworthy for ever! We were next at Stonybrook meeting, which was made precious in the renewing of Divine favour, and then at Trenton, with a people who have much lost the life and favour of truth. From thence going to Byberry and Philadelphia, I reached the quarterly-meeting at Concord, which began on the sixth of the eleventh month; the next day I went to Chichester, where I was enabled to speak to the states of the people in the love of truth; which may be useful if remembered in a right manner, and returned to the quarterly-meeting on second day, which was comfortable, the Divine presence being felt: our friend Elizabeth Robinson was there, and had good service. On third day I attended the general meeting at Chester, which was poor and dull; the expectations of the people being too much outward, they were disappointed: then attending the monthly-meeting at Wilmington, tarried their meeting the next day, and proceeded to our quarterly-meeting at London-Grove, at which we had the company

company of our friends Robert Walker, Elizabeth Robinson, and Mary Leaver, from Great Britain: it was a season of refreshment and comfort to many friends; I then went home, having travelled in this journey about three hundred and sixty miles.

In the third month, 1774, I attended our general spring-meeting in Philadelphia, the divers sittings whereof were divinely favoured; and, after it, the general meeting at Wilmington, which was held chiefly in silence, and on that account remarkable.

Having an engagement on my mind for some time to visit our friends on Long-Island, with some adjacent meetings, I laid it before my brethren, who gave me their certificate for that purpose; and on the third of the fifth month I set out on the journey, having the company of a friend from Wilmington: taking a meeting at Philadelphia, we reached New-York, attended their morning and afternoon meetings on first day, and had an opportunity with divers friends in the evening, which was (to me at least) instructive, and I believe, through Divine goodness, profitable to some others. We then had meetings at West-Chester, Mamaroneck, and the Purchase, the last being a monthly-meeting: these opportunities were close and searching, the testimony of truth was encouraging to the well-minded, but very sharp to the formalists, and my mind was made thankful for the blessing of peace in
the

the discharge of my duty. We next attended meetings at Flushing, on Long-Island, Cowneck, Westbury, Matinicock, Sequitogue, and Bethpage, then at Newtown, the monthly-meeting at Westbury, and the quarterly-meeting at Flushing, where the yearly-meeting began the next day, which held four days; and, on the whole, I believe it may be said, that the authority of truth was in some good degree felt to keep down forward spirits, both in the ministry and discipline; which was cause of thankfulness to the Lord, who rules among his children, and is worthy of all praise for ever. Here I had the company of our dear friends Robert Walker, Elizabeth Robinson, and Susanna Lightfoot, who intending for Rhode-Island, I parted with them, and went to the monthly-meeting at New-York, which, through merciful regard, was comfortable. From thence going to Rahway, had a meeting at Plainfield, which was satisfactory, through the extendings of Divine favour; then at Kingwood on first day, from whence crossing Delaware, we were at Buckingham monthly-meeting, where I thought the true spirit of discipline appeared to be much wanting in many. Here my companion returned homewards. The next day I was at Wright's-town monthly-meeting, which, through the Lord's blessing, was edifying to many, and we parted in peace and sweetness of spirit; the day following I attended the meeting

meeting at Pine-street in Philadelphia, also that at High-street on fifth day, which was a precious opportunity to such who loved to live near the Spirit of Truth. From thence I went to visit my brother-in-law, Daniel Brown, near Chester; was at New-town meeting on first day, and at an afternoon meeting near Amos Yarnal's; then went to the general meetings at Goshen and Uwchlan: after which, taking London-Grove meeting, I came home, having rode in this journey about six hundred miles, and feeling a degree of thankfulness that the Lord was pleased to give me ability to perform it.

I tarried much at home the remaining part of this summer; on the twenty-first of the ninth month I set out, in order to attend the yearly-meeting at Philadelphia, which was very large in the several sittings, continued a full week, and I thought it the most solid and weighty in transacting the affairs of truth that I ever knew: the testimony thereof against slave-keeping was wonderfully exalted, through the power and love of God, who is worthy of all praise for ever. In my way home I was at Providence meeting, in which the testimony of truth went forth by way of warning to the lukewarm and declining professors, and of encouragement to the youth.

Our general meeting at Nottingham next day was large, and I hope profitable to some; after which, having a desire to be at the
general

general meeting at Cæcil, in Maryland, I left home on the seventh of the tenth month, was at the quarterly-meeting of ministers and elders there on first day morning, which was profitably instructive, through Divine goodness: two publick meetings for worship were held on first and second days, both large and solid; several other friends from Pennsylvania were there. The business of the quarterly-meeting ended on third day morning; on the same day we had a comfortable publick meeting, from which we parted with friends in much love and nearness. On the following day was their monthly-meeting, to attend which several of us staid; then, having a desire to see friends at Chester-River, I went to their week-day meeting, Nicholas Waln bearing me company; the meeting was large, and, through the Lord's goodness, it was, I believe, made profitable to many. Then taking meetings at Saffafrafs, Duck-Creek, Motherkill, and Little-Creek, the two last being their preparative meeting at each place; the next day was their select meeting of ministers and elders, and their monthly-meeting the day following; which, with divers other friends from Pennsylvania, we attended, and on the first and second days of the next week the general meeting at Little-Creek: I believe there is a renewed visitation to friends, and some others, hereaway; but formal professors at present appear

pear to be as stumbling-blocks, by joining with the spirit of the world. I returned home with an easy mind.

Weakness and infirmity of body gradually increasing upon our beloved friend, he frequently mentioned, that many years past it was unexpected to him to live to his seventieth year, and to be favoured with health and strength sufficient to travel so much as he lately had; saying, that now he scarcely thought much more would be required of him: he however attended the western quarterly-meeting in the eleventh month this year, and in the second month, 1775, in both which he was favoured with strength and clearness to speak to the state of the church, as well in some of the select, as the more publick meetings, tending to the edification and comfort of many.

In the third month, 1775, he also attended the general spring meeting at Philadelphia, and in some of the sittings thereof was much favoured; on his return home from thence he was at Wilmington general meeting, in company with our friends Robert Walker and Elizabeth Robinson, from Great Britain.

His last journey was on a visit to most of the meetings on the Eastern-shore of Maryland,

land, and to attend the yearly-meeting at Third-haven, in Talbot county; for which purpose he set out from his own habitation on the twenty-second of the fifth month, having, according to his usual care, obtained the concurrence of his brethren, and was accompanied by a young man (William Jackson) a member of New-Garden monthly-meeting, who has given the following account of this journey.

' Our first day's ride was to George Ford's,
' near Back-Creek; the next morning being
' damp and foggy, was very trying to his
' weak constitution, yet we rode forty-five
' miles that day, to Hannah Turner's, in
' Queen Ann's county, which was thought
' to be a means of bringing on him a disor-
' der, which proved painful and afflicting,
' and encreased till near his end. Being ad-
' vanced in age, his bodily infirmity ap-
' peared great; but the fervency of his mind
' for the promotion of truth and righteous-
' ness, and his care as a father in Israel, was
' truly as prevalent as ever. On the twen-
' ty-fourth of the month he went to the
' preparative meeting at Tuckahoa, where-
' in he was concerned to exhort some to
' faithfulness in times of temptation and
' trial, that they might experience an over-
' coming, and be enabled to strengthen
' their brethren. Next day we attended
' Third-haven monthly-meeting, in which
' he was qualified to speak instructively to
' the

'the members thereof, particularly to such
' who were incumbered with much care
' about the things of this life; things which,
' although lawful in themselves, yet, when
' suffered to engross the minds and affec-
' tions of people, obstruct a progress in re-
' ligion. On the twenty-sixth a meeting at
' Choptank was a time of heavy exercise,
' on account of a lifeless, lukewarm, indif-
' ferent situation of mind, which seemed to
' attend divers there assembled: the next
' day we attended a burial at Third-haven,
' on which occasion a meeting was held,
' and he laboured honestly to arouse those
' that lived in the neglect of making timely
' preparation for their last awful and solemn
' change. On the twenty-eighth we were
' at Tuckahoa meeting, and on second day
' at the Bay-side, where were but few of
' our society; but several others attended,
' who behaved soberly, and some of the
' younger sort were reached and tendered
' by truth's testimony; to whom he was led
' instructively to shew, " That they need
" not give their money for that which is
" not bread, nor their labour for that
" which satisfieth not;" ' and opened to
' them the way of life and salvation, which
' is attained through " the Spirit, or free
" gift of grace, that is come upon all men
" for justification:" ' so that if they at-
' tended to the dictates thereof in their own
' hearts, it was sufficient to instruct them
' in

' in the way of godliness; but when people
' go from and neglect this inward teacher,
' seeking to or depending on learned men,
' they err.

' Next day we had a religious opportu-
' nity in the family of John Bartlett, and
' on fourth day went to Tuckahoa meeting
' again; where he had to speak of the suf-
' ficiency of the grace of God, and the in-
' consistency of people's living in a profes-
' sion thereof without being found in the
' faith, or fully believing in this principle
' as sufficient for salvation. We next at-
' tended the meetings at Third-haven and
' Marshy-Creek; the yearly-meeting began
' on seventh day, and continued until the
' fourth of the following week, which, al-
' though he was feeble and unwell, he at-
' tended the several sittings thereof, being
' nine in the five days, and the last held
' seven hours. He was enabled to appear
' for the cause and testimony of truth, both
' in the meetings for worship and discipline,
' and, like the good scribe, well instructed
' in the things of the kingdom, had to
' bring forth out of the treasury, things
' new and old, profitable and instructive,
' being seasoned with the love and virtue
' of truth. After the meeting on fourth
' day, we went to the house of Joseph Ber-
' ry, where next morning we had a religious
' opportunity in the family, and the day
' following a meeting in Queen Ann's Fo-
' rest;

'rest; from whence we went to Joshua
'Vansant's: here he was very poorly, hav-
'ing taken some fresh cold. The next day
'being very warm, he was much spent
'with riding, and said, as he had at seve-
'ral times before on this journey, " that
" he believed it would be his last, if he
" lived to reach home, which, at times, he
" thought seemed unlikely." ' On first day,
'the eleventh of the sixth month, he had a
'meeting in a school-house at Back-Creek,
'among a people who behaved with much
'sobriety, which was a satisfactory time,
'very instructive and open for doctrine,
'and that evening reached home, having
'travelled in this journey about two hundred
'and ninety miles.'

On the fourteenth of the sixth month, he went to the week-day meeting at London-Grove, to meet with a committee of our quarterly-meeting on particular business, and returned to our meeting at Nottingham the next day; on the first day of the week following was there also; in the same week he attended our preparative and monthly-meetings; but a fever daily encreasing upon him, he was afterwards chiefly confined at home.

On the fourth of the seventh month he expressed himself thus: 'I am glad I am at home; I have ever found it best, when my service abroad was over, to get home as quick as might be; and though I have felt great inward poverty and weakness, since my last journey, so that I can neither see my beginning nor ending, but seem as if all were hidden, yet I hope, if Providence shall see meet to remove me at this time, some light will appear again, and that it will be otherwise before I go.

At another time he spake to this purpose: 'I have found myself much stripped, as to a sense of good, and tried with poverty many days. I suppose I have been accounted by some, as one of the better sort of people, but have seen great occasion to beware of a disposition that would seek to feed upon the praise or commendations of others: a carnal selfish spirit is very apt to present, and creep in here, and I have seen it hurt many, who have had right beginnings; it always introduces dimness, and oppression, to the pure, precious, innocent life of truth, which only groweth up into dominion through deep abasement of soul, and the entire death of self.'

At several other times he signified to this effect: 'My present baptism of affliction hath tended to the further refinement of my nature, and to the bringing me more perfectly into the image of my Master.'

He frequently expreffed his full fubmiffion to the Divine will, either refpecting life or death; feveral times faying, 'I now expe-
'rience my life and my will to be flain, and
'I have no will left.'

In the two laft weeks of his time it appeared that his defire and hope, mentioned in the fore part of his illnefs, for light again to appear, were fully anfwered by the frefh influence thereof; fo that although his pain was often great, he would many times in a day break forth into a kind of melody with his voice, without uttering words; which, as he fometimes intimated, was an involuntary afpiration of his foul in praife to the Lord, who had again been pleafed to fhine forth in brightnefs, after many days of poverty and deep baptifm, which, though painful, had proved beneficial to him, being a means of further purifying from the dregs of nature; faying he was at times afraid to difcover that melody in the hearing of fome that vifited him, left they could not comprehend his meaning, and might therefore mifconftrue it.

On fecond day morning, the feventeenth of the feventh month, being afked by a friend how he was, he replied, 'I am here in the
' body yet, and when I go out of it, I hope
' there is nothing but peace:' and foon after further faid, 'I have feen that all the buf-
' tles, and noifes, that are now in the world,
' will end in confufion; and our young
'men,

'men, that know not an establishment in
'the truth and the Lord's fear, for a bal-
'last, will be caught in a trying moment.'
At another time he said, 'I feel nothing but
'peace, having endeavoured honestly to dis-
'charge myself in publick, and privately to
'individuals, as I apprehended was required;
'and if it be the Lord's will that I should
'go now, I shall be released from a great
'deal of trouble and exercise, which I be-
'lieve friends who are left behind will have
'to pass through.'

On the twentieth of the same month he thus expressed himself: 'I love friends who
'abide in the truth as much as ever I did,
'and I feel earnest breathings to the Lord,
'that there may be such raised up in the
'church who may go forth in humility,
'sweetness, and life, clear of all superfluity
'in expressions and otherwise, standing for
'the testimony, that they may be useful to
'the church in these difficult times.'

About three days before his death, several friends being in his room, he spake as follows: 'Friends in the beginning, if they
'had health and liberty, were not easily di-
'verted from paying their tribute of wor-
'ship to the Almighty on week-days as well
'as first-days; but after a while, when out-
'ward sufferings ceased, life and zeal decay-
'ing, ease, and the spirit of the world,
'took place with many; and thus it became
'customary for one or two out of a family to
'attend

'attend meetings, and to leave their children
'much at home. Parents also, if worldly
'concerns were in the way, could neglect
'their week-day meetings some times, yet
'be willing to hold the name, and plead
'excuse because of a busy time, or the like;
'but I believe that such a departure from
'primitive integrity ever did, and ever will,
'occasion a withering from the life of true
'religion.'

To a friend who came to visit him on the twenty-first of the seventh month, he said: 'I feel that which lives beyond death and
'the grave, which is now an inexpressible
'comfort to me, after a time of deep bap-
'tism that I have passed through: I believe
'my being continued here is in the will of
'Providence, and I am fully resigned.'

His illness encreasing, he said but little on seventh day, the twenty-second; in the afternoon he was very low, and speechless about twelve hours: early on first day morning he recruited a little, and gave directions about his coffin to a friend who sat up with him, being a joiner. Continuing rather easier the fore part of that day, and appearing chearful, he expressed divers weighty sentences, like farewell exhortations, to some who came to see him. On second day morning he sat up a considerable time; in the afternoon he appeared lively and sensible, though very weak, thus expressing himself; 'I am much refreshed with my Master's
'sweet

'sweet air; I feel more life, more light, more love, and sweetness, than ever before;' and often mentioned the Divine refreshment and comfort he felt flowing like a pure stream to his inward man; saying to those who were with him, 'I may tell you of it, but you cannot feel it as I do.'

In the evening, a young person coming into the room, looking at her earnestly and affectionately, he said, "Deborah arose a mother in Israel;" and shortly after, 'The sweetness that I feel:' then his difficulty of breathing encreased, and, being turned once or twice, he requested to be helped up, and was placed in his chair, in which he expired about the ninth hour, on second day night, the twenty-fourth of the seventh month, 1775, aged near seventy, a minister about forty-two years. He was buried on the twenty-sixth, in friend's graveyard at East-Nottingham, a large concourse of people attending, after which a solemn meeting was held.

THE END.

The following Memorial of our beloved friend Joseph White, who was endued with an eminent gift in the ministry, and uniformly concerned for the welfare of the churches, is here subjoined at the desire of divers friends; which, as no account of his labours and visits in the service of the gospel, appears to be preserved by himself, may, in some measure, supply that deficiency, and, we apprehend, will be an instructive and acceptable appendage to the foregoing journal; tending to revive and keep in remembrance his pious life, and the near fellowship of his brethren with him, and further animate survivors to faithfulness in the discharge of their several religious duties, in order that they also may be favoured with a well-grounded hope of attaining the like happy end.

A TESTIMONY *from the Falls monthly-meeting in Bucks Connty, concerning our friend* JOSEPH WHITE.

AS the memory of the just is pronounced blessed, we think it expedient to give forth a testimony concerning this our esteemed friend.

He was born at the Falls the twenty-eighth of the eleventh month, 1712-13: being young when his father died, he was brought up under the care of his relations and friends; and, through the extending of heavenly regard whilſt young, and attending to the teachings of divine grace, he was led and preſerved from many of the follies and extravagancies incident to unthinking youth. About the twentieth year of his age he appeared in publick teſtimony in our religious meetings, and, continuing in a good degree faithful to the meaſure of light and grace communicated, he grew in his gift, and became a lively and able miniſter.

He was naturally of an open chearful diſpoſition, and honeſty concerned for the promotion of piety and virtue, and for the ſupport and maintenance of good order in the church; for which ſervice he was eminently gifted, and truly ſerviceable amongſt us, being often concerned that the authority of truth might be kept up in all our meetings of diſcipline, and that true judgment might be placed upon the diſorderly and irreclaimable. He was exemplary in his life and converſation; a diligent and timely attender of our religious meetings, when health of body permitted; and was often favoured therein in publick teſtimony and ſupplication, much to the comfort and edification of the truly humble waiters. And although he had a large gift in the miniſtry, he many times ſat meetings in ſilence, waiting upon the Lord; not being haſty or forward in the exerciſe of his gift, but careful not to miniſter without the heavenly life and power

that

that firſt raiſed him up in the miniſtry; whereby his publick ſervice was greatly to the conſolation and refreſhment of many.

He ſeveral times had a concern to viſit the churches abroad, and, with the concurrence of this meeting, viſited many of the meetings of friends in this and ſeveral of the adjacent provinces, and once through ſome parts of Maryland, Virginia, and North-Carolina: and having for ſome conſiderable time been under a weighty concern to pay a religious viſit to friends in ſeveral parts of Europe, he, with the concurrence and unity of his friends, took ſhipping for that purpoſe in the year 1758, and, after a ſhort paſſage, landed in England; and having pretty generally viſited friends meetings in England and Ireland, and ſome parts of Wales, he returned to his family and friends, having been from home in truth's ſervice near three years. And at his return from theſe viſits, produced certificates of friends unity and good ſatisfaction with him, and his publick ſervice amongſt them.

He was divers times appointed and engaged in the ſervice of viſiting families, being well qualified for that weighty ſervice.

He much loved the company and converſation of his friends; was a loving and affectionate huſband, a tender parent, and a good neighbour, generally beloved by his friends and others that knew him, being in
ſeveral

several respects useful and serviceable in the neighbourhood where he lived.

He was attended from his youth at times with a pain at his breast, with intermissions of health, sometimes for years, and at other times but short; but as he advanced further in age, intermissions of health grew short, and pain encreased, which brought on other bodily infirmities, which he bore with patience and resignation, often craving he might not be off his watch when his pains were exquisite, nor his faith fail in the time of trial; believing it to be the goodness of God, through his thus dealing with him, more and more to wean him from all outward connections and nearest ties of nature, that, being as the pure gold, refined through the furnace, he might with triumph join the redeemed that were gone before, which he at times had a foretaste and evidence of; but the time when, as he himself sometimes expressed, he did not then see, believing it to be consistent with Divine wisdom to keep it hid from him.

The latter part of his time, for several months, he slept but little in the night season, being, at times, engaged in reverent intercessions and divine contemplation, and appeared to be waiting for the solemn moment.

He lived in the compass of the Falls particular meeting until a few years before his death, and then removed to Makefield, (a branch

branch of the fame monthly-meeting) and having for some months felt strong desires (if favoured with health) to go to the Falls meeting, on a monthly-meeting day he set out to go there; but the weather being cold, and he in a weak state of health, soon found himself unable to perform the journey, and returned home. But some time after, feeling his bodily strength somewhat restored, and love renewed, he set out, in company with his wife, one first day morning, and got to the meeting, where he was favoured with an open time in publick testimony, much to the satisfaction of those present. After the meeting was over, and friends gone out, a friend being desirous of speaking to him, not seeing him out of doors, returned into the house, and found him sitting on a seat, unable to move without help: the friend assisted him, and took him to his house, where he was taken care of. The fit being of the paralytick kind, was much more favourable than at some other times, though it continued ebbing and flowing for several hours; in which time he expressed several things, some of which, being then taken down, are nearly as follows.

Being asked by his son Samuel how it was with him, he answered, ‘ I don't know but ‘ that I am near my end. My desire at this ‘ time for thee is, that thou seek unto the ‘ Lord for assistance, to govern thee in thy ‘ conduct in this fluctuating life; for I have
‘ found

'found him to be a sure help and counsellor
'to me: and if thou follow after him in
'truth and sincerity, as I have endeavoured
'to do, he will be unto thee a sufficient
'director, a teacher that cannot be removed
'into a corner. I have not been anxious to
'gather a portion of this world, nor make
'to myself mammon of unrighteousness; for
'I think I have seen a snare that has at-
'tended many young people on these ac-
'counts. I have ever from my youth had
'a desire to be more in substance than in
'shew: let me appear as I might in the
'sight of men, their praise I sought not
'for; but I have sought the honour of God,
'therefore there is a place where no trouble
'shall annoy, prepared for me, as a reward
'for obedience. You that stay be more
'humble, and when trouble awaits you,
'look not upon nor trust to the arm of
'flesh for assistance, but stay yourselves up-
'on him who suffered for you, for me, and
'for all mankind: for I have for some time
'believed and lived in the hopes thereof,
'and am now in measure confirmed, of
'more glorious things yet to be revealed to
'the church of Christ, and that further and
'greater discoveries will yet be made, with
'respect to the Christian religion, than ever
'yet has been since the apostasy.'

And after a short pause, he broke forth in these expressions: 'The door is open, I see
'an innumerable company of saints, of an-
'gels,

' gels, and of the spirits of just men, which
' I long to be unbodied to be with, but not
' my will, but thy will be done, O Lord! I
' cannot utter, nor my tongue express, what
' I feel of that light, life and love, that
' attends me, which the world cannot give,
' neither can it take away from me. My
' sins are washed away by the blood of the
' Lamb, that was slain from the foundation
' of the world: all rags and filthiness are
' taken away, and in room thereof love and
' good-will for all mankind. O that we
' may become more united in the church
' militant, and nearer resemble the church
' triumphant! O that we might all make
' such an end as I have in prospect; for it is
' all light, all life, all love, and all peace:
' the light that I see is more glorious than
' the sun in the firmament. Come, Lord
' Jesus Christ, come when thou pleasest;
' thy servant is ready and willing: into thy
' hands I commit my spirit; not my will,
' but thy will be done, O Lord! Let this
' mortal body be committed to the dust: be
' with me, with my children, and my
' grandchildren; be with all them that love
' thee, that love thy appearance. O the
' pains that I feel, that attend this mortal
' body, they are more comely to me than
' jewels! I rejoice in my sighs and groans,
' for to me they are most melodious: I am
' near to enter that harmony with Moses
' and the Lamb, where they cry Holy, holy,
' holy;

'holy; I cannot express the joy I feel.
'My heart (if it were possible) would break
'for joy. If any enquire after me, after
'my end, let them know all is well with
'me.'

Many more weighty expressions he spoke, which, not being taken down, cannot be recollected.

The next day, his pain abating, and finding himself somewhat relieved from his disorder, he was taken to his own house, where he remained, in a weak state of health, for some time, being unable to go much abroad. And one night, some short time before his death, his pain had been sharp the fore part of the night, but the latter part it abating, his wife lay down by him, and fell asleep, but he, as usual, slept not, but, after some time called to his wife in these words: 'My
'dear, I believe I must take my leave of
'thee. I have never seen my end till now,
'and now I see its near, and the holy angels
'enclose me around, waiting to receive me.'
His wife asked him if she should call up the children; he said, he did not see any thing further he had to say to them, except to his son Joseph, who being called, and he having expressed what he had on his mind, was much spent, and appeared as though he was near his desired port; but after some time he revived, with these words:
'Life is yet strong in me, and will not
'yield.' Thus he continued the few concluding

cluding days, waiting in refignation and retirednefs of mind, until the repeated returns of the paralytick complaint reduced his faculties and fenfes fo, that he knew not what was done for fome days, and departed in much ftillnefs, as in a fleep, the tenth day of the third month, 1777, and was decently interred in friend's burying-ground at the Fall's meeting-houfe, the twelfth of the fame; his body being attended to the grave by a number of friends and neighbours.

May we, under the confideration of our great lofs of him, and many other faithful labourers in the Lord's vineyard, now removed from us, be excited fo to follow their footfteps, that, with them, we may be partakers of that incorruptible inheritance, which is referved for the righteous, when time here fhall be no more.

Aged fixty-four, and a minifter about forty-four years.

> Signed on behalf of faid monthly-meeting, held by adjournment the 12th of the 8th month, 1778.
>
> JOSEPH GILLINGHAM, Clerk.

" Bleffed are thofe fervants whom the
" LORD, when He cometh, fhall find watch-
" ing." Luke xii. 37.

LATELY PRINTED BY
JAMES PHILLIPS.

A Journal of the Life, Travels, and Labours, in the Work of the Miniftry, of JOHN GRIFFITH, 8vo. *Calf*, 4s.

The Works of JOHN WOOLMAN, containing a Journal of his Life, Gofpel-Labours, and Chriftian Experiences; with Confiderations on various Subjects, 8vo. *Calf* 3s. 6d.

The fame Work, large, 12mo. *Sheep*, 2s. 6d.

Select Pieces, by ISAAC PENNINGTON, *Stit.* 1s.

A Spiritual Diary, by JOHN RUTTY, M.D. late of Dublin, 2 vols. 6s. *bound*.

A Journal of the Life of JOHN GRATTON, giving an Account of his Exercifes when Young, and how he came to the Knowledge of the Truth; as alfo of his Labours, Travels, and Sufferings for the fame, 2s. *Bound*.

Some Confiderations relating to the Prefent State of the Chriftian Religion, in three Parts, by ALEXANDER ARSCOTT, *Bound*, 3s.

Alfo New and Neat Editions of the following Books.

The Sacred Hiftory of the Old and New Teftament, by THOMAS ELLWOOD, 3 vols. 8vo. 18s. *Calf, lettered*, and 15s. *Sheep, rolled*.

Fruits of Solitude, in Reflections and Maxims relating to the Conduct of Human Life, in two Parts, by WILLIAM PENN, *Sheep, rolled*, 2s.

Fruits of a Father's Love, being the Advice of WILLIAM PENN to his Children, relating to their Civil and Religious Conduct, *Stitched* 9d.

A Journal of Labours and Travels in the Work of the Miniftry of that faithful Servant of Chrift, DEBORAH BELL, *Stitched*, 1s.

Where may be had, gratis, Propofals for reprinting the Select Works of WILLIAM PENN, in Five Volumes, 8vo.

www.ingramcontent.com/pod-product-compliance
Lightning Source LLC
Chambersburg PA
CBHW020320240426
43673CB00039B/873